IMMUNITY AND INTERNATIONAL CRIMINAL LAW

Immunity and International Criminal Law

YITIHA SIMBEYE

ASHGATE

© Yitiha Simbeye 2004

All rights reserved. No part of this publication may be reproduced, stored in a retrieval system or transmitted in any form or by any means, electronic, mechanical, photocopying, recording or otherwise without the prior permission of the publisher.

The author has asserted her moral right under the Copyright, Designs and Patents Act, 1988, to be identified as the author of this work.

Published by
Ashgate Publishing Limited
Gower House
Croft Road
Aldershot
Hants GU11 3HR
England

Ashgate Publishing Company
Suite 420
101 Cherry Street
Burlington, VT 05401-4405
USA

Ashgate website: http://www.ashgate.com

British Library Cataloguing in Publication Data
Simbeye, Yitiha
    Immunity and international criminal law
    1. International Criminal Court 2. Criminal liability
    (International law) 3. Criminal jurisdiction 4. Privileges
    and immunities
    I. Title
    345'.01

Library of Congress Cataloging-in-Publication Data
Simbeye, Yitiha, 1972-
    Immunity and international criminal law / Yitiha Simbeye.
       p. cm.
    Includes bibliographical references and index.
    ISBN 0-7546-2433-1
      1. International Criminal Court. 2. Immunities of foreign states. 3. Criminal jurisdiction.
    I. Title.

    KZ6310.S55 2004
    345'.01--dc22

2004047677

ISBN 0 7546 2433 1
Printed and bound by Athenaeum Press, Ltd.,
Gateshead, Tyne & Wear.

Contents

Acknowledgements		*vi*
Abbreviations		*vii*
Introduction		1
1	The International Criminal Court	8
2	International Crimes	36
3	Individual Criminal Responsibility	67
4	Immunities	92
5	High- Ranking State Officials and Crime	109
6	The Need for Balance: The Pursuit of International Justice Versus Stable Inter-State Relations	135
Conclusion		158
Appendix		*160*
Bibliography		*164*
Index		*170*

Acknowledgements

This book is the result of my research into international criminal law and immunity that culminated in a PhD thesis titled: The Erosion of Sovereign and Diplomatic Immunity under International Criminal Law (University of Reading, 1999-2003). Without the consistent and patient assistance of my supervisor Dr J.C. Barker it would never have materialized. I would like to thank him for his dedication to my research, his kindness and sincerity in all his dealings with me, connected or unconnected, to the PhD I would also like to thank my parents, without whom, I most certainly would have been unable to meet the financial requirements of a PhD. I would especially like to thank them for their loving encouragement. A special thank you must be said to my sister and brother for their tireless patience of the nerd-like demeanour I displayed during my PhD years.

To the members of staff at the University of Reading, I would particularly like to thank Marilyn Hennessey for all her support. I would also like to extend my gratitude to Professor C.F. Stychin for his unwavering assistance. In addition, a warm thank you is extended to Deborah Edwards, Jane Mills and Julie Jones, who has now retired.

> The Lord is my Shepherd, I'll not want. He makes me down to lie. In pastures green; He leadeth me; the quiet waters by. *Psalms 23:1-2*

Abbreviations

Journals/Periodicals

AJIL	American Journal of International Law
An. Dig.	Annual Digest
AYIL	Australian Yearbook of International Law
BYIL	British Yearbook of International Law
Calif. L. Rev.	California Law Review
CLR	Criminal Law Reports
CYIL	Canadian Yearbook of International Law
Conn. JIL	Connecticut Journal of International Law
EJIL	European Journal of International Law
Emory LJ	Emory Law Journal
HJIL	Houston Journal of International Law
ICAO Doc.	International Civil Aviation Organization Documents
ICLQ	International and Comparative Law Quarterly
ICR	International Case Reports
ILM	International Legal Materials
IMO Doc.	International Maritime Organization Documents
JDIP	Journal de Droit International Privé
JMC	Journal of Modern Conservatism
LNTS	League of Nations Treaty Series
MLR	Modern Law Review
MSU-DCL JIL	Michigan State University-DCL Journal of International Law
New England L. Rev.	New England Law Review
NILR	Netherlands International Law Review
NJIL	Nordic Journal of International Law
NYIL & Pol.	New York Journal of International Law and Politics
Pace IL Rev.	Pace International Law Review
Tenn. L. Rev.	Tennessee Law Review
UN Leg Series	United Nations Legislative Series
UNTS	United Nations Treaty Series
US For. Rel.	Foreign Relations of the United States
Van. JTL	Vanderbilt Journal of Transnational Law
VJIL	Virginia Journal of International Law
YBILC	Yearbook of the International Law Commission

viii　　　　　　　　　*Immunity and International Criminal Law*

Law Reports

AC	Appeal Cases
All ER	All England Law Reports
F. Supp.	Federal Supplement
Fam.	Law Reports, Family Division
ICJ Reps.	International Court of Justice Law Reports
ILR	International Law Reports
KB	Law Reports, King's Bench Division
Leach	Leach
O.R.	Ontario Reports
PCIJ	Permanent Court of International Justice Reports
QB	Law Reports, Queen's Bench Division
RIAA	United Nations Reports of International Arbitral Awards
U.S. Dist	United States District Court
WLR	Weekly Law Reports

Other

Gen. Ass. Res.	General Assembly Resolution
HC Debs.	House of Commons Debates
HL Debs.	House of Lords Debates
SC Res.	Security Council Resolution

Introduction

Two very significant events occurred in 1998. The Diplomatic Conference of Plenipotentiaries in Rome[1] adopted the Statute for the International Criminal Court,[2] and, General Pinochet, former head of state of Chile was arrested in London for, *inter alia*, crimes against humanity.[3] The establishment of a permanent international criminal court and the pursuit of a former head of state in a foreign domestic court for the commission of international crimes, are events that marked a turning point for international criminal law.

The *Pinochet Case* and the establishment of the International Criminal Court (ICC) are a culmination of the aspirations of many in the world seeking legal processes that could bring an end to impunity for state officials who commit international crimes. The case against Pinochet demonstrated that state officials could be called to account for their acts at some point in time after the cessation of their official functions. The diplomatic conference leading to the establishment of the ICC is apparently a demonstration of the world community's combined resolve to establish a permanent international criminal court to deal with state officials whether or not their functions have ceased.

A significant aspect of the ICC, in relation to state officials, is its Article 27, which states:

> 1. This statute shall apply equally to all persons without distinction based on official capacity. In particular, official capacity as Head of State or Government, a member of Government or parliament, an elected representative or a government official shall in no case exempt a person from criminal responsibility under this Statute, nor shall it, in and of itself, constitute a ground for reduction of sentence.

---

[1] Hereinafter the Diplomatic Conference. Representatives from states, IGOs and NGOs met in Rome, Italy, between the 15 June and 17 July to discuss and finalize a draft statute for an international criminal court.

[2] Hereinafter the Rome Statute. UN Doc.A/CONF.183/9. For the full text of the Rome Statute see: www.icc-cpi.int.

[3] The arrest warrant was issued by a Spanish judge. *Reg. v. Bow Street Metropolitan Stipendiary Magistrate, Ex. P. Pinochet Ugarte (No. 1)* [1998] 3 WLR 1456, and *(No. 3)* [1999] 2 All ER 97. (Hereinafter *Pinochet (No. 1) or (No. 3)*. *Pinochet (No. 2)* dealt with the issue of bias regarding one of the judges in the first case, and is not relevant to the issues discussed herein. Reference to *Pinochet (No. 1)* in this article does not imply that it is a binding precedent but is referred to where it is deemed persuasive in illustrating a point of view.

2 *Immunity and International Criminal Law*

2. Immunities or special procedural rules which may attach to the official capacity of a person, whether under national or international law, shall not bar the Court from exercising its jurisdiction over such person.[4]

State officials and diplomats are not, therefore, immune from the court's jurisdiction by virtue of their status.

However, when it comes to the issue of their arrest, detention and surrender, status becomes imperative. According to Article 98:

1. The Court may not proceed with a request for the surrender or assistance which would require the requested State to act inconsistently with its obligations under international law with respect to the State or diplomatic immunity of person or property of a third State, unless the Court can at first obtain the cooperation of that third State for the waiver of the immunity.

2. The Court may not proceed with the request for surrender which would require the requested State to act inconsistently with its obligation under international agreements pursuant to which consent of a sending State is required to surrender a person of that State to the Court, unless the Court can first obtain the cooperation of the sending State for the giving of consent for the surrender.

Whilst disallowing the status of an individual to act as a bar to proceedings, the Rome Statute then makes status an issue pertinent to the possibility of such proceedings actually taking place. Without the suspect in custody the ICC cannot proceed, as the Rome Statute does not permit a trial without the presence of the accused.[5]

Proceedings against state officials and diplomats can only occur if they are apprehended and surrendered to the ICC with the consent of their home states. A state can surrender any of its officials to the ICC without violating international law, but it is suggested that states will be averse to surrendering their own officials to the ICC. As a result, foreign states could play a greater role in the apprehension of persons of status as the UK did with Pinochet. However, foreign states must grant visiting state officials and resident diplomats immunity from their civil and criminal jurisdiction.[6]

Heads of state and government are accorded immunity in foreign jurisdictions according to international customary law.[7] The immunity that diplomats enjoy in their receiving states is regulated by the Vienna Convention on Diplomatic Relations 1961.[8] Official acts of such state agents are considered acts of state and the domestic courts of foreign states are prevented from adjudicating.[9]

---

[4] Rome Statute, Article 27.

[5] Rome Statute, Article 63.

[6] Watts, 'The Legal Position in International Law of Heads of State, Heads of Government and Foreign Ministers' (1994) *247 Hague Recueil des Cours 13*.

[7] Watts, *op cit*. Head of state and government immunity is discussed in detail in Chapter 4.

[8] Vienna Convention on Diplomatic Relations 1961 (500 UNTS 95) (hereinafter the Vienna Diplomatic Convention).

[9] This issue is examined in further detail in Chapter 5.

Introduction 3

In addition, both diplomats in their receiving states and visiting heads of state and government are inviolable and cannot, therefore, be arrested and detained. Inviolability and immunity for acts of state are international doctrines that exist for good reason. Holding state officials or diplomats accountable in foreign domestic courts could hinder relations between the states concerned. The individual's state may interpret court action against its official as an infringement of its sovereignty.

The doctrine of sovereignty is understood to involve a sovereign government that is the supreme authority within the state.[10] It is independent of any earthly authority, within and without the borders of its country.[11] For a state to be sovereign it must not be dependent on another state, thus states are sovereign and equal to each other in the international community.[12] Absolute sovereignty infers that in international relations states' rights are actualized according to their will, a will that supersedes any universal will. The universal will does not progress beyond the 'ought to' stage as the will of states is deemed greater and can,

---

[10] The term 'sovereignty' comes from the Latin word *superanitas*, which means of the topmost position. Although the term is derived from this Latin word, the concept did not have its roots in the Roman world, but evolved in Europe in feudal times, to denote the supreme ruler as kingdoms became more centralized. The Romans did not have the notion of sovereignty. Their notion of the state: *Res Publica* denoted the people. As the notion of the state developed, so did the concept of sovereignty. The state as we know it was not evident during the early Middle Ages, nor was the notion of sovereignty in the sense of an ultimate territorial organ that knows no superior. It would appear that any historical examination of the development of the concept of sovereignty would not be complete without looking at the state and analysing how its establishment led to the conceptualization of the doctrine of sovereignty. According to Hinsley the concept of sovereignty will not be found in societies in which there is no state. Hinsley, *Sovereignty* (1986), p. 22. Sovereignty is so caught up with the question of state that to try and examine sovereignty without examining the state is impossible. Theories abound as to how states originated, from the social contract theory expounded by Hobbes, Locke and Rousseau, to the theories of class struggle; Morgan, Engels and to the social Darwinians. Hobbes' social contract theory is discussed below, p.107. An analysis of the development of the state involves an examination not only of the historical aspects of the emergence of states, but also the anthropological and political aspects. The subject of state development is wide and complex and certainly beyond the scope of this book. But, briefly, a state through government has been defined as 'a body of people who are authorized to make and enforce rules that are binding on everyone who comes under their jurisdiction. They also have the power to settle disputes arising between them and to organize defences against external enemies and, the power to impose taxes or other economic contributions upon them.' Mair, *Primitive Government* (1964), p. 11.

[11] Oppenheim identifies sovereignty with a government, and puts sovereignty as a criterion for a state proper. Without sovereignty, amongst other things, a state proper would not exist. Oppenheim, *International Law A Treatise* Jennings & Watts eds. (1995), p. 118-119.

[12] Malanczuk, *Akehurt's Modern Introduction to International Law* (1997), p. 17-18. For Malanczuk it would be far better if the word 'sovereignty' was to be replaced by the word 'independence'. In the *Austro-German Customs Union Case* Judge Anzilotti held that an independent state 'has over it no other authority than that of international law', that it is not dependent on a superior state that can legally impose its will over it, a will that it is legally compelled to submit to. (1931) PCIJ Ser. A/B No. 41 at p. 57.

therefore, overpower the universal will.[13] States make mutual stipulations as autonomous entities but are believed to remain superior to such stipulations.[14]

From this absolute position it is assumed that total power is consolidated in the state as an independent entity. Independence denotes the right of states to exercise within their territories 'to the exclusion of any other state, the functions of state'.[15] On the international stage, however, states have to balance their power with those of other independent states.[16] Although the absolute perspective argues that where states disagreed in their attempts to harmonize their wills, war became inevitable,[17] states are prevented from imposing their power onto other states by international law. International law regulates the separate 'wills' of states that are subject to it, and as an example, it has placed limits on a state's right to wage war.[18]

International law is a legal system that regulates sovereign and equal entities. It requires that they do not impose their jurisdiction to proscribe and enforce laws on other states, but leaves them free to do so within their territories. Nevertheless, even within their territories states have to concede their jurisdiction over foreign heads of state and government, high-ranking government officials and diplomats.[19] Accordingly, if a defendant's status as head of state or government, or as a diplomat, is raised in court proceedings, it will act as a bar to such procedures, indeed inviolability will prevent such individuals from being arrested. The International Court of Justice (ICJ) has so ruled in a recent case: *Democratic Republic of Congo v. Belgium*, where it held that a foreign minister was immune from arrest whilst in office.[20] Belgium issued an arrest warrant against an incumbent foreign minister for alleged crimes constituting serious violations of international humanitarian law.[21]

However, it appears that recent developments in the UK could lead to heads of state or government and diplomatic inviolability being restricted. A law has been passed that appears to enable the UK's legal authorities to arrest and detain inviolable individuals for surrender to the ICC.[22] The UK's International Criminal Court Act 2001 enables inviolable individuals who are nationals of states party to

---

[13] Hegel, *The Philosophy of Right* (1942 translation), p. 213, para. 333.

[14] *Ibid*, p. 212, para. 330, p. 297, para. 330.

[15] *Islands of Palmas Case* (1928) 2 RIAA 829, Judge Huber.

[16] For issues on equality of states, see: Shaw, *International Law* (1997), p. 152-153.

[17] *Ibid*, p. 214, para. 334.

[18] Barker, *International Law and International Relations* (2000), p. 44. International legal personality is discussed in Chapter 3. By limiting recourse to war international law can be said to restrict the 'will' of states. Limiting recourse to war is analysed below in Chapter 2.

[19] Malanczuk, *Akehurst's Modern Introduction to International Law, op cit*, p.118.

[20] *Democratic Republic of Congo v. Belgium*, Judgment of 14 February 2002, www.icj-cij.org. Hereinafter the *Arrest Warrant Case*. Case is discussed in further detail below.

[21] *Ibid*.

[22] UK statute: International Criminal Court Act 2001, Part 2 s.23(1). Butterworths UK statutes, www.butterworths.co.uk. This act would appear to supplant provisions of the Diplomatic Privileges and Immunities Act 1964.

Introduction 5

the Rome Statute to be arrested in order to facilitate ICC surrender requests. It states that:

> 'Any state or diplomatic immunity attaching to a person by reason of a connection with a state party to the ICC Statute does not prevent proceedings under this Part [Part 2 Arrest and Surrender] in relation to that person.'[23]

In effect the UK legislature has produced a statute that appears to put aside inviolability in favour of an ICC surrender request. Subsequently, if a sitting head of state of country A (a party to the Rome Statute) travels to the UK whilst an ICC arrest warrant against him is active, he may find himself being arrested by British police and detained at her Majesty's pleasure pending transportation to The Hague. That this situation will give rise to tensions between the UK and country A is more than apparent.

For British courts an 'Act of Parliament is supreme', and they are bound to follow its terms.[24] In interpreting statutes, they assume that Parliament does not draft statutes that are contrary to international law. But, where a statute appears to contradict international law, they are bound by the Act of Parliament, and will effect such enactment.[25] Likewise, the US courts apply international law only where there is no contravening federal law.[26] Consequently, although customary international law and conventional law provide to certain persons absolute inviolability in foreign states, the UK will not adhere to this position where the person in question is an official of a state party to the Rome Statute and is wanted by the ICC.

However, customary and conventional rules on inviolability provide for no exceptions, an opinion held by the ICJ in the *Arrest Warrant Case*.[27] The person in question in this case was a foreign minister, who was accused of having committed crimes for which the ICC would have had jurisdiction. Yet, in attempting to issue an arrest warrant, Belgium was held to have acted contrary to binding international law. If Belgium was prevented from implementing its warrant, how is the UK going to effect arrest? Irrespective of the fact that the arrest warrant is from an international court, it is the domestic legal authorities of a state that will realize the actual arrest and detention prior to transfer.

Where the suspect is a diplomat, this clause is also contrary to the Vienna Diplomatic Convention's Article 29 obligation on receiving states to refrain from arresting and detaining diplomatic agents, which states:

---

[23] *Ibid.*

[24] *Mortensen v. Peters* 14 S.L.R. 227, Lord Dunedin.

[25] *Maclaine Watson v. Department of Trade and Industry* [1989] 3 All ER 523, 531, Lord Oliver.

[26] *US v. Sissoko* (1977) U.S. Dist., Lexis 22115, p. 25. It is acknowledged that the approach is more complex than suggested here.

[27] *Arrest Warrant Case, op cit.*

> The person of a diplomatic agent shall be inviolable. He shall not be liable to any form of arrest and detention...[28]

The Vienna Diplomatic Convention does not provide for any exceptions which would allow for the arrest and detention of a diplomat in a receiving state. That the arrest is at the behest of an international court does not alleviate the UK's obligation under this convention, a convention that codified customary international norms.[29]

It is suggested that inviolability serves to protect international peace and to maintain good relations between states, goals which are evidently not promoted by arrest warrants against incumbent heads of state and government and high-ranking state officials. The world we know is still one based primarily on rights and duties of states in international law. Immunities are there to keep inter-state relations running smoothly. It must be borne in mind that such inter-state relations are vital, and short of changing the actual structure of international law and international relations, the system will continue to demand immunities. International peace and security will suffer where a state, by virtue of being a member of the Rome Statute, could find its leader being arrested and detained by British authorities. Just what kind of effect the UK's arrest clause will have in the future with regard to rules of inviolability remains unclear.[30]

Nonetheless it is acknowledged that pursuing international crimes irrespective of the status of the accused is one of international criminal law's prime objectives, hence the inclusion of Article 27 in the Rome Statute.[31] It is arguable that the pursuit of state officials through domestic channels has the potential to destabilize inter-state relations and the system of laws that regulate such affairs. International law seeks to ensure that each state is afforded rights and duties as an independent and sovereign state, and in effect sustain international peace and security.[32] Sovereignty is, therefore, a necessary doctrine.[33] As a consequence, Article 98's addition to the Rome Statute is explicable. But with Article 98 in place, Article 27 may become a provision on paper only. It may never produce results.

This book will, therefore, attempt to propose methods that could be employed to enable Article 98 to be circumvented, without violating international

---

[28] Vienna Diplomatic Convention, *op cit.*

[29] More on this issue in Chapter 4.

[30] It is possible that the drafter of the UK statute, with political appeasement to human rights pressure groups, included this provision, knowing full well that the operation of the Rome Statute's Article 98 will prevent them having to arrest a sitting head of state or diplomat.

[31] Evidence of international criminal law's indifference to status can be traced back to Nuremberg and the Tokyo Tribunals. The status of an individual was not a bar to proceedings for international crimes. The Charter of the International Military Tribunal at Nuremberg (hereinafter The Nuremberg Charter) Article 7 The Charter of the International Military Tribunal for the Far East (hereinafter The Tokyo Charter) Article 6.

[32] Shaw, *International Law, op cit*, p. 10.

[33] Hegel, *The Philosophy of Right, op cit*, p. 213-214, para. 333.

Introduction 7

law. Accordingly, the challenge is to present solutions that could provide a balance between maintaining stable inter-state relations and the pursuit of international justice. Acknowledging that immunities are essential on one hand, one must balance, on the other, the need to pursue international crimes.

Chapter 1

The International Criminal Court

The international criminal justice system is a dual faceted system. One aspect deals with the development of norms prohibiting international crimes and the other with holding individuals responsible for such crimes. The establishment of the ICC is based on the second feature. It is intended that as a court it will act as the last resort when states fail to proceed.[1] Thus states retain the power to deal with international crimes at the domestic level, given that they still proscribe and enforce rules in their territories.[2] Their competence to deal with persons suspected of breaching their rules endures.

The History

The idea of a permanent international criminal court has been in circulation for decades. Ever since the Second World War various groups and the UN have been engaged in debate as to how, when, and what kind of international criminal court could be established.

Efforts to Establish an International Criminal Court before the United Nations

The concept of an international criminal court, albeit one to arbitrate inter-state disputes, was evident as far back as 1899. It was put forward during the First Peace Conference in The Hague, where it was acknowledged that an international tribunal was a good way to settle disputes, and proposed the establishment of a permanent Court of Arbitration.[3] It was not, however an ordinary court, but a list of non-professionals who were available to arbitrate if called upon by the state parties.[4] During the Second Peace Conference in 1907, the US resurrected the idea

---

[1] Ferencz, 'International Criminal Courts: The Legacy of Nuremberg' (1998) *10 Pace IL Rev. 203, 215*. The Rome Statute does not give the ICC primacy over domestic jurisdictions. It has to wait for national legal authorities to proceed first. Rome Statute, Article 17, *op cit.*

[2] Shaw, *International Law*, *op cit*, p. 452.

[3] Final Act of the International Peace Conference 1899. Article 16 states that in questions of a legal nature, and especially in the interpretation or application of international conventions, arbitration is recognized by the signatory powers as the most effective and at the same time the most equitable means of settling disputes which diplomacy has failed to settle. Ferencz, *An International Criminal Court A Step Toward World Peace (Vol. 1)* (1980), p. 114.

[4] *Ibid*, p. 8-9.

The International Criminal Court 9

of a permanent court by suggesting a court with 15 professional judges who in their 12-year terms would work towards building up a body of international law.[5] But states placed so many reservations that this proposal proved unworkable.

In 1926 the International Law Association (ILA) drafted a statute for an International Penal Court.[6] It was envisioned that the International Penal Court would have jurisdiction over violations of international obligations of a penal character, violations of treaties or conventions regulating methods and conduct of war and violations of the laws and customs of war generally.[7] In 1937 the League of Nations produced its Convention for the Creation of an International Criminal Court to deal with the crime of terrorism as put forward by the League's Convention for the Prevention and Punishment of Terrorism.[8] The court was to be a permanent body, sitting only when seized of proceedings for an offence within its jurisdiction.[9]

During the Second World War the London International Assembly,[10] created under the auspices of the League of Nations, called for international criminal law to be codified and war of aggression to be recognized as a crime. The London Assembly appealed for those militarily responsible for aggressive war to be held personally accountable.[11] It wanted certain crimes, such as those committed against the Jews, to be recognized as crimes against mankind although they were not crimes under domestic law. To further these goals it drafted a convention for an international criminal court to be established by the United Nations having jurisdiction over those who had committed war crimes irrespective of rank.[12] The draft gave primacy to domestic courts:

> no case shall be brought before the Court when a domestic court of any one of the United Nations has jurisdiction to try the accused and it is in a position and willing to exercise such jurisdiction.[13]

The draft convention gave member states the choice to either prosecute or commit the accused for trial by the international criminal court.[14] The London Assembly's draft included a novel idea of an international constabulary capable of executing the court's orders. Member states were to confer on the international

---

[5] Hereinafter the 1907 Conference. Ferencz, *A Step Toward World Peace (Vol. 1)*, *op cit*, p. 11-12.

[6] International Law Association 34 Conference 1926, *ibid*, p. 252.

[7] ILA Draft Statute, Article 21, *ibid*.

[8] League of Nations Terrorism Convention, Article 1 from: Ferencz, *A Step Toward World Peace (Vol. 1)*, *op cit*, p. 389.

[9] ILA Draft Statute, Article 3.

[10] Hereinafter the London Assembly.

[11] Ferencz, *A Step Toward World Peace (Vol. 1)*, *op cit*, p. 57-58.

[12] Articles 1 and 2 Draft Convention for the Creation of an International Criminal Court London International Assembly (1943). (Hereinafter London Assembly Draft Convention.)

[13] London Assembly Draft Convention, Article 3(1), *ibid*.

[14] London Assembly Draft Convention, Article 4(1), *ibid*.

constabulary the power to request the help of local police where necessary, to assist it in the performance of its duties.[15]

Although not permanent, the International Military Tribunal at Nuremberg and the International Military Tribunal for the Far East were the first international criminal tribunals. The Allies, subsequent to the defeat of Germany and Japan, established them in 1945. The objective was to punish those responsible for the international crimes of crimes against peace, war crimes and crimes against humanity.[16] However altruistic the thinking behind the two tribunals may have been, both the Nuremberg and Tokyo Tribunals were accused of being 'victors' courts; an accusation denied by the United States amongst others. The USA's representatives maintained that the trials were intended to marshal in a new era that would make international crimes punishable under binding international law.[17] Such statements did not easily assuage the cries of 'victors' courts' especially when taken in context with Japan's inability to raise its complaint about the USA's use of nuclear weapons against it before the tribunal.[18] However, Nuremberg's openness and adherence to the law has ensured that it 'has withstood the test of time as a fair articulation of evolving international law'.[19] On the other hand, questions as to the Tokyo Tribunal's complete openness were raised as it failed to look at the Emperor's responsibility.[20] Nevertheless, the prosecutor did argue that the Emperor could not have been tried and convicted because under the Japanese constitution he did not have the power to make or stop the war.[21]

The United Nations and its Attempts to Create an International Criminal Court

The idea of an international criminal court was taken up thereafter by the UN when its Economic and Social Council (ECOSOC) included an international criminal court in its draft convention on genocide.[22] The contracting parties were to commit persons guilty of genocide under the convention for trial by an international court where they were unwilling to try or extradite the offenders, or where the acts were

---

[15] London Assembly Draft Convention, Article 25, *ibid.*

[16] The Tribunals are discussed in further detail in the next chapter.

[17] Ferencz, 'International Criminal Courts: The Legacy of Nuremberg', *op cit*, p. 217.

[18] Cassese, *International Criminal Law* (2003), p. 332-333. See: Onuma 'The Tokyo Trial: Between Law and Politics' in *The Tokyo War Crimes Trial: An International Symposium* (1986).

[19] Ferencz, 'International Criminal Courts: The Legacy of Nuremberg', *op cit*, p. 212.

[20] Brackman, *The Other Nuremberg The Untold Story of the Tokyo War Crimes Trials* (1989), p. 95-96.

[21] *Ibid.*

[22] Secretary General drafted a convention at the behest of ECOSOC, A/AC.10/41, A/AC.10/42 and A/AC.10/Rev.1. Historical Survey of the Question of International Criminal Jurisdiction (1949), p. 30. The draft was debated and amended by the Ad Hoc Committee in 1948; a new draft was then presented, E/794.

committed by persons acting as organs of the state or where there was support or toleration of the state for the acts in question.[23]

ECOSOC presented different views on an international court in two separate drafts:

(i) an international court having jurisdiction in all matters connected with international crimes, and

(ii) an international criminal court only having jurisdiction over genocide.[24]

This court could be either permanent[25] or ad hoc.[26] States reviewed the first draft and raised various concerns.[27] A few countries seemed unwilling to see their sovereignty infringed, whilst others saw it as being too unrealistic.[28] Consequently, the General Assembly voted to remove any reference to an international criminal court from the Genocide Convention.[29] Nevertheless, at the same time that it adopted the revised convention the General Assembly invited the International Law Commission (ILC) to look at the question of an international criminal jurisdiction. At that time the ILC was looking to formulate the Nuremberg principles through a draft code of offences against peace and security and it seemed logical to combine the two efforts.[30] The rapporteur dealing with the code of offences and the Nuremberg principles produced his report, which was discussed by the ILC in 1949.[31] Prior to this report, the ILC in 1948 appointed two rapporteurs, Alfaro and Sandström, to look specifically at the issue of an international criminal court.[32]

The rapporteurs reported back to the ILC in 1950 with opposing views. Alfaro, looking back historically, concluded that there was desire and support amongst states for the establishment of an international criminal court.[33] He was of the opinion that it was possible to set up an international organ of penal justice.[34]

---

[23] ECOSOC Draft Genocide Convention, (1946), Article 9(1) (2).

[24] ECOSOC Draft Genocide Convention, (1946), Article 10; Ferencz, *A Step Toward World Peace (Vol. 2)*, *op cit*, p. 129, 132.

[25] ECOSOC Draft Genocide Convention, (1946), Appendix 1 to Article 10, Article 3, *ibid*, p. 134.

[26] ECOSOC Draft Genocide Convention, (1946), Appendix 2, *ibid*.

[27] Communications received by the Secretary General Documents A/401 (1947).

[28] Former Soviet Union and Venezuela respectively, *ibid*.

[29] Gen. Ass. Res. 260(iii) (1948).

[30] A special rapporteur was appointed to look at these two points and report back in 1949.

[31] Rapporteur Spiropoulos; Ferencz, *A Step Toward World Peace (Vol. 2)*, *op cit*, p. 22. The ILC dropped the issue of an international criminal jurisdiction in its work on the draft codes of offences against peace and security in 1953.

[32] The difficult and contentious nature of the question of an international criminal court warranted two rapporteurs. Ferencz, *A Step Toward World Peace (Vol. 2)*, *op cit*, p. 23.

[33] Alfaro's Report: Document 3 March (1950) A/CN.4/15. Ferencz, *A Step Toward World Peace (Vol. 2)*, *op cit*, p. 241-258.

[34] Alfaro's Report, *ibid*.

His point of view was based on the judicial organs created by the Geneva Conventions of 1937 for the trial of persons responsible for acts of terrorism, and the two military tribunals set up after the Second World War. He put forward the argument that only an international court could properly try certain international crimes that are committed by governments.[35] According to him, the notion of absolute sovereign rights of nations was in part relinquished by the very existence and function of the UN. Accordingly, the sovereignty of states is subordinated to the supremacy of international law.[36] Sandström, on the other hand, was of the opinion that states were not ready to have an international criminal court that would in effect erode their sovereignty.[37] For Sandström the time was not right.[38] Although he agreed with Alfaro that there was a desire to establish an international criminal court, he concluded that the issues of sovereignty and criminal jurisdiction hindered the establishment of an effective inter-state criminal jurisdiction.[39]

Although faced with the two opposing views, the ILC managed to vote in favour of the establishment of an international criminal court and presented its recommendations to the General Assembly. Its Sixth Committee recommended that the General Assembly pass a resolution to create a special committee to meet and prepare a preliminary draft convention and proposals for the establishment of an international criminal court.[40] The resolution was passed and the seventeen-member Committee on International Criminal Jurisdiction met and produced proposals and a preliminary convention in August 1951.[41]

The international criminal court, envisaged by this seventeen-member committee, was to have jurisdiction over persons accused of crimes as provided in conventions or special agreements between states.[42] Jurisdiction was to be conveyed to the court by the states whose nationals were suspects, or by the state in whose territory the offence took place, with the General Assembly's approval.[43] Proceedings were to be initiated by either the General Assembly, any organization of states approved by the UN, or a state party to the statute which had conferred jurisdiction.[44]

The Sixth Committee met again in 1952 to review and discuss the proposals made in the draft statute, taking into consideration views of states. Based on these

---

[35] Alfaro's Report, *ibid*, Part iv (2) (129), *ibid*, p. 256.

[36] Alfaro's Report, *ibid*.

[37] Sandström's Report, 30 March 1950: A/CN.4/20. Ferencz, *A Step Toward World Peace (Vol. 2)*, *ibid*, p. 259-264.

[38] Sandström's Report, *ibid*.

[39] Sandström's Report, *ibid*, Part iv (14) & (15).

[40] Report of the Sixth Committee Doc: 1950 A/1639.

[41] Gen. Ass. Res. 489 (v) (1950). Report of the 1951 Committee on International Criminal Jurisdiction Doc: 1951 A/2136. The USSR and Poland refused to take part in this Committee.

[42] Report of the 1951 Committee on International Criminal Jurisdiction Draft Statute for an International Criminal Court, Annex I, Article 1, *ibid*.

[43] Committee on International Criminal Jurisdiction Draft Statute, Articles 27 and 28, *ibid*.

[44] Committee on International Criminal Jurisdiction Draft Statute, Article 29, *ibid*.

discussions the General Assembly passed a resolution reappointing the seventeen-member committee in 1953 to review the proposals and the draft statute, and present another report in 1954.[45] In the second seventeen-member committee discussions, certain alterations were made to some of the articles of the draft statute. Of particular interest were changes made to the articles conferring jurisdiction on the court. In the revised draft, jurisdiction is not presumed and if conferred on the court would not automatically remove authority from national courts to look into the case in question.[46] General Assembly approval of jurisdiction was deleted and, instead, states were given the opportunity, with a year's notice, to withdraw jurisdiction.[47]

In 1954 the Sixth Committee recommended that a General Assembly resolution be passed to postpone consideration of an international criminal court. The committee was of the opinion that the issue of an international criminal court should be looked at alongside the issues of aggression and codes of offences against peace and security, which were being addressed by other bodies.[48] The General Assembly concurred and passed a resolution to that effect.[49] There followed decades of inactivity. One possible explanation for this course of action is that states were not prepared to see an international tribunal that would, to some extent, infringe on their sovereignty. There was a great need in the world for such a court, but no great will among states to assist in its creation. The war between Bangladesh and Pakistan in 1972, for example, would have provided the right situation for an international criminal court to exercise its jurisdiction. But the ICJ, the only international court at the time, was not the most suitable forum.[50]

In the post-Cold War atmosphere of the late 1980s, a coalition of Latin American and Caribbean states raised the issue of an international criminal court before the General Assembly in 1989. In response to this initiative the General Assembly passed a resolution requesting the ILC to return to the issue of an international criminal court.[51] The ILC had been engaged in the draft codes of offences against peace and security. However, a working group of the ILC was

---

[45] Gen. Ass. Res. 687(vii) (1952).

[46] Report of the 1953 Committee on International Criminal Jurisdiction revised draft Statute of an International Criminal Court 1954 A/2645. Annex, new Article 26: (1) Jurisdiction of the Court is not presumed. (2) A State may confer jurisdiction upon the Court by convention, by special agreement or by unilateral declaration. (3) Conferment of jurisdiction signifies the right to seize the Court, and the duty to accept its jurisdiction subject to such provisions as the State or States have specified. (4) Unless otherwise provided for in the instrument conferring jurisdiction upon the Court, the laws of a State determining criminal jurisdiction shall not be affected by that conferment.

[47] 1953 Committee on International Criminal Jurisdiction Revised Draft Statute, Annex, Article 28, *ibid*.

[48] Sixth Committee Report 1954 A/2827.

[49] Gen. Ass. Res. 898 (ix) (1954).

[50] This issue is discussed further in Chapter 3.

[51] Gen. Ass. Res. 44/39 (1989). For the recent chronology of events leading up to the Rome Statute see: Appendix.

established to produce a draft statute for an international criminal court in 1993. The ILC's working group was able to draft a statute, which it adopted in its 1994 session.[52] In drafting their second attempt, the working group took into account the legal advances made by the International Criminal Tribunal for the Former Yugoslavia (ICTY). They also considered the investigations the Security Council was conducting on Rwanda following the genocide of 1993. It submitted this draft to the General Assembly for feedback and in 1994 the Sixth Committee met to discuss the draft. The main concerns that emerged during those discussions included: the 'scope of the court's subject-matter jurisdiction, the state consent requirements for the exercise of jurisdiction, the court's inherent jurisdiction over genocide as an exception to the consent requirements, the role envisioned for the Security Council in determining the existence of an act of aggression and referring matters of the court, the relationship between the court and the United Nations'.[53]

In 1995 the General Assembly established a Preparatory Committee to look into the draft statute produced by the ILC. The Preparatory Committee reviewed and revised the draft statute in 1996 and 1997, and submitted a draft text in 1998. Between 15 June and 17 July in that same year, a diplomatic conference finally adopted the Rome Statute.

Under the Rome Statute individuals will be held responsible for international crimes if the state in whose territory the crime took place is a member state, or where the state of the offender's nationality is a party to the treaty.[54] Where a state is not a member of the treaty its acceptance of the court's jurisdiction may be required for the court to exercise its jurisdiction.[55] The court will exercise its jurisdiction when there is a referral to the Prosecutor by a state party, where the Security Council acts under its Chapter VII powers, or where the Prosecutor initiates investigation.[56] Like the Ad Hoc Tribunals the ICC will not view immunity as a bar to its jurisdiction.[57]

It was envisaged in the 1994 Draft that the ICC would not have primacy over national legal authorities.[58] According to the 1994 Draft, cases could be held inadmissible at the request of either the accused or an interested state. A case would have been inadmissible for three reasons. First, where the authorities in a state with jurisdiction investigated it, and it was properly decided that there would be no proceedings; second, where the state with jurisdiction is investigating and the court has no reason to carry on with proceedings; and third, where the crime in

---

[52] Hereinafter the 1994 Draft. (1994) Vol. 2 Part 2 YBILC.

[53] Morris and Bourloyannis-Vrailas, 'Current Development: The Work of the Sixth Committee at the Forty-Ninth Session of the UN General Assembly' (1995) *89 AJIL 607, 614.*

[54] Rome Statute, Article 12(2) (a) & (b). Under 12(2)(a) territory would include a vessel or aircraft registered to the member state in question.

[55] Rome Statute, Article 12.

[56] Rome Statute, Article 13(a), (b) and (c).

[57] Rome Statute, Article 27.

[58] 1994 Draft, Article 35, *op cit.*

question is not grave enough to warrant action. These provisions were retained in the Rome Statute.

The Establishment of the International Criminal Court

The ICC is a tool of international criminal law through which it is hoped that those who have committed international crimes will be prosecuted where a state with jurisdiction has failed to act. It is open to question just how effective the ICC will be as a legal system created to operate when another has failed. Any system devised by man must have flaws. Indeed, the first judicial tools realized under international criminal law, the Nuremberg and Tokyo Tribunals, had their own distinctive problems, as mentioned above. In the case of the ICC, it is submitted that its imperfections stem from a primary weak point: the manner in which it was established. It was set up by a Diplomatic Conference to allow state participation. During the conference, states were able to air their views, thus moulding the Rome Statute and creating a court acceptable to their own individual designs. For almost a month states were able to put forward their views. For example, Denmark, through its Minister of Justice, was of the opinion that:

> What is important is not only the creation of an International Criminal Court, but ensuring that it will be an effective institution, capable of adequately responding to needs of today's international society. In short, we should ensure that we have a Court that acts in the same way in which we have come to expect from national justice systems.[59]

The Rome Statute was shaped out of the myriad of ideals of different states with varying agendas. Thus the content and context of the ICC is very much influenced by the manner in which it was created. It is a body that is sensitive to the needs of states and their sovereignty. In this respect it contrasts greatly with the ICTY and the International Criminal Tribunal for Rwanda (ICTR). They are the only other international tribunals set up under international criminal law after Nuremberg and Tokyo. Like their predecessors they were not set up through a state-sensitive diplomatic conference. The ICTY and the ICTR were established by the Security Council utilizing its powers under Chapter VII of the UN Charter.[60] The first Ad Hoc Tribunal was established after the conflict in the Balkans in 1993.

---

[59] www.un.org./icc/pressrel/lrom15.htm.

[60] The ICTY and the ICTR when mentioned jointly hereafter will be referred to as the Ad Hoc Tribunals. The ICTY was set up under SC Res. 808 (1993), and the ICTR, under SC Res. 955 (1994). Under Chapter VII the Security Council can take measures where it perceives a situation as a threat to peace in order to maintain or restore international peace and security, Art. 39, be it by military means, Art. 42, or by other means not involving the use of armed forces, Art. 41. UN Charter (557 UNTS) 143. See Sarooshi, *The United Nations and the Development of Collective Security: The Delegation by the United Nations Security Council of its Chapter VII Powers* (1999).

16 *Immunity and International Criminal Law*

This tribunal was followed by a second, set up subsequent to internal strife in Rwanda in 1994. It is suggested that the Ad Hoc Tribunals are powerful judicial organs that are the appropriate tools to tackle international crimes. The manner in which they were instituted is the factor that makes them so compelling. As a result of their formation they have primacy over national jurisdictions and extensive as well as flexible operational powers.

The Ad Hoc Tribunals were the first, and so far the only, Security Council criminal tribunals. The ICTY was the first tribunal and being the first of its kind it initially raised various concerns. Particular points of interest included the legality of its establishment, its primacy and its broad procedural powers. In 1995 the defence for Dusko Tadic, in *Prosecutor v. Tadic*, filed a preliminary motion challenging the ICTY's powers to try the accused.[61] The defence claimed that the ICTY was not properly established. They questioned the legality of Security Council action in establishing a subsidiary judicial organ under Chapter VII, arguing that it had exceeded its authority.[62] The defence was in fact asking the ICTY to judicially review the actions of the Security Council.

In response to this challenge the Trial Chamber held that it is not a constitutional court set up to review the actions of UN organs.[63] Rather, it is a criminal tribunal having clear and specified powers that limit it to criminal affairs.[64] Consequently, it stated that it did not have the authority to investigate the legality of its creation.[65] However, the Trial Chamber felt that the issue was of such importance that it had to pass comment.

> [The] Trial Chamber considers that it would be inappropriate to dismiss without comment the accused's contentions that the establishment of the International Tribunal by the Security Council was beyond power and an ill-founded political action, not reasonably aimed at restoring and maintaining peace, and that the International Tribunal is not duly established by law. [66]

Basing their observations on the Security Council's broad discretionary powers under Chapter VII, the judges found that the Security Council had not acted arbitrarily in establishing the tribunal.[67] Under Article 39 of the UN Charter, the Security Council can 'determine the existence of any threat to the peace, breach of the peace, or act of aggression and shall make recommendations, or decide what measures shall be taken in accordance with Articles 41 and 42, to maintain or

---

[61] *Prosecutor v. Dusko Tadic* (IT-94-I), *Decision on the Defence Motion on Jurisdiction* (Trial Chamber) (1995), (hereinafter the *Tadic Jurisdiction Challenge Case (Trial Chamber)* www.un.org/icty/tadic/trialc2/decision-e/100895.

[62] *Ibid.*

[63] *Ibid*, para. 5.

[64] *Ibid.*

[65] *Ibid.*

[66] *Ibid*, para. 6.

[67] *Ibid*, para. 16.

restore international peace and security'.[68] The Security Council can decide to take measures not involving the use of armed force in order to give effect to its decisions, and may call upon the members of the United Nations to apply such methods. It has the option to include complete or partial interruption of economic relations and rail, sea, postal telegraphic, radio, and other means of communication, and the severance of diplomatic relations.

The Trial Chamber maintained that the Security Council is not limited in its use of non-military measures by Article 41, and that such action could include the establishment of a judicial organ whose purpose is to adjudicate and punish those responsible for a notorious situation that was clearly a threat to international peace and security.[69] Tadic's defence had concentrated on the examples of action actually stated in Article 41 arguing that a judicial organ was not mentioned per se. Counter to that point of view, the Trial Chamber felt that the Article 41 list was not exhaustive.[70] Although the course the Security Council took to restore peace and maintain security in the former Yugoslavia was novel, the purpose behind the tribunal was not.[71] Further, it was the opinion of the Trial Chamber that Article 29 of the UN Charter enables the Security Council to establish subsidiary organs that it may deem necessary for the performance of its functions.[72] According to the Trial Chamber this article is broad enough so as not to limit the scope of the Security Council in establishing a subsidiary judicial organ.[73]

The Appeal Chamber fully supported the Trial Chamber's point of view and found that the UN Charter gives the Security Council sufficient basis for establishing subsidiary judicial organs.[74] According to the Appeal Chamber, the 'language of Article 39 is quite clear as to the channelling of the broad and exceptional powers of the Security Council under Chapter VII through Articles 41 and 42'. This article leaves it with 'such wide choice' allowing it to resort to establishing 'a judicial organ in the form of an international criminal tribunal as an instrument for the exercise of its own principal function of maintenance of peace and security, i.e., as a measure contributing to the restoration of peace in the former Yugoslavia'.[75]

The Security Council's power to establish subsidiary judicial organs is an advantage for international criminal law. The benefits are evident in the power that subsidiary judicial organs derive from the Security Council's authoritative position

---

[68] UN Charter, Article 39.

[69] *Ibid*, paras. 26 and 27.

[70] *Ibid*, para. 28.

[71] The *Tadic Jurisdiction Challenge Case (Trial Chamber)*, para. 22.

[72] UN Charter, Article 29: The Security Council may establish such subsidiary organs as it deems necessary for the performance of its functions. *Tadic Jurisdiction Challenge Case (Trial Chamber)*, para. 35.

[73] *Tadic Jurisdiction Challenge Case (Trial Chamber)*, ibid.

[74] *The Prosecutor v. Tadic, Decision on the Defence Motion for Interlocutory Appeal on Jurisdiction* ICTY (hereinafter the *Tadic Jurisdiction Challenge (Appeal Case)* IT-94-1-AR72, 2 Oct 1995 RP D6413-D6491.

[75] *Ibid*, paras. 31 and 38.

in the international community. The Security Council was set up to maintain international peace and security through peaceful settlements of disputes or enforcement measures. In doing so it acts on behalf of UN member states as a whole under Article 24 of the UN Charter:

> In order to ensure prompt and effective action by the United Nations, its members confer on the Security Council primary responsibility for the maintenance of international peace and security, and agree that in carrying out its duties under this responsibility the Security Council acts on their behalf.[76]

Acting on their behalf, its decisions bind them, according to Article 25:

> The members of the United Nations agree to accept and carry out the decisions of the Security Council in accordance with the present Charter.[77]

So where action is deemed a threat to international peace and security the Security Council can act through peaceful settlement or take enforcement measures. Any action it decides to take will bind all UN member states. The process by which it decides to take action, and the type of action to be undertaken, does not involve the input of all member states. With just fifteen members, of whom five are permanent, its actions bind more than 200 states.[78] It was envisaged that in order for the UN to take prompt and effective action in grave situations, members had to confer the responsibility on the Security Council to maintain international peace and security and act on their behalf.[79] Thus action is taken without the need to take into consideration the views of every member state. It is supposed to be a rapid response system that is not slowed down by lengthy negotiations in diplomatic conferences. By using its Chapter VII powers the Security Council avoided the protracted diplomatic process that created the ICC.

The Security Council and the International Criminal Court

The Security Council has been given a role in the ICC process.[80] Acting under its Chapter VII powers it can refer cases to the court.[81] Under this procedure the ICC will have territorial and personal jurisdiction, not only in respect of state parties and their citizens, but also over all UN member states according to Article 24 of the UN Charter.

---

[76] UN Charter, Article 24.

[77] UN Charter, Article 25. Shaw, *International Law, op cit*, p. 827.

[78] UN Charter, Article 23(1): The Security Council shall consist of fifteen Members of the United Nations. The Republic of China, France, the Union of Soviet Socialist Republics, the United Kingdom of Great Britain and Northern Ireland, and the United States of America shall be permanent members of the Security Council.

[79] UN Charter, Article 24(1).

[80] Rome Statute, Article 13(b).

[81] UN Charter, Article 13(b).

The International Criminal Court

As a general rule, only parties to a treaty are bound by its obligations.[82] This principle is expressed in the maxim *pacta tertiis nec nocent nec prosunt*.[83] According to the Vienna Convention on the Law of Treaties, a treaty is 'an international agreement concluded between States in written form and governed by international law' that is binding on states that are parties to it.[84] A party to a treaty consents to be bound by the treaty upon ratification.[85] Third states, or states not party to the treaty,[86] do not have obligations or rights under treaties without their express consent.[87] Rules in a treaty can bind third states only when they become part of international custom.[88]

It would appear that by including the Security Council option the framers have created a paradox. As a treaty, the obligations in the Rome Statute bind its parties only, whereas Security Council action under Chapter VII binds all UN member states. When the Security Council refers a case under Chapter VII, states not party to the Rome Statute, nor accepting the ICC's jurisdiction, may find that they have to accept its jurisdiction because they are members of the UN. It would appear that this provision violates the Treaty Convention as third states will find themselves having to accept treaty obligations for a treaty they have not ratified. However, their obligation stems from the Security Council resolution rather than the Rome Statute. Nonetheless states will be placed in a difficult situation and just how this problem will be resolved is open to question. Perhaps if all UN member states ratified the Rome Statute, it need not become a problem.

The International Criminal Court: Strengths and Weaknesses

Primacy over National Judicial Authorities

The Rome Statute adhered to the draft's vision of an ICC complementary to national systems. As a result states have the first opportunity to investigate and prosecute a suspect. Cases will only be admissible if a state with jurisdiction is genuinely unwilling or unable to investigate or to prosecute.[89] The ICC will not have simultaneous jurisdiction with national courts. In other words it will not commence proceedings where a national court is also taking action. Nor will it

---

[82] Brownlie, *Principles of Public International Law* (1990), p. 694.

[83] *Ibid.*

[84] Vienna Convention on the Law of Treaties 1969, Article 2(1)(a). (Hereinafter Treaty Convention) (1155 UNTS 331).

[85] Treaty Convention, Article (2)(1)(g), *ibid.*

[86] Treaty Convention, Article 2(1)(h), *ibid.*

[87] Treaty Convention, Article 34, *ibid.* Article 35 provides for obligations for third states where the parties to the treaty intended its provisions to be a means of establishing the obligation and the third party expressly accepts the obligation.

[88] Treaty Convention, Article 38, *ibid.*

[89] Rome Statute, Article 17. A case can also be held inadmissible where it is deemed that it lacks gravity to justify action by the Court: Article 17(1)(d).

have primacy over national courts. Thus where a national court is proceeding against an individual, the ICC will not be able to compel the national court to cease proceedings and hand over the suspect. In the Preamble, the Rome Statute reminds states: that it is their duty to exercise their criminal jurisdiction over those responsible for international crimes,[90] emphasising that the ICC will be complementary to national criminal jurisdictions.[91]

The Ad Hoc Tribunals and Primacy In contrast to the ICC, the Ad Hoc Tribunals do not adhere to the complementary position. Notably, both Nuremberg and Tokyo as forerunners had primacy as they were imposed upon the states in question. Germany and Japan were both occupied by the victorious Allied forces after the war ended. Having set up international tribunals it would have been problematic for the Allies if their only function were to act as a last resort, picking up where either Germany or Japan failed to prosecute. The two post-Second World War tribunals were a spontaneous reaction to an immediate and compelling situation. Much can be said about the similarity between those post-Second World War events and the circumstances after the Balkan war of the late 20th century. The intense conflict in the former Yugoslavia and then in Rwanda both required immediate reaction. It must have been with this immediacy in mind that the framers of the Ad Hoc Tribunal's statutes gave them primacy over national jurisdictions. Arguably, this immediacy was a reflection of the lack of a functioning impartial domestic system. The Ad Hoc Tribunals have concurrent jurisdiction with national courts but they have primacy over them.

Thus the ICTY statute states that:

> The International Tribunal shall have primacy over national courts. At any stage of the procedure, the International Tribunal may formally request national courts to defer to the competence of the International Tribunal in accordance with the present Statute and the Rules of Procedure and Evidence.[92]

The ICTR's statute states:

> The International Tribunal for Rwanda shall have primacy over national courts of all States. At any stage of the procedure, the International Tribunal for Rwanda may formally request national courts to defer its competence in accordance with the present Statute and the Rules of Procedure and Evidence of the International Tribunal for Rwanda.[93]

National legal systems are obliged at any time to defer competence to the Ad Hoc Tribunals. Hence where a national court is in the process of adjudicating

---

[90] Rome Statute, Preamble para. 6.

[91] Rome Statute, Preamble para. 10.

[92] ICTY Statute, Article 9(2). The Statute provides for concurrent jurisdiction with the tribunal having primacy.

[93] Article 8(2) ICTR Statute annexed to SC Res. 955 (1995) UN Doc S/Res/955.

The International Criminal Court 21

on a particular case that an Ad Hoc Tribunal has an interest in, and the tribunal signals its interest in the person concerned, the national court will be obliged to surrender its suspect to the tribunal. The ICTY, with regard to the *Tadic Case*, was able to request a state to put off a future trial in order to hand over the accused. Tadic was arrested in Germany on 13 February 1994 and transferred to the ICTY on 24 April 1995.[94] He was just one of over 350,000 Balkan refugees that Germany took in after the conflict,[95] and was arrested after another refugee recognized him and accused him of having committed offences that are also crimes under German law.[96] Germany has jurisdiction over a selection of acts perpetrated abroad that violate certain international legal norms. These include, *inter alia*, the prohibition of genocide.[97] Upon his arrest by German authorities, the ICTY issued a formal request to Germany on 8 November 1994 to defer its planned prosecution in order to hand him over to the tribunal. Legislation to enable his transfer was enacted by Germany and he was transferred to The Hague in 1995. Nonetheless, Germany had been willing and was able to pursue the case against Tadic. In this situation the ICC would have had to declare the case inadmissible.

The ICTY's primacy over national legal systems was challenged in the *Tadic Case*, where it was argued by the defence team that primacy has no basis in international law.[98] They argued that the national courts of Bosnia and Herzegovina, or alternatively the Bosnian Serb Republic, had primary jurisdiction. The Trial Chamber, in disregarding this challenge to the tribunal's primacy, acknowledged that the issue involved state sovereignty. Tadic being an individual could not, therefore, raise the issue of primacy.[99] The Appeal Chamber disagreed:

> Whatever the situation in domestic litigation, the traditional doctrine upheld and acted upon by the Trial Chamber is not reconcilable, in this International Tribunal, with the view that an accused, being entitled to a full defence, cannot be deprived of a plea so intimately connected with, and grounded in, international law as a defence based on the violation of State sovereignty. To bar an accused from raising such a plea is tantamount to deciding that, in this day and age, an international court could not, in a criminal matter where liberty of an accused is at stake, examine a plea

---

[94] www.un.org/icty/glance/tadic.

[95] William Walsh, M. 'A Tribunal in a Time of Atrocities' *L.A. Times* 30 August 1995.

[96] German Penal Code, www.redress.org/annex.html.

[97] s6 German Penal Code, *ibid*.

[98] The Trial Chamber regarded the issue as being that of sovereignty. It referred to *Attorney-General of the Government of Israel v. Eichmann* (1961) *36 ILR 5* (hereinafter *Eichmann Case*) in deciding that the accused not being a state, he could not enter a plea that the sovereignty of a state had been violated as a result of the primacy given to an international tribunal over national ones. *Tadic Jurisdiction Challenge (Appeal) Case*, paras. 41, 52. In the *Eichmann Case* the Israeli Supreme Court reaffirmed the Trial decision that the 'right to plead violation of the sovereignty of a State is the exclusive right of that State. Only a sovereign State may raise the plea or waive it, and the accused has no right to take over the rights of that State'. Israeli Supreme Court Judgment (1962) *36 ILR 27, Eichmann Case*, p. 62.

[99] *Ibid*.

22 *Immunity and International Criminal Law*

> raising the issue of violation of State sovereignty. Such startling conclusion would imply a contradiction in terms which this Chamber feels it is its duty to refute and lay to rest.[100]

The Appeal Chamber concluded, however, that although it recognized that the accused has the right to plead state sovereignty, it does not mean that his plea must be favourably received.[101]

The basis upon which the plea was dismissed was first mentioned at the trial stage, where the Trial Chamber emphasized that the 'sovereign rights of states cannot and should not take precedence over the right of the international community to act appropriately' when dealing with crimes that are 'universal in nature' and 'transcend the interest of any one state'.[102] Consequently, sovereignty of a particular state cannot be allowed to interfere with an international tribunal properly constituted to try those accused of having committed international crimes on behalf of the international community.[103] At the appeal it was decided that the tribunal 'being empowered and mandated' to 'deal with trans-boundary matters' or issues, although domestic in nature, affecting 'international peace and security', it would be 'a travesty of law and a betrayal of the universal need for justice' if the concept of state sovereignty is 'allowed to be raised successfully against human rights'.[104] 'Borders should not be considered as a shield against the reach of the law and as a protection for those who trample underfoot the most elementary rights of humanity.'[105] In addition the Appeal Chamber stated that:

> when an international tribunal such as the present one is created, it must be endowed with primacy over national courts. Otherwise, human nature being what it is, there would be a perennial danger of international crimes being characterised as "ordinary crimes", or proceedings being "designed to shield the accused", or cases not being diligently prosecuted. If not effectively countered by the principle of primacy, any one of these stratagems might be used to defeat the very purpose of the creation of an international criminal jurisdiction, to the benefit of the very people whom it was designed to prosecute.[106]

For these reasons, the Appeal Chamber was of the opinion that the principle of primacy of the ICTY over national courts must be affirmed and dismissed the plea of state sovereignty.[107]

---

[100] *Tadic Jurisdiction Challenge (Appeal Case)*, para. 55.

[101] *Ibid*, para. 56.

[102] *Tadic Jurisdiction* Challenge *(Trial Chamber)*, para. 42.

[103] *Ibid*.

[104] *Ibid*, para. 58.

[105] *Ibid*.

[106] *Ibid*. Under Article 10 (2)(a) and (b) of the ICTY Statute, persons tried at the national level may then be tried at the Tribunal only if the crimes tried at the domestic level were ordinary crimes, or the domestic procedure was not impartial or independent, or sought to shield the accused or was not diligently prosecuted.

[107] *Tadic Jurisdiction Challenge (Appeal Case)*, para. 58.

The Trial and Appeal Chambers' view, that the crimes which international tribunals are created to try are of such importance that a state's sovereignty cannot and should not interfere with the administration of international justice, is very perceptive. The crimes which the ICC has jurisdiction over are crimes that are 'invariably committed by or with the connivance of a national state, which can hardly be expected to try itself'.[108] Primacy is, therefore, necessary to ensure that international crimes transcend states' interests. It is therefore unfortunate that the ICC has not been given primacy over national courts.

Primacy Versus Complementarity As a minimum the ICC could have been given the capacity to determine when it should have priority.[109] States should have considered this as a compromise between the need to have a powerful court and their need for it to be complementary to national jurisdictions. Undoubtedly, state representatives at the Diplomatic Conference conveyed their desire for a powerful court. Delegates expressed the desire for an 'effective',[110] 'just and fair'[111] court that is 'impartial',[112] 'independent'[113] and 'free from political interference'.[114] If the ICC is to fulfil all these requirements it is suggested that it should have been given primacy. However, it was clear during the conference that states equally wanted an international court that would be complementary to their national legal systems. In support of the complementarity principle the Danish considered it vital, and the Maltese thought it a pivotal point of the court's jurisdiction.[115] According to Haiti and Yemen the ICC must be complementary to national penal jurisdictions.[116] Iraq stated that the statute must contain an acceptable balance between national and international institutions through the principle of complementarity.[117]

States appear to want a powerful judicial organ that is complementary to their judicial systems. Yet it does not appear possible for both elements to coexist. It is questionable just how effective, impartial, fair, just, independent and free from political interference the ICC will be when it will be hampered by the cumbersome admissibility process. This procedure involves the ICC taking into account any

---

[108] Ferencz, 'International Criminal Courts: The Legacy of Nuremberg', *op cit*, p. 227.

[109] *Ibid.*

[110] W. Sadi (Jordan), J. Prlic (Bosnia and Herzegovina), D. Opertii Badan (Uruguay), M. Al Badri (Yemen), F. Jensen (Denmark), C. Agius (Malta), M. Kleopas (Cyprus), V. Kirabokyamaria (Uganda), www.un.org/icc/pressre/lrom15.htm.

[111] J. Prlic (Bosnia and Herzegovina), *ibid.*

[112] J. Dorneval (Haiti), D. Opertii Badan (Uruguay), *ibid.*

[113] A. De Abreu (Angola), T. Sinunguruza (Burundi), P. Nze (Congo), M. Kleopas (Cyprus), C. Larrea (Ecuador), Y. Al-Admi (Iraq), W. Sadi (Jordan), V. Kirabokyamaria (Uganda), M. Al Badri (Yemen), *ibid.*

[114] C. Agius (Malta), C. Larrea (Ecuador), *ibid.*

[115] *Ibid.*

[116] According to Yemen: 'The Court must be created on the principle of complementarity. It must act in cases where national courts are unable to do so', *ibid.*

[117] *Ibid.*

investigations being carried out by, or prosecutions taking place in, a state that has jurisdiction over it. Where a case has been investigated and the state in question has decided not to prosecute, the case will not be admissible to the ICC, unless there is unwillingness or inability on the state's part to genuinely prosecute.[118]

In order to determine that a state is unwilling to pursue the case in question, the ICC will examine whether or not there is an attempt to shield the person in question.[119] The ICC may also consider a situation where there is a prolonged delay in deliberating a case so as to render such delay inconsistent with the intent to bring the person in question to justice, or where proceedings conducted were not independent or impartial. In both situations the ICC may conclude that the state in question is unwilling and declare the case admissible.[120] But just how it will come to its decision is not made clear. According to Article 17, the court will be guided in making these determinations by 'principles of due process recognized by international law'. But what does this phrase mean? Schabas notes that this expression suggests 'an assessment of the quality of justice from the standpoint of procedural and perhaps even substantive fairness'.[121] According to the ICC's Rules of Procedure and Evidence, the state in question may bring to the court information showing that its courts meet internationally recognized norms and standards for the independent and impartial prosecution of similar conduct.[122]

The ICC will also have to ascertain if a case is admissible due to a state's inability to proceed. In order to do so it will have to consider whether, due to a total or substantial collapse or unavailability of its national judicial system, a state is unable to obtain the accused or the necessary evidence and testimony or otherwise be unable to carry out its proceedings.[123] Once again, just how the ICC will make this determination is not clear. Furthermore, the Rome Statute makes no provisions for admissibility where a state is unable to obtain the accused or necessary evidence because the accused is immune from its jurisdiction.

As noted in the introduction, states have the power to lay down the law and to enforce the laws within their territories. The power to proscribe law is called prescriptive jurisdiction and the power to enforce such laws is referred to as enforcement jurisdiction. According to Malanczuk, states have through their courts adjudicative jurisdiction, the power to adjudicate over cases.[124] In a situation where a crime is committed in state A and the accused flees to state B, state A has prescriptive and adjudicative jurisdiction whereas state B has enforcement jurisdiction that is custodial. In order for state A to adjudicate, under its criminal jurisdiction, state B must make use of its enforcement jurisdiction.[125] Adjudicative

---

[118] Rome Statute, Article 17(1)(d).

[119] Rome Statute, Article 17(2)(a).

[120] Rome Statute, Article 17(2)(b) and (c).

[121] Schabas, *An Introduction to the International Criminal Court* (2001), p. 68.

[122] Rule 51 Finalized Draft Text of the Rules of Procedure and Evidence PCNICC/2000/1/Add.1 (hereinafter ICC Rules of Procedure) www.icc-cpi.int.

[123] Rome Statute, Article 17(3).

[124] Malanczuk, *Akehurst's Modern Introduction to International Law, op cit*, p. 109.

[125] *Ibid.*

and prescription jurisdiction cannot operate legitimately without custodial enforcement jurisdiction, which requires the physical presence of the accused. Trials in absentia are contrary to the International Covenant on Civil and Political Rights' requirement that a suspect is entitled to be tried in his presence in order to defend himself in person.[126]

Once the situation is referred to the ICC, the prosecutor must notify all state parties and those states which would normally exercise jurisdiction.[127] The prosecutor must then wait a month to hear from the states in question. Upon hearing from these states, he is to wait a further six months before he can review their actions.[128] During the month-long wait the prosecutor will have deferred the case to the state with jurisdiction and will continue to do so unless there is unwillingness or inability to act on the part of the state after the six months. It is not clear which state with jurisdiction will qualify for the admissibility test. It is simply stated that a case will be inadmissible where a state with jurisdiction has investigated and prosecuted the case in question. The lack of clarity as to the type of jurisdiction required creates two main problems that challenge the ICC's objective of being a deterrent. The first relates to the number of states that can lay claim to jurisdiction over a particular crime. Using the scenario mentioned above, the prosecutor in that setting would have had to notify state A and B as they both have jurisdiction. However, if a national of state C was injured or killed during the commission of the crime, the prosecutor will also have to notify that state. If the accused is a national of state D, he is required to notify that state as well.[129]

Neither the relevant articles nor applicable rules make it apparent if more than one state can claim such a deferral.[130] Article 18(3) simple refers to the prosecutor's deferral to *a state*. Consequently more than one state can prevent admissibility for a given situation. The prosecutor will then perhaps have to sift through each potential individual claim of jurisdiction. How he will decide as to which state has the right to jurisdiction is uncertain. Whichever method he employs and whatever the outcome, the states that he thinks have a better claim must be notified. If more than one state is notified, for example A and B, each can then make a request to have the case deferred to them. The combined wait for prosecutory review for these two states could be 12 months. This is enough time for witnesses to be intimidated and evidence to disappear.

The second problem centres on the ICC's capacity to effect individual accountability. Continuing with our case scenario, state A as the state in whose territory the act was committed can investigate and proceed against the accused who is corporeally present in state B. Putting aside the fact that state A's action may fall foul of the ICCPR if there is a trial in absentia, the case may be deemed

---

[126] International Covenant on Civil and Political Rights 1966, (999 UNTS 171) (hereinafter the ICCPR), Article 14 (3)(d).

[127] Rome Statute, Article 18 (1).

[128] Rome Statute, Article 18 (2).

[129] It is assumed that all states in the scenario have prescriptive jurisdiction over the offence. The basis upon which states lay claim to a crime is discussed in further detail in Chapter 3.

[130] Rome Statute, Articles on admissibility: 17,18 and 19, Rules: 51-62.

inadmissible to the ICC if there is only an investigation. As the relevant provision mentions investigation or prosecution, it would appear that states are not required to carry out both for ICC admissibility purposes. As a result, although the case has been pursued by a state with jurisdiction, state A, it is possible that the accused will never stand trial and the case will be inadmissible to the ICC. If the custodial state does not act he will remain free.

The current position under the Rome Statute leads one to conclude that if a country with prescriptive jurisdiction investigates or proceeds against someone who is corporeally present elsewhere the case would be inadmissible to the ICC. However, if the ICC aims to act as a powerful deterrent the jurisdiction required must be custodial enforcement jurisdiction. A case should be deemed admissible only where a state with custodial enforcement jurisdiction is unable or unwilling to proceed. It seems logical that if a state with custodial enforcement jurisdiction proceeds, inasmuch as the accused will have to face up to his responsibility, the ICC's objective will be met. He or she will live through the investigation and possible trial, knowing that the process is a direct reaction to his or her conduct. As a result, where a custodial state is unable or unwilling to investigate or proceed against an individual, the case should be admissible to the ICC.

The ICC's lack of primacy will result in a court that is cumbersome, lacking the effectiveness and efficiency of the Ad Hoc Tribunals. Perhaps by confining a state's jurisdiction for admissibility purposes to custodial jurisdiction it can try and compensate for its lack of primacy. If custodial enforcement jurisdiction is the only jurisdiction applicable, the number of states capable of rendering a case admissible in a given scenario is whittled down. Referring back to the situation mentioned above, where a suspect escapes the jurisdiction of state A where he committed a crime to the jurisdiction of state B: the ICC should concentrate on state B where the suspect is corporeally present. Admissibility based on state B's inability or unwillingness to proceed rather than that of state A appears more logical. Thus by narrowing down the range of states capable of rendering a case admissible it is hoped that the process of admissibility will be more efficient and effective. By directing its attention to state B, the ICC may be able to put pressure on it to take action.[131]

A state must be made aware that where a suspect is in its territory the ICC will divert its attention to it to encourage it to act. That state will know that its national legal authorities will come under scrutiny as the ICC decides if the case is admissible. But in order to have such effect the ICC will have to have extensive investigatory powers. Although supporting the ICC's lack of primacy, Georgia warned during the Diplomatic Conference that the ICC 'should not be reduced to a residual mechanism for dispensing justice'.[132] Georgia was concerned that if the court is not 'truly empowered to step in where national systems prove incapable or unwilling to punish the perpetrators of serious crimes, its establishment will be of

---

[131] This line of argument does not absolve a state with prescriptive jurisdiction from its obligation under universal jurisdiction to investigate.

[132] www.un.org/icc/pressrel/lrom.htm.

limited value'.[133] Bearing in mind the court's lack of primacy, if it is to be of some consequence, it must have persuasive and flexible powers of operation.

Operational Powers

The ICC's operational powers are outlined in its Rules of Procedure. These rules must empower the court to act decisively and resourcefully if it is to have any influence on international justice. The Ad Hoc Tribunals rely on rules of evidence and procedure that have been adopted by their judges, amended as the need arises.[134] The rules are, therefore, flexible in order to facilitate the work of the tribunals. They have been sufficiently adaptable to enable the tribunal to investigate within a state's territory and to issue binding orders to states.

The Power to Conduct Investigations within a State's Territory According to the Ad Hoc Tribunals' statutes:

> The Prosecutor shall have the power to question suspects, victims and witnesses, to collect evidence and to conduct *on-site investigations*. In carrying out these tasks, the Prosecutor may, as appropriate, seek the assistance of the State authorities concerned.[135]

Their rules state that in the conduct of an investigation, the Prosecutor may:

> (ii) summon and question suspects, victims and witnesses and record their statements, collect evidence and conduct *on-site investigations*;[136]

The prosecutor for the Ad Hoc Tribunals is thus empowered to conduct his investigation within the territory of a state. It appears that both the statute and the rules do not require state permission and cooperation for on-site investigations.

The ICC's prosecutor, on the other hand, must have state cooperation to conduct his enquiries and collect evidence on state territory.[137] State parties are obliged to cooperate fully with the court in its investigations and prosecutions of crimes within the court's jurisdiction.[138] Investigations can be conducted on a state's territory without its cooperation only where the Trial Chamber has ascertained that the state is 'unable to execute a request for cooperation due to unavailability of any authority or any component of its judicial system competent to execute the request for cooperation'.[139] For that reason the ICC Rules empower

---

[133] *Ibid.*

[134] Cassese 'The Statute of the International Criminal Court: Some Preliminary Reflections' (1999) *10 EJIL 144, 165.*

[135] ICTY Statute, Article 18(2), ICTR Statute, Article 17(2). Italics not in statute.

[136] ICTY and ICTR Rules, Rule 39(ii). Italics not in statute.

[137] Rome Statute, Article 54(2)(a).

[138] Rome Statute, Article 86, Part 9.

[139] Rome Statute Article 57(3) (d), *ibid.*

28   *Immunity and International Criminal Law*

the pre-Trial Chamber to issue an order specifying procedures to be followed in carrying out the collection of evidence.[140] According to Schabas these provisions will enable the prosecutor to 'undertake specific investigative steps in the territory of a State *without* having previously obtained its consent and cooperation'.[141] The article is of limited value however as it constrains the Trial Chamber to situations where there is a lack of judicial component capable of acting. However, the orders that the Trial Chamber will be able to issue might not be binding, nor compel a state to cooperate if the prosecutor seeks to conduct his investigation on its territory, even though it is party to the statute.

The Power to Issue Binding Orders Ultimately the question remains: can the ICC issue binding orders? Are its rules capable of empowering its chambers to issue obligatory orders? The ICTY has determined that its operational powers are flexible enough to enable it to issue binding orders to states to produce documents.[142] The Ad Hoc Tribunal's rules have a broad provision covering the issuing of, *inter alia*, orders, warrants and subpoenas. The relevant rule states that:

> At the request of either party or *proprio motu*, a Judge or Trial Chamber may issue such orders, summonses, subpoenas, warrants and transfer orders as may be necessary for the purposes of an investigation or for the preparation or conduct of the trial. [143]

The ICTY's Appeal Chamber in the *Prosecutor v. Blaskic, Decision on the Objection of the Republic of Croatia to the Issuance of Subpoenae Duces*, confirmed that the tribunal had the power to issue binding orders to states.[144] Orders which the tribunal issues to states are binding because states are obliged to lend cooperation and judicial assistance to the tribunal under Article 29 of the statute and Security Council Resolution 827 of 1993.[145] According to the Appeal Chamber, the Security Council is a body entrusted with the primary responsibility for maintaining international peace and security, and has thus solemnly enjoined all

---

[140] ICC Rules, Rule 115, *op cit.*

[141] Schabas, *An Introduction to the International Criminal Court, op cit*, p.104.

[142] ICTY Rules, Rule 54 *bis*.

[143] ICTY and ICTR Rules, Rule 54.

[144] *Prosecutor v. Blaskic* (IT-54-14) *Decision on the Objection of the Republic of Croatia to the Issuance of Subpoenae Duces*, (1997) para. 23. (Hereinafter the *Blaskic Croatian Subpoena Decision*) www.un.org/icty.
Prosecutor v. Blaskic, Judgement on the Request of the Republic of Croatia for Review of the Decision of the Trial Chamber II of 18 July 1997, (29 October 1997) (hereinafter *Blaskic Croatian Subpeona Decision (Appeal)*. The Appeal Chamber's verdict maintains that orders to state officials are not to be addressed to them personally, rather they are to be addressed to the state concerned. It is then up to the state to identify the person responsible. Para. 44.

[145] ICTY Statute, Cooperation and Judicial Assistance, SC Res. 827, Article 29. See: Warbrick, 'Co-Operation with the International Criminal Tribunal for Yugoslavia' (1996) *45 ICLQ 947.*

member states to comply with orders and requests of the ICTY.[146] This obligation is *erga omnes partes* and every member state of the UN has a legal interest in fulfilling the obligation to cooperate under Article 29.[147] As mentioned above, UN member states are obliged to accept and carry out the decisions of the Security Council.

Although lacking a comparable broad rule, the ICC's Rome Statute does provide the Trial Chamber with the power to order 'the production of evidence in addition to that already collected prior to the trial or presented during the trial by the parties'.[148] It can require the 'attendance and testimony of witnesses and production of documents and other evidence by obtaining, if necessary the assistance' of states.[149] Where there is a lack of state assistance the prosecutor may seek authorization from the Trial Chamber to issue 'orders and warrants as may be required for the purposes of an investigation'.[150]

The orders the ICC will be capable of issuing to states will not be binding in the same way, unless the case was a referral from the Security Council. Where the Security Council makes a referral, the binding nature of its action under Chapter VII will compel member states to comply. In ordinary cases, where a state fails to comply with a request to cooperate by the court, thus preventing it from exercising its functions and powers, the ICC may make a finding to that effect and refer the matter to the Assembly of States Parties.[151] Where the Security Council initiates the case, the matter will be referred back to it.

Notwithstanding the ICC's lack of express coercive powers to bind states that the Ad Hoc Tribunals have, it can, perhaps, attempt to extend its powers by implication.

The Powers of Arrest and Surrender The Ad Hoc Tribunal's operational powers include the capacity to issue indictments against citizens of sovereign states.[152] They can seek the arrest, detention and the surrender or transfer of suspects.[153] States are obliged to cooperate with arrest warrants,[154] but where they fail to execute their arrest warrants the matter is then referred to the Security Council for

---

[146] *Ibid.*

[147] The equivalent article in the ICTR's Statute is 28. See: ICTR Trial Chamber II Decision on the Defence Motion seeking a Request for Cooperation and Judicial Assistance from States Pursuant to Article 28 of the Statute, *Proscutor v. Kajelijeli Case* No. ICTR-98-44A-T. *Ibid.*

[148] Rome Statute, Article 64(6) (d), *op cit.*

[149] Rome Statute, Article 64(6)(b), *ibid.*

[150] Rome Statute, Article 54(20)(b) and 57(3)(a), *op cit.*

[151] Rome Statute, Article 87(7), *op cit.*

[152] ICTY and ICTR Rules, Rules on indictment: 47-53.

[153] ICTY and ICTR Rules, Rules on arrest 55-9. See: *Prosecutor v. Musabyimana Case* (ICTR-2001-62-I) *Warrant of Arrest and Order for Transfer and Detention,* www.un.org/icty.

[154] ICTY and ICTR Rules, Rule 56.

action.[155] The fact that the citizen in question is a head of state or government, or high-ranking government official, has not prevented the Ad Hoc Tribunals from issuing indictments.[156] In 1999 the ICTY indicted a sitting head of state.[157] Slobadan Milosevic was indicted when he was still the head of state of Yugoslavia, but was transferred to the tribunal after his removal from office.

The Rome Statute does not provide for indictments, but the pre-Trial Chamber can at any time after the initiation of an investigation issue a warrant of arrest at the behest of the prosecutor.[158] A request for the arrest and surrender of the person is then transmitted to the state on the territory of which that person may be found, and the court shall request the cooperation of that state in the arrest and surrender of such person.[159] The state is obliged to comply with the requests in accordance with national laws,[160] and must immediately inform the registrar of the court when the person sought is available for surrender.[161] The court is to take measures to ensure that it is informed of the arrest and detention of the suspect.[162]

Like the Ad Hoc Tribunals the ICC does not acknowledge immunities for heads of state or government. According to the Rome Statute:

> Immunities or special procedural rules which may attach to the official capacity of a person, whether under national or international law, shall not bar the Court from exercising its jurisdiction over such person.[163]

This is contrary to Schabas' conclusion that the court 'is prevented from exercising its jurisdiction in the case of defendants who are immune to prosecution'.[164] The court will find that it may not be able to apprehend an individual with immunity, but that does not mean that it cannot exercise its jurisdiction over him. As domestic judicial authorities are required to grant immunity for criminal cases to certain individuals, the ICC will be unable to proceed with a demand for surrender, where such a request will make the requested state act inconsistently with its obligations under national and international law with respect to the state or diplomatic immunity of another state.[165] The ICC requires a waiver from that third state.[166] A head of state or government or diplomat's immunity in a foreign state is discussed in Chapter 5 below. Suffice to say at this point that a state with custodial enforcement jurisdiction will be unable to apprehend such persons in order to

---

[155] ICTY Rules, Rule 61. ICTR Rules, Rule 59 and 61.

[156] ICTY Statute, Article 7(2). ICTR Statute, Article 6(2).

[157] Initial Indictment 24 May 1999. www.un.org/icty.

[158] Rome Statute, Article 58(1).

[159] The custodian state. Rome Statute, Article 89 (1).

[160] *Ibid.*

[161] ICC Rules, Rule 184(1).

[162] ICC Rules, Rule 117.

[163] Rome Statute, Article 27.

[164] Schabas, *An Introduction to the International Criminal Court, op cit*, p. 64.

[165] Rome Statute, Article 98.

[166] *Ibid.*

The International Criminal Court 31

surrender them to the ICC unless its courts can make determinations as to the scope of the individual's immunity. Primarily they will have to ascertain if the norms prohibiting the crimes that the ICC has jurisdiction over are superior to the norms regulating immunities.

At variance with the ICC's position, there is nothing in their statutes that purports to prevent the Ad Hoc Tribunals from requesting the arrest and transfer of a head of state or government, or high-ranking state official, from his own state, or indeed a third state. There is no equivalent of the Rome Statute's Article 98 in either the ICTY or the ICTR's statutes. It is arguable that because they are able to issue an international arrest warrant,[167] they can request the transfer of heads of state in host countries when they travel outside their countries. Where a state refuses or fails to cooperate with an arrest warrant, the tribunals can refer the matter to the Security Council.[168]

Extending Operational Powers by Implication

The lack of flexible operational powers could prevent the ICC from attempting to subpoena state governments, as the ICTY attempted to do in 1997.[169] Although the ICTY has the power to subpoena individuals, its capacity to subpoena states and their officials is not expressly provided for in either its statute or its rules. However, in *Prosecutor v. Blaskic* it ordered a *subpoena duces tecum* against the Croatian Government and its defence minister that was challenged by the Croatian Government.[170] In its decision regarding this objection, the Trial Chamber was of the opinion that the power to issue subpoenas against governments and their officials could be implied.[171] Its conclusion was based on the assumption that Security Council subsidiary judicial organs must have a certain degree of independence to enable them to fulfil their functions properly.[172] As 'a subsidiary organ of a judicial nature, ... fundamental prerequisite for its fair and effective

---

[167] ICTY and ICTR Rules, Rule 61 (D).

[168] ICTY and ICTR Rules, Rule 61 (E). See: Sarooshi, 'The Statute of the International Criminal Court' (1999) *48 ICLQ 387*. The Security Council passed two resolutions in 1992 with regard to Libya's refusal to hand over its nationals who were suspects in the Lockerbie Pan Am bombing, in which it requested Libya to provide a full and effective response to the UK and USA's requests. Libya took its case to the ICJ. (1992) *ICJ Rep. 3*.

[169] The ICTY Trial Chamber ordered Bosnia and Herzegovina to produce documents that were deemed necessary for reaching the truth. The order was based on the Tribunal's Statute's Article 29 and Rule 54. Bosnia and Herzegovina was given a deadline within which it had to submit the documents in question. *Prosecutor v. Blaskic, Trial Chamber Decision on the Prosecutor's Request for the Issuance of a Binding Order to Bosnia and Herzegovina for the Production of Documents 18 July 1998.* (Hereinafter *Blaskic Bosnia Case.*)

[170] *Subpeona duces tecums* are issued to compel those mentioned to appear in person to hand over documents to the court.

[171] *Blaskic Croatian Subpoena Decision*, paras. 18-23.

[172] Principle of implied powers and effectiveness must relate to the UN Charter's Article 2(1): sovereign equality and Article 2(2): domestic jurisdiction of states. *Ibid.*

32   *Immunity and International Criminal Law*

functioning is its capacity to act autonomously'.[173] The Trial Chamber was in fact attempting to extend the tribunal's powers by implication.

In the *Reparation for Injuries Suffered in the Service of the United Nations Case (Reparations Case)* in 1949, the ICJ held that 'the rights and duties of an entity such as an Organization must depend upon its purpose and functions as specified or implied in its constituent documents and developed in practice'.[174] Further, in reference to the UN, the ICJ believed that under international law, it 'must be deemed to have powers, which though not expressly provided for in the Charter, are conferred upon it by necessary implication as being essential to the performance of its duties.'[175]

Brownlie notes that in practice the reference to implied powers might be linked to a principle of institutional effectiveness.[176] When faced with ambiguous provisions as to the binding nature of its provisional measures in the *Germany v. USA (LaGrand Case)*,[177] the ICJ referred to the object and purpose of the court's statute in order to reach its decision that such orders are binding:[178]

> The context in which Article 41 has to be seen within the Statute is to prevent the Court from being hampered in the exercise of its functions because the respective rights of the parties to a dispute before the Court are not preserved. It follows from the object and purpose of the Statute, as well as from the terms of Article 41 when read in their context, that the power to indicate provisional measures entails that such measures should be binding, inasmuch as the power in question is based on the necessity, when the circumstances call for it, to safeguard, and to avoid prejudice to, the rights of the parties as determined by the final judgment of the Court. The contention that provisional measures indicated under Article 41 might not be binding would be contrary to the object and purpose of that Article.[179]

However, the ICTY's Appeal Chamber disagreed with the Trial Chamber on this issue of its implied powers to issue a subpoena to a state.[180] It was of the

---

[173] *Blaskic Croatian Subpoena Decisions*, para. 23.

[174] *Reparation for Injuries Suffered in the Service of the United Nations Case* (1949) ICJ Reps. 174, 180.

[175] *Ibid.*

[176] Brownlie, *Principles of Public International Law, op cit*, p. 690.

[177] *Germany v. USA (LaGrand Case)* 27 June 2001 www.icj.cij.org. The case involved two brothers, Karl and Walter LaGrand, who were German nationals at the time of their conviction in the USA for attempted armed robbery and murder. They were denied their consular rights and the German Government was alerted some time later. After Karl was executed, Germany was able to get a Provisional Order under Article 41 of the ICJ's Statute requesting the USA, *inter alia*, to take all measures at its disposal to ensure that Walter LaGrand is not executed pending the final decision in these proceedings, and inform the court of all the measures which it has taken in implementation of this order. However, Walter was still executed.

[178] *Ibid*, para. 102, 109, 110.

[179] *Ibid*, para. 102.

[180] *Blaskic Croatian Subpoena Decisions (Appeal)*, www.un.org/icty.

opinion that the capacity to give such orders cannot be regarded as inherent in the tribunal's function, primarily because the tribunal does not 'possess the power to take enforcement measures against States'.[181] According to the Appeal Chamber if the drafters had wanted it to have such powers they would have expressly provided for it.[182] The Appeal Chamber acknowledged that the penalty attached to a subpoena is penal in nature and that states are not subject to criminal sanctions.[183] Thus subpoenas cannot be applied or addressed by the Ad Hoc Tribunals to states or their officials by implication.[184]

Perhaps the ICC will determine that its powers to issue certain binding orders are not inherent. However, if it is to operate effectively, a time will come when it will have to rely on implication to extend its capacity to act. A particular area where this may occur is with the surrender of suspects.

The Surrender of Suspects Entitled to Immunity

The Ad Hoc Tribunals follow what has been identified as the 'supra-state' model.[185] International tribunals that follow the supra-state model have far-reaching powers over states and individuals and can issue binding orders to states and can enforce compliance.[186] In order to be effective they act autonomously. They can carry out acts not necessarily outlined in their statutes by implication, in order to carry out their function proficiently. Being 'supra-state' they have primacy over national courts.[187] Having primacy they can request a domestic court to halt proceedings in favour of them and request the individual be transferred. The situation is not so for the ICC. It has been deemed to follow the 'intra-state' model.[188] According to this theory tribunals that are intra-state do not have a higher status then state national legal authorities. They cannot force state cooperation, nor can they enforce coercive powers over a state's sovereign territory.[189] In that respect it does not have an elevated position over national legal systems.

As outlined above, the Ad Hoc Tribunals have immense power based on the nature of their establishment, primacy and their capacity to operate. They are

---

[181] *Ibid*, para. 25,

[182] *Ibid*.

[183] *Ibid*.

[184] *Ibid*, para. 38. As for subpoenas to state officials, the Appeal Chamber held that as they act in their official capacity they have functional immunity, hence the tribunal cannot subpoena state officials.

[185] Cassese, 'The Statute of the International Criminal Court', *op cit*, p. 164-165.

[186] *Ibid*.

[187] ICTY Statute, Article 9(2). ICTR Statute, Article 8(2). For both articles: The International Tribunal shall have primacy over national courts. At any stage of the procedure, the International Tribunal may formally request nations courts to defer to the competence of the International Tribunal in accordance with the Rules of Procedure and Evidence of the International Tribunal.

[188] Cassese, 'The Statute of the International Criminal Court', *op cit*, p. 164-165.

[189] *Ibid*.

34 *Immunity and International Criminal Law*

capable of operating in a manner that the ICC will not be able to emulate. Based on this supposition it is possible to say that this weaker system will hinder the ICC in its attempts to apprehend suspects, in particular those with immunities.

The scope of this book is limited to the review of a state's inability or unwillingness to proceed against an individual who ordinarily enjoys immunity. Notwithstanding the general principles of state jurisdiction summarized in the preceding pages, a state has to concede enforcement and adjudicative jurisdiction within its territory to certain individuals who are immune. The extent of the analysis is further restricted to a state's custodial enforcement jurisdiction against a head of state or government and diplomat.

Most states are sensitive to accusations that their heads or senior officials are in any way implicated in the commission of international crimes. This is particularly so where the head enjoys broad-based support as a democratically elected leader. What occurred in Yugoslavia with Milosevic is not common. He was head of state of Yugoslavia during the Balkan wars and was still head when indicted by the ICTY in 1999, but was handed over to the tribunal after a change of government and, accordingly, ceased to hold such office. Had he been the current head of state it would have been most difficult for the ICTY to apprehend him.

Although a civil case, an illustrative example is that of the Israeli Prime Minister in Belgium. On 28 November 2001, a Belgian court of appeal was asked to look at the possibility of claimants pursuing a compensatory claim against Ariel Sharon, the Israeli Prime Minister, for war crimes committed when he was defence minister.[190] It is alleged that he was involved in the massacre of civilians in Sabra and Shatila in Lebanon in 1982 whilst he was defence minister. The Israeli Government vehemently opposed the case and criticized Belgian authorities for allowing the case to continue as far as it did.[191] The Belgian government's response has been interpreted as showing some embarrassment with regards to the whole affair.[192]

In a situation where a head of state or government is being shielded by his state, the ICC may find that the case is admissible, but that it is unable to apprehend the suspect. Few states will be agreeable to handing over a serving head of state or government. It is suggested that the ICC will not be able to exert pressure on the state concerned to hand over their head as the ICTY, a Security Council tribunal, did with Yugoslavia. Rather, the ICC could seek to apprehend

---

[190] Inside Story *The Guardian 28 November 2001*. A case against Sharon was also initiated in the Lebanon for the same charges. See: 'Lebanon Hears Case against Sharon' at www.bbc.co.uk/1/hi/word/middle_east/1817749.stm.

[191] The Israeli Government reaction to the Belgian case against Ariel Sharon: Peres' comments *Jerusalem Post 7 November 2001*.

[192] 'Belgium was somewhat embarrassed recently when Sharon declined to visit the European Union headquarters in Brussels, probably out of concern from either an interrogation or arrest. The Sharon investigation has furthermore hurt Israeli relations with Belgium, which now holds the rotating EU presidency and as such has taken lead of the EU's post-11th of September efforts to push for peace in the Middle East.' Hand, 'The Belgian Follies' *3 December 2001 JMC*, www.enterstageright.com.

him in a foreign state, when he travels outside his country. The host state will have temporary custodial enforcement jurisdiction and it is to this state that the ICC may have to issue a surrender request. Once that state receives a surrender request it will have to make determinations as to the individual's immunity.

Even though an international criminal court exists, domestic legal systems will still have to grapple with the problem of individuals with immunities and the ensuing issues of sovereignty, equality and stable inter-state relations. In order to legally circumvent Article 98 to effect ICC surrender requests so as to breathe life into Article 27, domestic courts will have to strike a balance between the needs of international justice and maintaining stable international relations. In attempting to maintain just such a balance, a domestic court will have to review the situation in three stages. The first stage involves a look at international crimes and the second, an analysis of immunities. The third and last stage involves determining which takes precedence: immunities or international crimes. In doing so it is proposed that a foreign domestic court with temporary custodial enforcement jurisdiction will conclude that it does not have the jurisdiction to arrest and surrender a sitting head of state or government or foreign minister, nor will the courts of a diplomat's receiving state.

Chapter 2

International Crimes

This chapter focuses on the crimes over which the ICC has jurisdiction. The Rome Statute covers four international crimes: aggression, war crimes, crimes against humanity and genocide. The reason why the ICC covers only a limited number of crimes may be explained by, *inter alia*, the differences between two main groups of international crimes: those created by international customary law and those by international treaty.

The two categories of international crimes differ substantively, procedurally and even descriptively. Distinctions are made between the various international crimes without there being a general consensus amongst writers. According to Bassiouni the four ICC crimes of crimes against peace/aggression, genocide, crimes against humanity and war crimes are crimes affecting the peace and security of mankind or crimes which disturb human conscience.[1] For Bassiouni other crimes such as aircraft hijacking, the taking of hostages, trafficking in drugs and the unlawful use of the mail affect only limited international concerns. He asserts that the difference between the two categories lies in the interest to be protected, thus leading to the distinction he makes between 'international crimes *stricto senso*' (crimes involving the threat of peace and security and those that 'shock human conscience') with 'international crimes *largo senso*' (crimes that affect 'a narrower international interest and involve an inter-state element').[2] The causes or effects of international crimes *stricto senso* need not cross borders. For example, the international crime of genocide is most likely to be contained within a state's borders.[3]

Goodwin-Gill makes the distinction between international crimes and serious crimes of international concern,[4] although he notes that the Rome Statute itself uses the two terms interchangeably.[5] Nonetheless he sets apart the ICC

---

[1] Paust, Bassiouni, Scharf, Gurulé, Sadat, Zagaris, and Williams, *International Criminal Law Cases and Materials* (2000) p. 13-14. (Hereinafter Paust, Bassiouni et al.)

[2] *Ibid.* Crimes *largo senso* are also sometimes referred to as transnational crimes causing a confusing overlap with municipal crimes that have inter-state elements.

[3] Transnational crimes are crimes that are not in breach of the laws of nations but are violations of national laws having causes or effects across national borders. Money laundering is a transnational crime. International agreements come into play with transnational crimes with regards to the issues of jurisdiction, extradition and enforcement, among others.

[4] Goodwin-Gill, 'Crime in International Law: Obligations *Erga Omnes* and the Duty to Prosecute' (1999) p. 205.

[5] *Ibid*, footnote 24.

crimes as being international crimes and designates other crimes as serious crimes of international concern.

It is suggested that the distinction could also be made in terms of the legal source of the international crime for example one can distinguish between international crimes that are based on custom and those that are based on treaty. The ICC's four crimes are international customary crimes based on international customary rules. International customary crimes are prohibitive norms that are intended to protect values that the entire world community considers important. They have universal jurisdiction and accord no immunity to those in authority.[6] This is distinct from treaty-based crimes, or Bassiouni's international crimes *largo senso*. International treaty crimes are violations of prohibitive conventions that have not evolved into customary law. Jurisdiction for international treaty crimes is limited to the provisions of the relevant treaty binding states party to it.

There is debate as to which crimes are customary and which are treaty-based. In order to try and resolve this issue, an examination of how customary norms evolve is crucial.

International Customary Crimes

In order to be a international customary crime, the act in question must violate a prohibitive norm of international customary law. International customary norms have been defined as rules built on the general practice of states accepted and observed as law, i.e. from a sense of legal obligation.[7] For a rule to become part of international customary law there has to be constant state practice with states accepting that they have an obligation to act.[8] A single instance cannot establish a customary rule. The ICJ in the *Columbia v. Peru (Asylum Case)* was of the opinion that international custom was 'constant and uniform usage, accepted as law'.[9] In other words, international custom is evidence of a general practice accepted as law,[10] or the 'actual practice and *opinio juris* of States'.[11]

State Practice

Practice need not be for a specific length of time but it must occur for a long enough time to establish a custom. That custom must be applied in a uniform and constant fashion. Complete uniformity between states is not essential as long as

---

[6] Cassese, *International Law* (2000), p. 246.

[7] Meron, *Human Rights and Humanitarian Norms as Customary Law* (1989), p. 3.

[8] *Opinio juris* is also a requirement that is discussed below.

[9] *Columbia v. Peru* (1950) ICJ Reps. 266, 277.

[10] *Nicaragua v. USA (Merits)* (1986) ICJ Reps. 14, 97. (Hereinafter *Nicaragua (Merits) Case.)*

[11] Italics: writer's own. *Libya v. Malta (The Continental Shelf Case)* (1985) ICJ Rep. 13, 29-30, para. 27.

practice is 'extensive and virtually uniform'.[12] Not all states need practice the rule rigorously and consistently provided conduct in general is continuous and that contradictory practice is deemed as a breach of the rule rather than an indication of a new rule.[13] Major inconsistencies in the practice prevent the rule in question from becoming a customary rule.[14] Arguably, therefore, widespread practice contrary to a given norm will prevent it from becoming a customary norm.

Consequently, 'general practice' or 'constant and uniform usage' are the first factors one must look for when determining if a norm is part of custom. Evidence of a state's practice can be deduced from current affairs reports on state action, the work of its legislature and judiciary, pronouncements made by governments through their representatives at the UN, during conferences and to the press. It has been suggested that states' claims and statements are a way in which they communicate their perceptions of the status of international norms, hence they operate in this respect in the same way as physical acts.[15] 'Whether *in abstracto* or with regard to a particular situation, they constitute the raw material out of which may be fashioned rules of international law.'[16] Shaw's conclusion that the formulation that state practice covers any act or statement by a state from which views about customary law may be inferred is substantially correct.[17] Thus what states say and do are both important in establishing practice.

However, it should be a matter of what states say supported by what they do physically. This is important as states can say one thing and do another. In particular, when dealing with prohibitive norms, physically not doing a certain act is undoubtedly of great importance, over and above statements, for the deduction of practice. 'A state can act in only one way at one time, and its unique actions, recorded in history, speak eloquently and decisively.'[18] Thus physical acts must be the decisive element of practice.

Opinio Juris

Opinio juris is the second factor required in the creation of a customary norm. Psychologically, states must feel legally obliged to obey customary norms according to the maxim: *opinio juris sive necessitatis* or *opinio juris* in short.[19] The ICJ, in the *North Sea Continental Shelf Cases*, held that either the states taking action, or other states in a position to react to a given norm, must behave in such a

---

[12] *Federal Republic of Germany v. Denmark, Federal Republic of Germany v. The Netherlands (The North Sea Continental Shelf Case)* (1969) ICJ Reps. 3, 43. The ICJ was looking at a treaty norm becoming part of custom.

[13] *Nicaragua (Merits) Case*, p. 98.

[14] Malanczuk, *Akehurst's Modern Introduction to International Law, op cit*, p. 41-42.

[15] Shaw, *International* Law, *op cit*, p. 66.

[16] *Ibid.*

[17] Shaw quotes Akehurst 'Custom as a Source of International Law' (1974-1975) *47 BYIL 1, ibid.*

[18] D'Amato, *The Concept of Custom in International Law* (1971), p. 51.

[19] Malanczuk, *Akehurst's Modern Introduction to International Law, ibid*, p. 44.

International Crimes

39

way so that their conduct is 'evidence of a belief that this practice is rendered obligatory by the existence of a rule of law requiring it. The need for such belief, i.e. the existence of a subjective element, is implicit in the notion of the *opinio juris sive necessitates*.'[20] By believing that they have a legal duty to act, states turn a usage into custom.[21] The way in which they act or fail to act will help show state *opinio juris* on a matter. However, there is no consensus amongst writers as to how *opinio juris* should be deduced.

States have been saying for a long time that torture is prohibited, yet they practise torture routinely. States have consistently maintained that the prohibition of torture is a customary norm. Garnett has argued that the near unanimous support for the Convention Against Torture and Other Cruel, Inhuman or Degrading Treatment or Punishment is indication of the emergence of custom prohibiting torture.[22] But states have consistently tortured their citizens. According to Amnesty International, each year no less than 100 states will have committed torture by failing to prevent torture in their territories.[23] In 2002 people were reportedly tortured or ill-treated by security forces, police or other state authorities in 106 countries.[24] Going back to 1996 the number never drops below 100.[25]

To counter this problem, Garnett argues that states rarely acknowledge nor admit that torture occurs within their territory but consistently reaffirm their opposition to the practice.[26] Thus, according to him, their continued use of torture is in breach of a customary rule prohibiting the practice, rather than being a challenge to the law itself.[27] He relies on the ICJ's decision in the *Nicaragua (Merits) Case*, where it was held that a customary norm remains in force even if a number of states frequently violate it.[28] Where states justify their acts with reference to exceptions to the rule rather than contesting the rule, they thereby strengthen the rule rather than weakening it.[29] This may be the case for the norm that has already achieved the status of a customary norm.

It is difficult to see just how relevant the ICJ's pronouncement on custom in the *Nicaragua (Merits) Case* is to torture. At the time that the Torture Convention was being drafted, more than half of all states were practising torture. For a norm to become a customary norm there must be state practice. Conduct that is constant and uniform. In his dissenting opinion, Judge Read in the *UK v. Norway (Fisheries*

---

[20] *North Sea Continental Shelf Case*, p. 4.

[21] Shaw, *International* Law, *op cit*, p. 66.

[22] Garnett 'The Defence of State Immunity for Acts of Torture' (1997) *Australian YBIL 97, 102.* Convention Against Torture and Other Cruel, Inhuman or Degrading Treatment or Punishment 1984 (1465 UNTS 85) (hereinafter the Torture Convention).

[23] www.amnesty.org.

[24] Amnesty International Report (2001), Summaries, *ibid*.

[25] See Chart on Torture in Appendix, p. 163.

[26] Garnett 'The Defence of State Immunity for Acts of Torture', *op cit*, p.103.

[27] *Ibid*.

[28] *Nicaragua (Merits) Case*, p. 14.

[29] *Nicaragua (Merits) Case*, *ibid*. Garnett, 'The Defence of State Immunity for Acts of Torture', *op cit*, p. 103.

40   *Immunity and International Criminal Law*

Case), appeared to infer that customary norms cannot be created without enforcement.[30] This is not a widely held view but is most logical with regards to international crimes. At the time that the Torture Convention received near unanimous support, torture as a crime could not have crystallized into a customary norm unless states, not necessarily all, had ceased to commit torture. Reference to torture in this context is of the individual crime rather than crimes perpetrated against the civilian population in a systematic way. Systematic torture was already a international customary crimeas a crime against humanity. The ICJ in the *Nicaragua (Merits) Case* was dealing with a norm that had already so crystallized, hence it was possible to declare that states acting contrary to it do not challenge the norm, which remains in force.

How can *opinio juris* be deduced where the majority of states declare that they are legally bound not to carry out certain acts, but consistently commit such acts? Once again, the unique circumstances regarding torture provide a good illustrative point. As outlined above, more than 100 states commit torture each year. That is well over half the world community. In statements states condemn the act, but in practice they continue to commit acts of torture. It is conceivable, given the publicity that torture has managed to gain over the last decades, that states are aware that they have a legal duty not to commit torture. But *opinio juris* requires their acceptance as to this legal duty. Just how can this acceptance be deduced? Can it be inferred from state willingness to verbally condemn the act, or from the numerous ratifications of the Torture Convention, or from actual cessation of torture in states?

According to Garnett, states do not acknowledge acts of torture but reaffirm their opposition to it and it is this consistent and public repudiation of torture that has helped create a norm of custom.[31] It is true that this could be an indicator of states' *opinio juris*. But is it enough? Garnett's argument that torture as a customary norm emerged post the near universal ratification of the Torture Convention is more acceptable. It is reasonable to expect that practice thereafter is in breach of the norm rather than a challenge to it. However, ratification would reflect the *opinio juris* of member states only. If torture is part of custom the majority of states must accept this legal duty including non-member states. Broad-based acceptance of such duty cannot be established when well over half of states habitually torture their citizens, even states party to the Torture Convention. Only when a state ceases to torture can it be said that it has accepted its legal duty.

Higgins notes that:

> Where there is substantial non-compliance, over a period of time, the norms concerned begin to lose their normative character. What has been lost is the community expectation that claimed requirements of behaviour reflect obligation.[32]

---

[30] *UK v. Norway (Fisheries Case)* (1951) ICJ Reps. 116, 191.

[31] Garnett, 'The Defence of State Immunity for Acts of Torture', *op cit*, p. 103.

[32] Higgins, *Problems and Process. International Law and How We Use It* (1994), p. 19.

Where states can allude to their statements as actual practice without enforcement they are allowed to become complacent. After all, having signed all the requisite conventions and consistently affirmed how heinous the act in question is, they need not go further. They are able to say that the crime is now part of international customary law and the various human rights organizations can rest assured that as a crime it will, henceforth, receive their highest attention. Thus denigrating its importance. To make the prohibition of torture part of international customary law states must say and do consistently, thus ensuring that it takes its place as a norm of international law of significance.[33] To rely on statements over and above physical acts creates the situation where crimes are deemed part of customary law when they are committed on a broad-based and systematic scale. A situation that is illogical. If international customary norms are to bind all states, crimes that are part of custom must not only be seen to be prohibited but must also, at the physical level, cease to occur.

When customary rules are created, universality of practice is not a requirement. It is enough if the practice has been followed by a small number of states without contrary acts occurring. It has been outlined above that for the creation of customary norms in international criminal law, practice should be in both statements and physical acts. Where a state has in both statements and enforcement shown consistent practice in the prohibition of an international crime it can then show that it acknowledges and accepts its legal obligation. However, custom should not be evident where only a few states reach such a position with the majority still unable to show practice through enforcement. Thus the prohibition of torture is not a norm of international customary law.

There are only five international customary crimes: piracy, war crimes, genocide, crimes against humanity and the crime of aggression. Only piracy is excluded from the Rome Statute. It is discussed in detail here in order to provide an historical context of these crimes. The other crimes are examined in detail in a separate section below.

Piracy is perhaps the oldest international customary crime. Looking back in history it is possible to say that the act of piracy was outlawed as far back as the Greek civilization, and possibly even further back than that.[34] The first mention of piracy in texts is traced back to ancient Greek society, in particular Thucydides. He claimed that the powerful ruler of Crete, Mino, cleared the sea of piracy as far as

---

[33] It is acknowledged that practice can be found in domestic legal framework and public statements, but it is argued here that in relation to international crimes, practice must also include physical acts. Public statements, domestic legal framework and cessation of the act in question must all be present if an international crime is to become a international customary crime.

[34] De Souza, *Piracy in the Graeco-Roman World* (1999), p. 15. De Souza acknowledges that piracy emerged as a concept in itself in roughly 800-500 BC, basing his views on Homeric Poems as reasonable sources of evidence of Greek social history. He does not, however, accept that the concept of piracy was differentiated from that of warfare at this period in time.

42   *Immunity and International Criminal Law*

he was able in order to improve his profit.[35] This would have been around 1700-1400 BC.[36] The term pirate was used during classical Greek times in reference to anyone involved in attacking others by means of the sea. The act of piracy was an act deplored by them but still used as part of war.[37] The term piracy was highly politicized during this period as powerful entities used it to denounce their enemies in their struggle to gain control. They used the term to justify their actions and to question the legitimacy of others.

By the time the Romans became a powerful force, piracy had indeed become an act that all nations were concerned with. Rome pledged to suppress piracy under the *lex de provinciis praetoriis*[38] in 100 BC and expected her allies and friends to cooperate. All those concerned, according to Rome, were to deny pirates bases from which they could mount their attacks.[39] Pirates were the common enemy of all, and were international public enemies.[40] The notoriety of pirates helped establish the beginnings of an international crime as we know it. The elements of an international crime can be seen in the Roman expectation of international cooperation with all allies and friends, to do what they could to suppress the act.[41] The international crime of piracy was eventually codified in the 20th century.[42] It is defined as any illegal act of violence, detention or any act of depredation committed for private ends by the crew or passengers of a private ship or aircraft on the high seas against other ships or aircraft or persons aboard.[43]

---

[35] *Ibid.*

[36] *Ibid.*

[37] *Ibid*, p. 41.

[38] *Lex de Provinciis Praetoriis*: 'The senior consul is to send letters to the peoples and states to whom he may think fit, to say that the Roman people <will have> care, that the citizens of Rome and allies and the Latins, and those of the foreign nations who are in relationship of friendship with the Roman people may sail in safety, and that on account of this matter and according to this statute they have made Cilicia a praetorian province.' Crawford & Cloud, *Rome Statutes* (1996), p. 253-7.

[39] De Souza, *Piracy in the Graeco-Roman World*, *op cit*, p. 108, 135.

[40] Pirates were so despised that Cicero, in his discussions on the importance of keeping promises, stated that: 'If, for example, you do not hand over to pirates the amount agreed upon as the price of your life, that is not perjury, even if you have sworn an oath and do not do so, for a pirate is not included in the category of lawful enemies, but is the common enemy of everyone. In his case good faith and sworn oaths should not be recognized.' Cicero, *On Duties*, (1990, Griffin and Atkins eds.).

[41] Rome was the most powerful state at the time, and its position may not be too dissimilar to that of the Allied nations after the Second World War when the Nuremberg principles were established. This expectation of international cooperation was perhaps the rudiments of universal jurisdiction.

[42] The Geneva Convention on the High Seas 1958 (450 UNTS 11). (Hereinafter, the High Seas Convention.) The treaty prohibited piracy under international law or piracy *jure gentium*. Article 14: 'All States shall co-operate to the fullest possible extent in the repression of piracy on the high seas or in any place outside the jurisdiction of any State.'

[43] High Seas Convention, Article 15(1) (a) The act need not be committed only on the high seas but anywhere outside the jurisdiction of any state, and acts of inciting or intentionally

Acts of piracy are not necessarily sanctioned governmental action, but are more likely to be committed by private individuals for private financial gain. Acts of piracy will most likely occur on the high seas. [44] Hence, state sovereignty is not gravely threatened by this crime. States have always acted in a constant and uniform manner, and have accepted their legal duty with regards to the application of universal jurisdiction over pirates. From the Greeks to the Romans to the present day, pirates have been and are the enemies of mankind. The extension of this jurisdictional basis to other crimes has not occurred with such singular international cooperation.

As part of international customary law, war crimes and the crime of aggression have their origins in war under two categories: *jus ad bellum*, the rules that govern the legality of war, and *jus in bello*, or the rules that regulate the conduct of war.[45] States have the power to decide when to wage war; this power, manifest in their sovereignty, is weakened when recourse to war is limited. Although states have final authority within their territories to make and enforce laws, on the international sphere their authority is limited by virtue of the fact that all states are sovereign and equal. If one state is equal to another it has the right not to have its territory invaded by the other. Restricting state recourse to war ensures that this balance is maintained. Sovereignty cannot be seen to give states the right to assault other states. There is, therefore, a great need to regulate the legality of war: *jus ad bellum*. This need has directed international discourse on limiting aggressive war.

Rules that regulate the conduct of war, *jus in bello*, give rise to war crimes. War crimes are internationally prohibited acts that may occur during an armed conflict. Such acts include murder and deportation as well as acts of torture aimed at primarily civilians and prisoners of war. Torture, although an international treaty crime in its own right, was for many years a crime falling under *jus in bello*.[46] Genocide and crimes against humanity would have fallen under this category as well. For these crimes to be international crimes there was a requirement that they be committed in an armed conflict. On their own merit they were not international crimes because for centuries sovereigns could not be held accountable for acts committed on their own soil against their own subjects. To hold a sovereign accountable would have resulted in a challenge to his sovereign power and authority.

---

facilitating piracy are also considered as acts of piracy: High Seas Convention, Article 15(1) (b) & (3). Convention on the Law of the Sea 1982 (1994 UNTS 42). Article 101 gives a definition of piracy.

[44] This is a broad assertion as piracy did have government sanction in some cases during its history. Many governments profited from this act and many committed acts of piracy for their own financial gain, but they could distance themselves when it suited them.

[45] Aggression or crimes against peace and war crimes fall under the two categories of *jus ad bellum* and *jus in bello*. They are examined in full below.

[46] Torture Convention, *op cit*. See: Roberts and Guelff, *Documents on the Laws of War* (1989) for the Hague Conventions and Regulations 1907, and torture under the Geneva Conventions 1949. See below, p. 84-8.

International Treaty Crimes

International treaty crimes include: torture,[47] slavery,[48] hostage-taking,[49] aircraft hijacking and sabotage,[50] apartheid,[51] international drug trafficking[52] and maritime violent acts.[53] Slavery as an international treaty crime lies in the birth of slavery as a crime in the African slave trade, and British efforts to abolish it in the 18th and 19th centuries.[54] By 1926 it was well known that slavery was an international

---

[47] Torture Convention, *op cit.*

[48] Slavery Convention 1926 (60 LNTS 253), Protocol Amending the Slavery Convention 1953 (182 UNTS 51), Supplementary Convention on the Abolition of Slavery, the Slave Trade, and Institutions and Practices Similar to Slavery 1956 (266 UNTS 3).

[49] International Convention Against the Taking of Hostages 1979 1983 (1316 UNTS 205), Convention on the Prevention and Punishment of Crimes Against Internationally Protected Persons, Including Diplomatic Agents 1977 (1035 UNTS 167).

[50] Tokyo Convention on Offences and Certain Acts Committed Onboard Aircraft 1963 (704 UNTS 219), Hague Convention for the Suppression of Unlawful Seizure of Aircrafts 1970, (860 UNTS 105), Montreal Convention for the Suppression of Unlawful Acts Against the Safety of Civil Aviation 1971 (974 UNTS 177), Protocol for the Suppression of Unlawful Acts of Violence at Airports Serving International Civil Aviation 1971 (ICAO Doc. 9518).

[51] International Convention on the Suppression and Punishment of the Crime of Apartheid 1973, (1974) *13 ILM 50.*

[52] Convention on the Suppression of the Illicit Traffic in Dangerous Drugs 1936 (12 UNTS 179), Single Convention on Narcotics Drugs 1961 (520 UNTS 151), Geneva Protocol of 1972 Amending the Single Convention on Narcotics Drugs (UN Doc. E/CONF.6319), UN Convention Against Illicit Traffic in Narcotic Drugs and Psychotropic Substances 1988 (UN Doc E/CONF.82/15).

[53] Convention for the Suppression of Unlawful Acts Against the Safety of Maritime Navigation 1988 (IMO Doc. SUA/CON/15/Rev.1), Protocol for the Suppression of Unlawful Acts Against the Safety of Fixed Platforms on Continental Shelf (IMO Doc. SUA/CONF/15/Rev.1).

[54] Secular and religious doubts raised during this period led to the Quakers forming an Abolition Committee in 1787. They took on abolition, which became a political issue, and sought to eradicate the trade. After many years of propaganda and campaigning, the Foreign Slave Trade Bill was drafted and passed in 1807. (This was followed by the Reform Act 1832.) The 1807 Act prohibited the British trade in slaves to foreign and newly acquired territories. Sentiments in other countries followed suit resulting in the Berlin Conference Concerning the Congo where a General Act was passed in 1885. Countries that were part of the conference included the US, Germany, Prussia, Austria, Bohemia, Hungary, Belgium, Denmark, Spain, France, UK, The Indies, Italy, the Netherlands, Luxembourg, Portugal, Russia, Sweden and Norway and the Ottomans. This was followed by the General Act between the United States of America and other Powers for the repression of the African Slave Trade, etc. signed in 1890. Countries that participated included the US, German Empire, Austria, Belgium, Denmark, Spain, the Congo, France, UK, Italy, the Netherlands, Persia, Portugal, Russia, Sweden and Norway, the Ottomans and Zanzibar. Craton, Walvin and Wright, *Slavery, Abolition and Emancipation* (1976), p. 231-2.

crime.[55] In 1927 the First International Conference for the Unification of Penal Law met and passed a resolution that looked at the *delits du droit des gens* or offences under international law.[56] The resolution considered crimes such as piracy, counterfeiting, slave trade, *inter alia*, as crimes against the laws of nations.

Treaty-based crimes fall under Bassiouni's description of international crimes *largo senso*. As jurisdiction for these crimes is limited by the relevant treaty's provisions, and the Treaty Convention, it is arguable that they do not have universal jurisdiction. The deciding factor in the determination as to which crimes are international customary crimes is universal jurisdiction.

International Crimes and Universal Jurisdiction

International treaty crimes are prohibited by treaties under which member states are obliged to take measures to submit an individual for prosecution or extradite under the maxim *aut dedere aut judicare*. This is not universal jurisdiction.

Universal Jurisdiction

According to the universal jurisdiction principle, it does not make a difference where a crime took place and against whom it was committed as all states have an obligation to initiate proceedings and prosecute suspects.[57] There is a form of universality of jurisdiction between states party to the various international crime treaties, but this is not universal jurisdiction. Non-member states without links to the crimes are not obliged to prosecute or extradite. Under the Treaty Convention, provisions of a treaty can only bind states party to the treaty.[58]

The Aut Dedere Aut Judicare Principle   Universal jurisdiction has often been confused with treaty-based jurisdiction. This was evident in the *Pinochet Case (No. 3)* where Lord Browne-Wilkinson held:

---

[55] The Slavery Convention 1926 helped establish slavery as an international crime. The treaty was put together under the auspices of the League of Nations. It was amended by a Protocol in 1953. Slavery featured in the Universal Declaration of Human Rights, Article 4: 'No one shall be held in slavery or servitude; slavery and the slave trade shall be prohibited in all their forms.' It also featured in the High Seas Convention, Article 13: 'Every State shall adopt effective measures to prevent and punish the transport of slaves in ships authorized to fly its flag, and to prevent the unlawful use of its flag for that purpose. Any slave taking refuge on board any ship, whatever its flag, shall, *ipso facto*, be free.' See also ICCPR Article 8.

[56] The First International Conference for the Unification of Penal Law, Warsaw 1927 held under the auspices of the International Association of Penal Law.

[57] See: Bassiouni, 'Universal Jurisdiction for International Crimes: Historical Perspectives and Contemporary Practice' (2001) *VJIL 81*.

[58] Treaty Convention, *op cit.*

46   *Immunity and International Criminal Law*

> I gather the following points from the Torture Convention...(3) if the states with the most obvious jurisdiction (the art. 5(1) states) do not seek to extradite, the state where the alleged torturer is found must prosecute or, apparently, extradite to another country, ie there is universal jurisdiction.[59]

The Latin phrase *aut dedere aut judicare* refers to a state's obligation to either prosecute or extradite. The principle appears in many international treaties prohibiting certain acts. Under the Treaty Convention the principle is applicable only to member states.[60] It appears in different ways in various treaties:

> Each State Party shall likewise take such measures as may be necessary to establish jurisdiction over these crimes in cases where the alleged offender is present in its territory and it does not extradite him.[61]

> The Contracting State in the territory of which the alleged offender is found, shall if it does not extradite him, be obliged, without exception whatsoever and whether or not the offence was committed in its territory, to submit the case to its competent authorities for the purpose of prosecution. These authorities shall take their decision in the same manner as in the case of any ordinary offence of a serious nature under the law of that State.[62]

Where a convention obliges member states to prosecute or extradite, it cannot oblige non-member states to do the same. A treaty is binding only to states party to it. Rules in a treaty can only bind third states if they become customary rules.[63] Where a crime is treaty-based and is not a customary norm warranting universal jurisdiction, only states members to that treaty have the duty to extradite or prosecute under that treaty.

There appears to be much confusion over certain treaty-based crimes having universal jurisdiction. It is difficult to maintain that the prohibition of torture is a international customary crime especially when its jurisdiction is ardently attached to the treaty that created it. In *Pinochet (No. 3)* the scope of Pinochet's responsibility was narrowed to post-ratification of the Torture Convention by Chile and the UK.[64] For example Lord Hope was of the opinion that:

---

[59] *Pinochet (No. 3)*, Lord Browne-Wilkinson, *op cit*, p. 111.

[60] A treaty does not create either obligations or rights for a third state without its consent. Article 34, Treaty Convention, *op cit*.

[61] Convention on the Prevention and Punishment of Crimes Against Internationally Protected Persons, Including Diplomats, *op cit*, Article 3(2). This article is repeated in the International Convention Against the Taking of Hostages 1979, Article 5(2).

[62] Hague Convention on the Unlawful Seizure of Aircraft 1970. This article is reproduced in the Montreal Convention for the Suppression of Unlawful Acts against the Safety of Civil Aviation 1971, Article 7,

[63] Treaty Convention, Article 38.

[64] *Pinochet (No. 3)*, *ibid.* Lord Browne-Wilkinson, p. 115, Lord Hope, p. 152, Lord Hutton, p. 167

the date as from which the immunity *ratione materiae* was lost was 30 October 1988, which was the date when Chile's ratification of the Torture Convention of 30 September 1988 took effect. Spain had already ratified the convention. The convention was ratified by the United Kingdom on 8 December 1988 following the coming into force of s134 of the [Criminal Justice] 1988 Act.[65]

If the prohibition of torture is a international customary crime this would have been unnecessary. Pinochet's responsibility would have been established by international customary law, prior to, during, and after the Torture Convention. Lord Millett, in *Pinochet (No. 3)*, appreciated this point. He emphasized that systematic torture on a large scale, as an instrument of state policy is a international customary crime; a crime against humanity.[66] If it is a international customary crime, he concluded, UK courts possessed universal jurisdiction and did not need a statute to exercise it.[67] However, where torture occurs on a small scale, that is, against only a few individuals, it is an international treaty crime, and as such its jurisdiction is dependent on the Torture Convention. Treaties dealing with hijacking are said to 'address domestic jurisdiction over hijacking where it was not...subjected to the universality principle under customary law before'.[68]

It has been argued that evidence of the universality principle promulgated by treaty law over hijacking is evident in the USA's Restatement of Foreign Relations Law, its Hostage Taking Act 1984, the Hague and Montreal Conventions and the Hostage-Taking Convention.[69] Further, it is maintained that the universality of jurisdiction under international agreements over hijacking is confirmed in the case of *US v. Yunis*[70] and in *US v. Rezaq*.[71] It was held in the *Yunis Case* that a 'majority of states in the world community...have signed three treaties condemning aircraft piracy'; with such 'global efforts to punish aircraft piracy and hostage taking, international legal scholars unanimously agree that these crimes fit within the category heinous crimes for purposes of asserting universal jurisdiction'.[72] According to the court (aircraft) 'hijacking may well be one of the few crimes so clearly condemned under the law of nations that states may assert universal jurisdiction to bring offenders to justice, even when the state has no territorial connection to the hijacking and its citizens are not involved'.[73] Based on these

---

[65] *Pinochet (No. 3)*, *ibid*, Lord Hope, p.152. Lord Hope refers to immunity *ratione materiae* (italics are the author's own), which is a type of immunity accorded heads of state and governments, and accredited diplomats to cover acts of state. This is discussed in detail in Chapter 5.

[66] *Op cit*, p. 178.

[67] *Ibid*.

[68] Jordan, 'Universal Jurisdiction in a Dangerous World: a Weapon for all Nations against International Crime', (2000) *9 MSU-DCL JIL 1,19*.

[69] *Ibid*, p. 19-20.

[70] *US v. Yunis* (1988) 681 F. Supp. 896.

[71] *US v. Rezaq* (1995) 899 F. Supp. 687.

[72] *US v. Yunis*, p. 900-901.

[73] *Ibid*.

48 *Immunity and International Criminal Law*

assumptions the court in *Rezaq* found that its universal jurisdiction over the hijackers in question was clear.[74]

The use of the phrase universal jurisdiction in this context is misleading. Universal jurisdiction based on international customary law is the only form of universal jurisdiction. The jurisdiction in a treaty cannot be universal, no matter how many states it binds, unless and only when it becomes a customary norm binding all states, members and non-members alike. It would be better if the shared jurisdiction amongst states party to a treaty was referred to as multi-state jurisdiction rather than universal jurisdiction. Shaw concludes that treaties that prohibit international crimes:

> provide for the exercise of state jurisdiction but not for universal jurisdiction. Some conventions establish what may be termed a quasi-universal jurisdiction in providing for the exercise of jurisdiction upon a variety of bases by as wide a group of state parties as possible.[75]

The courts in both *Yunis* and *Rezaq* were perhaps asserting universal jurisdiction for international customary crimes as the true and only form of universal jurisdiction, but erred in their choice of international crime to apply it.

As advantageous as it may be to extend universal jurisdiction to hijacking, states are not obliged to prosecute or extradite hijackers where they have absolutely no interest in the hijacking. For example, a commercial airliner registered to country A is hijacked by a national of country C. He escapes and is discovered many years later in country B, a country that did not have nationals on board and whose airspace the aircraft never entered. If country B is not party to any of the hijacking treaties, it is inconceivable that it will feel obliged under the universal jurisdiction principle to prosecute or extradite. Even if the state wanted to pursue the case, it would be prevented from doing so by international principles of jurisdiction.[76] Nor would it feel compelled to proceed against the hijacker *in absentia*, for the simple reason that hijacking is an offence against all states. Hijacking may be a heinous crime covered by several treaties, but it has not attained the lofty heights of an international customary crime with universal jurisdiction.

The same could be said about terrorism. Cassese has put forward that terrorism is a international customary crime.[77] According to him 'transnational, state-sponsored or state-condoned terrorism amounts to an international crime, and is already contemplated and prohibited by international customary law as a distinct category of such crimes'.[78] The UN's General Assembly passed a resolution to this

---

[74] *US v. Rezaq*, p. 709.

[75] Shaw, *International Law, op cit*, p. 473.

[76] Jurisdiction is discussed in further detail in Chapter 3.

[77] Cassese, *International Law, op cit*, p. 246.

[78] Cassese, 'Terrorism is Also Disrupting Some Critical Legal Categories of International Law' (2001) *12 EJIL 993*.

International Crimes

effect in 1985.[79] Nonetheless, terrorism is not a international customary crime. Certain acts of terrorism are international treaty crimes, such as aircraft hijacking. If acts of terrorism were committed during an act of piracy, terrorism would then become a international customary crime. The act of hijacking commercial airlines is an international treaty crime. Where such planes are flown into heavily occupied civilian buildings with the intent to kill civilians in order to facilitate a state or group's policy, the acts become crimes against humanity. In that situation, acts of terrorism become international customary crimes.[80]

Terrorism as a broad-based definition of various acts is not, therefore, in itself a international customary crime or a treaty crime. A US court in 1984 correctly concluded that:

> The divergence as to basic norms of course reflects a basic disagreement as to legitimate political goals and the proper method of attainment. Given such disharmony, I cannot conclude that the law of nations – which, we must recall, is defined as the principles and rules that states feel themselves bound to observe, and do commonly observe – outlaws politically motivated terrorism, no matter how repugnant it might be to our own legal system.[81]

Thus if not outlawed as a crime by nations, it cannot attract universal jurisdiction; it is not a international customary crime.

The confusion surrounding universal jurisdiction and international crimes perhaps stems from the unique character of genocide as both a customary and treaty international crime. Judge Weeramantry of the ICJ, in the case of *Bosnia and Herzegovina v. Yugoslavia (Genocide Case)*, concluded that the principles in the Genocide Convention protect human rights and humanitarian values that are 'principles of international customary law'.[82]

The Convention on the Crime of Genocide does not give genocide universal jurisdiction.[83] However, as the prohibition of genocide is an international customary norm, the duty to prosecute or extradite is superseded by its universal jurisdiction. The territorial jurisdiction in the Genocide Convention was held not to be exhaustive. Thus the Israeli District Court was of the opinion in the *Eichmann Case* that 'every sovereign state may exercise its existing powers within the limits

---

[79] UN Gen. Ass. Res. No. 40/61 (1985).

[80] 11 September 2001: US civilian airplanes were hijacked and flown into the two World Trade Center towers in New York with the loss of thousands of lives, for the political benefit of an extremist Islamic group called Al Qaeda.

[81] *Tel Oren v Libyan Arab Republic (1984)* 726 F2d 774, 796 per Judge Edwards.

[82] *Bosnia and Herzegovina v. Yugoslavia (Case Concerning Application of the Convention on the Prevention and Punishment of the Crime of Genocide)*, 11 July 1996, Judge Weeramantry, para. 5, www.icj-cij.org.

[83] Under Article VI of the Convention on the Prevention and Punishment of the Crime of Genocide 1948 (78 UNTS 277), persons charged with genocide are to be tried in the state where the offence took place, or in an international criminal court, (hereinafter the Genocide Convention.)

50   *Immunity and International Criminal Law*

of international customary law'.[84] Customary universal jurisdiction for genocide was also recognized in Nuremberg.

In conclusion therefore there are only five crimes that have universal jurisdiction. They are: piracy, crimes against peace/aggression, war crimes, crimes against humanity and genocide. These crimes have come under the jurisdiction of the Nuremberg and Tokyo Tribunals, the ICTY,[85] the ICTR,[86] and now, the ICC's Rome Statute.[87] International treaty crimes, or international crimes *largo senso*, have tended not to be included in international tribunals.

The International Criminal Court's Crimes in Detail

In UN discussions leading to the establishment of the ICC there was much debate about the crimes the court would have jurisdiction over. Countries put forward differing views; for example Austria, Sweden, Malaysia, Republic of Korea and the Netherlands argued that treaty-based crimes should be left to national jurisdictions.[88] Algeria, on the other hand, asserted that treaty-based crimes and terrorism should be included in a less restrictive approach to the ICC's jurisdiction

---

[84] *Eichmann Case*, p. 18.

[85] Grave breaches of the Geneva Conventions: Article 2, violations of the laws or customs of war: Article 3, genocide: Article 4, and crimes against humanity: Article 5.

[86] Genocide: Article 2, crimes against humanity: Article 3 and violations of Common Article 3 of the Geneva Conventions and Additional Protocols Article 4. Common Article 3: In case of armed conflict not of an international character occurring in the territory of one of the High Contracting Parties, each Party to the conflict shall be bound to apply, as a minimum, the following provisions: (1) Persons taking no active part in the hostilities, including members of the armed forces who have laid down their arms and those placed *hors de combat* by sickness, wounds, detention or any other cause, shall in all circumstances be treated humanly, without any adverse distinction founded on race, colour, religion or faith, sex, birth or wealth, or any other similar criteria. To this end, the following acts are and shall remain prohibited at any time and in any place whatsoever with respect to the abovementioned persons: (a) violence to life and person, in particular murder of all kinds, mutilations, cruel treatment and torture; (b) taking hostages; (c) outrages upon personal dignity, in particular humiliating and degrading treatment; (d) the passing of sentences and the carrying out of executions without previous judgment pronounced by a regular constituted court, affording all the judicial guarantees which are recognised as indispensable by civilized peoples. (2) The wounded and sick shall be collected and cared for. An Impartial humanitarian body, such as the International Committee of the Red Cross, may offer its services to the Parties to the conflict. Reprinted in Roberts and Guelff , *Documents on the Laws of War*, *op cit*, p. 172, 195, 217, 273.

[87] Genocide: Article 6, crimes against humanity: Article 7, war crimes: Article 8 and aggression: Article 5. The crime of aggression, listed as falling under the Court's jurisdiction, has yet to be fully provided for: Article 5(1).

[88] Preparatory Committee Press Release L/2766 27 March 1996, www.un.org.

over crimes.[89] Belgium wanted to see trafficking in human beings as an ICC crime,[90] whilst the DRC and Russia argued for the court to have jurisdiction over terrorism.[91] Indeed, terrorism and drugs trafficking proved to be quite contentious in the deliberations leading to the Rome Statute.[92] There were objections to their inclusion as ICC crimes from, *inter alia*, the USA and France. According to the US government the fact that both had an international dimension was not rationale enough to include them.[93] France argued that it is best if terrorism is dealt with at the national level through domestic prosecutions and inter-government cooperation.[94] States such as Lebanon, Libya and Qatar wanted distinctions made as to terrorism and struggles for national liberation, with Pakistan inferring that foreign domination was itself a form of terrorism.[95]

However, it appears that limiting the scope of the ICC's criminal jurisdiction to the most serious crimes of international concern was the best option and was approved. Nevertheless, the possibility of a review mechanism to include other crimes in the future was put forward.[96] For the moment, although there are numerous crimes of an international nature, the ICC has jurisdiction over only four international customary crimes.

Crimes against Peace or the Crime of Aggression

The history behind the crime of aggression lies in the limits sought for state recourse to war. Efforts to restrain and curtail the use of force by states have included attempts to control the basis upon which states can legitimately use military force to secure a specific objective.[97] *Jus ad bellum*, the right of states to wage war, was and is still a contentious issue.[98] Attempts in history to limit resort to war saw the creation of the 'just war' theory. It is impossible to examine the entire development of the just war idea in this book; however, a brief outline of the

---

[89] Algerian Representative, Gen. Ass. Sixth Committee (Legal) Press Release GA/L/3011, *ibid.*

[90] www.un.org/icc/pressrel/lrom.

[91] www.un.org/icc/pressrel/lrom.

[92] The inclusion of international drugs trafficking was proposed by Barbados, Dominica, Jamaica and Trinidad and Tobago. A/CONF.183/2/ADD.1 (1998). Arguably, drugs trafficking is sufficiently provided for by conventions mentioned earlier, working under the *aut dedere aut judicare* principle.

[93] US Representative to the Preparatory Committee, *ibid.*

[94] French Representative to the Preparatory Committee, *ibid.* Indeed, it would have proved too difficult to include terrorism, which is a controversial crime.

[95] *Ibid.*

[96] Poland, Gen. Ass. Sixth Committee Press Release, *op cit.*

[97] Efforts have also been made through the regulation of conduct during armed conflicts, *jus in bello.*

[98] Kaplan and Katzenbach 'Resort to Force: War and Neutrality The Strategy of World Order' (Falk and Mendlovitz eds.) *International Law* (1966).

52   *Immunity and International Criminal Law*

idea is necessary to give a better understanding of the notion of the crime of 'crime against peace' or aggression that has evolved as a consequence.

By the 16th century state-centred sovereignty developed as a result of the collapse of the unifying authority of the Church. The development of the idea that war was an essential element of that sovereignty did not diminish the need to justify war. Just causes for war included self-defence, action in retaliation for wrongs done to citizens and the protection of property. Recourse to war in order to expand territory, to subjugate people against their will or to gain political independence from another state was deemed unjust.[99] Writing in the 16th century, De Vitoria was of the opinion that wars should be waged only to remedy a wrong.[100] According to him, where a subject is convinced of the injustice of war, he may take no part in it, in spite of the sovereign's orders.[101] However, the just war doctrine lost influence as the balance of power system developed in a divided international community, with states considering their national interest as the predominant factor in the decision to wage war. By the 19th century war was seen as a continuation of state policy.[102]

Wars of aggression remained a controversial issue in the international community thereafter, and in 1927 the Assembly of the League of Nations adopted the Declaration on Aggressive War, acknowledging it as an international crime.[103] According to this declaration 'all wars of aggression are, and shall always be, prohibited, and [that] every pacific means must be employed to settle disputes of every description, which may arise between states'.[104] Subsequently in 1928 the Kellog-Briand Pact renounced war 'as an instrument of national policy'. exempting the resort to war in self-defence.[105] The pact did not disallow war altogether, only prohibiting recourse to war where effective substitute measures were available. It thus sought to prohibit wars of aggression.

The world was slowly moving towards an all-out ban on aggressive war. By 1945 it was generally recognized that aggressive war was prohibited, but just what constituted aggressive war was not clear. Nonetheless, in the post-Second World War atmosphere it was deemed essential to pursue those it was believed had waged aggressive war. As a result both the Nuremberg and Tokyo Tribunals included aggression as an international crime.[106] The Nuremberg Tribunal looked at wars of aggression in its definition of crimes against peace. Crimes against peace,

---

[99] *Ibid*, p. 282.

[100] De Vitoria, *On the Law of War* (E. Nys ed., translated by J. Pawley Bate) (1917).

[101] *Ibid*.

[102] The concept of war is only a branch of political unity... war is simply a continuation of political intercourse. Clauswitz, *On War* (Howard and Paret eds.) (1993), p. 731.

[103] 24 September 1927, Publications de la Société des Nations IX. Désarmement 1927 IX. 14.

[104] *Ibid*.

[105] Also known as the Pact of Paris. The pact was acceded to or ratified by 63 states. The pact did not state that aggression was a crime, nor did it place responsibility on individuals for the act.

[106] Tokyo Charter and Nuremberg Charter, *op cit*.

according to the Nuremberg Charter, included 'the planning, preparation, initiation or waging of a war of aggression, or a war in violation of international treaties, agreements or assurances, or participation in a common plan or conspiracy for the accomplishment of any of the foregoing'.[107] According to the Tokyo Charter some of the accused had planned, prepared, initiated and waged wars of aggression, which were also wars in violation of international treaties, agreements and assurances.[108] The Nuremberg and Tokyo Charters were the first international legal texts to detail crimes against peace. However, they failed to define aggressive war.

It has been argued that the category of crimes against peace was created *ex post facto* by an international tribunal; that it did not exist in international law prior to Nuremberg.[109] Although individual responsibility for acts of aggressive war had not been previously fully provided for in legal texts, advances up to that point in time could lead one to believe that waging aggressive war was contrary to the laws of nations. The 1927 League Declaration, and the 1928 Kellog-Briand Pact[110] showed international consensus that aggressive war was not to be encouraged as being lawful. Indeed individual accountability for this crime was evident in the Treaty of Peace with Germany, 1919.[111]

The UN seemed to take up the issue of aggressive war when it outlined to its members in its Charter that they should refrain from the use of force against the territorial integrity and political independence of any state, but again failed to give a definition of aggressive war.[112] The UN General Assembly, in a resolution in 1974, declared aggression as 'the most serious and dangerous form of the illegal use of force'.[113] Once again full details on what aggressive war is were not

---

[107] Nuremberg Charter, Article 6.

[108] Tokyo Charter, Article 5 (c). It is interesting to note that the Tokyo Tribunal Charter had elements of the concept of just war legitimisation of war. This Charter, unlike the Nuremberg Tribunal, did not limit its crimes against humanity to civilians but included military personnel, the intention being the inclusion of mass killings and detention of military personnel in an illegal war. It would therefore appear that according to its creators the killing of military personnel was legitimate only where the war was justified. Röling, *The Tokyo Tribunal and Beyond* (1993), p.57-8.

[109] Justice Röling, one of the Tokyo Tribunal judges, held this view. Röling, *The Tokyo Tribunal and Beyond, ibid*, p. 66.

[110] This treaty did not, however, deal with individual responsibility, but sought to outlaw war as an instrument of state policy.

[111] Article 227-230, Penalties, Treaty of Peace with Germany (Versailles, 28 June 1919).

[112] The UN Charter, Article 2(4). The ILC in its work to codify laws on treaties voiced their opinion that 'the law of the Charter concerning the prohibition of the use of force in itself constitutes a conspicuous example of a rule in international law having the character of *jus cogens*'. (1966) 2 *YBILC* 247. Accordingly it would appear that recourse to war for the sake of war is prohibited and that it may be a rule of *jus cogens*, but we have yet to find out just what aggressive war entails. The UN Charter does not 'impair the inherent right of individual or collective self-defence if an armed attack occurs' under Article 51.

[113] Gen. Ass. Res. 3314 (XXIX) 14 December 1974.

54 *Immunity and International Criminal Law*

given.[114] The issue of aggression is still outstanding. No definition was given in the Rome Statute; in fact the matter was left open, to be resolved at a later date.[115]

War Crimes

War crimes are acts committed in violation of the rules of armed conflict; *jus in bello*. The law regulating conduct during war is also referred to as international humanitarian law. The purpose of this branch of international law is to limit the methods and means of warfare in order to lessen the effects of war.[116] This objective has prevailed over many centuries, thus leading to the rules of armed conflict as we know them being incorporated into various treaties. From the Lieber Code of 1863[117] to the Hague Convention of 1907,[118] the Geneva Conventions of 1949[119] and their Additional Protocols of 1977.[120] The treaties cover the acts, methods and means of combat, weapons and occupation of territories as well as conduct towards civilians and their protection.

The Hague Conventions of 1907, although focusing primarily on combatants, has provisions covering treatment of civilian populations in occupied territories.[121] The Preamble to the Regulations, in its famous 'Martens Clause',

---

[114] Aggressive war is yet to be defined in full. Hopefully when the time comes for its full inclusion into the Rome Statute, it will be defined.

[115] Rome Statute, Article 5(2). See: Report of the ILC on the Work of its Fifth Session (1998) Suppl. No. 10, A/53/10.

[116] Paust, Bassiouni, et al, *op cit*, p. 806-7.

[117] The Lieber Code: The Instructions for the Government of Armies of the United States in the Field, General Orders No. 11. This was perhaps the first codification of customary rules of conduct during armed conflicts.

[118] Hague Convention Respecting the Laws and Customs of War on Land, Hague Convention Respecting the Rights and Duties of Neutral Powers and Persons in Case of War on Land, Hague Convention Relating to the Status of Enemy Merchant Ships at the Outbreak of Hostilities, Hague Convention Relating to the Conversion of Merchant Ships into Warships, Hague Convention Relative to the Laying of Automatic Submarine Contact Mines, Hague Convention Concerning Bombardment by Naval Forces in Time of War, Hague Convention XIII Concerning the Rights and Duties of Neutral Powers in Naval War, 1907. Roberts and Guelff, *Documents on the Laws of War, op cit*, p. 43-120.

[119] Geneva Convention I for the Amelioration of the Condition of the Wounded and Sick in Armed Forces in the Field, Geneva Convention II for the Amelioration of the Condition of Wounded, Sick and Shipwrecked members of the Armed Forces at Sea, Geneva Convention III Relative to the Treatment of Prisoners of War, Geneva Convention IV Relative to the Protection of Civilian Persons in Time of War, 1949. *Ibid*, p. 169-338.

[120] Geneva Protocol I Additional to the Geneva Conventions of 12 August 1949, and Relating to the Protection of Victims of International Armed Conflicts, Geneva Protocol II Additional to the Geneva Conventions of 12 August 1949, and Relating to the Protection of Victims of Non-International Armed Conflicts, 1977. *Ibid*, p. 387-468.

[121] Regulation IV Respecting the Laws and Customs of War by Land, Article 46 requires occupying forces to honour and protect the rights of families, people's lives, private property and religious practices and convictions. Roberts and Guelff, *Documents on the Laws of War, op cit*, p. 56.

International Crimes 55

states that the 'inhabitants and belligerents remain under the protection and the rule of the principles of the law of nations, as they result from the usages established among civilised peoples, from the laws of humanity, and the dictates of public conscience'.[122]

The Geneva Conventions are considered to represent international customary law,[123] in particular their Common Article 3, the grave breaches provisions,[124] and Article 11 and 85 of Additional Protocol I.[125] Just prior to the Geneva Conventions, the Nuremberg Charter identified war crimes as 'violations of the laws or customs of war including but not limited to, murder, ill-treatment or deportation to slave labour, or for any other purpose, of civilian population of or in occupied territory, the murder or ill-treatment of prisoners of war or persons on the seas, killing hostages, plunder of public or private property, wanton destruction of cities, towns, villages, or devastation not justified by military necessity'.[126]

After the Nuremberg Tribunal and the Geneva Conventions, Israel was able to convict Eichmann for, *inter alia*, war crimes based on its Nazi and Nazi Collaborators (Punishment) Law.[127] The crime of war crimes in this statute is very similar to the crime as defined in the Nuremberg Charter outlined above.[128]

It would be illogical to think of war crimes being committed without a situation of hostilities. It is obvious from the explanations of war crimes given above that hostilities are a prerequisite. In *Fédération Nationale des Déportés et Internés Résistants et Patriotes and Others v. Barbie*,[129] Barbie, head of the Gestapo in Lyons during the Second World War, was charged with war crimes *in absentia* by French authorities after the war and sentenced to death. He was apprehended many years later in 1983 after being expelled by Bolivia where he

---

[122] Preamble to the Hague Regulations, *Ibid*, p. 45.

[123] The U.N. Secretary General, in his report regarding the establishment of the ICTY, acknowledged that the Geneva Conventions, as well as Hague Convention IV, are part of international customary law. Report of the Secretary General Pursuant to Paragraph 2 of S.C. Res. 808 (1993) U.N. Doc S/25704. See Paust, Bassiouni et al, *International Criminal Law, op cit*, p. 807.

[124] A grave breach under Geneva Convention IV, Article 147 involves the wilful killing, torture or inhuman treatment, wilfully causing great suffering or serious injury, extensive destruction of property not justified by military necessity and carried out unlawfully and wantonly, unlawfully deporting or transferring or confining a protected person, wilfully depriving a protected person of the right to a fair trial and taking hostages. Roberts and Guelff, *Documents on the Laws of War, op cit*, p. 323.

[125] Additional Protocol I, Articles 11 and 85. Roberts and Guelff, *Documents on the Laws of War, op cit*, p. 396 and 437 respectively.

[126] Nuremberg Charter, *op cit*, Article 6.

[127] Israeli Nazi and Nazi Collaborators (Punishment) Law. Under s1(a) of this Act a person who has committed an act constituting a war crime is liable to the death penalty provided that the act in question was committed during the Second World War in a hostile country. *Eichmann (District Court)*, p 7.

[128] The Israel war crime under this act substitutes 'slave labour' for 'forced labour'.

[129] *Fédération Nationale des Déportés et Internés Résistants et Patriotes and Others v. Barbie* (1985) ILR 125. Hereinafter: *Barbie Case*.

had taken refuge. The French Court of Cassation held that war crimes are directly connected with the existence of a situation of hostilities declared between the respective states to which the perpetrators and the victims of the acts in question belong.[130]

It has almost always been assumed that the hostilities in question involve inter-state conflicts. Apart from Common Article 3 of the Geneva Conventions and their Additional Protocol II, not much has been stated about hostilities of a non-international conflict, for example civil wars. However, the ICTR was able to use Common Article 3 and the Additional Protocol II in its Statute for a conflict that was purely internal in character.[131] This was perhaps the first time where a purely internal conflict gave rise to war crimes in the 20th century, thus paving the way for the ICC to have jurisdiction over war crimes for both international conflict and non-international conflicts.[132]

It would appear that contemporary war crimes include crimes committed by states on their citizens where there is some kind of conflict. This narrows the difference between war crimes and crimes against humanity.[133] Previously, when inter-state hostilities were a prerequisite for war crimes, the boundaries between war crimes and crimes against humanity seemed clear. However, now that war crimes can be committed in civil war situations, and perhaps during major civil disturbances, the demarcation between the two crimes is unclear as they both involve acts against a civilian population. Where acts are committed against combatants, the difference is clear; such acts are war crimes, as are acts committed against prisoners of war and those under occupation.

Crimes Against Humanity

Prior to the Nuremberg Tribunal there was not much written about this crime. According to the Nuremberg Charter this crime includes:

> murder, extermination, enslavement, deportation, and other inhumane acts committed against any civilian population, before or during war, or persecutions on political, racial or religious grounds in execution of or in connection with any crime within the jurisdiction of the Tribunal, whether or not in violation of the domestic law of the country where perpetrated.[134]

This is a rather broad category that appears to overlap with other crimes such as genocide and torture.[135] However, the acts in question must be committed before or during an armed conflict. The Nuremberg Tribunal limited the scope of this crime

---

[130] *Ibid.*

[131] ICTR Statute, Article 4.

[132] Rome Statute, Article 8(1)(b) and (c).

[133] This can be attributed to the Protocol II Additional to the Geneva Conventions which deals with non-international armed conflicts.

[134] Nuremberg Charter, Article 6.

[135] There is now an overlap with war crimes as detailed below.

International Crimes

by linking it to armed conflicts and other crimes it had jurisdiction over, hence only crimes against humanity committed alongside crimes against peace or war crimes could be tried.

This crime can cover a range of acts connected to an armed conflict. Recently, but prior to the Rome Statute, the French Court of Cassation in the *Barbie Case* included the crimes committed against the French Résistance by the German occupying forces as falling within the definition of politically motivated persecution, thereby making it a crime against humanity.[136] It has not been limited to civilians either, as was the case in the Tokyo Tribunal where it included military personnel.[137] Details of the crime were reaffirmed most recently in the definition under the Statute of the ICTY. There is much similarity between the ICTY classification and that of the Nuremberg Charter.[138] The main difference in the ICTY's statute is the specific inclusion of imprisonment, torture and rape.[139] Torture is an international crime in its own right, but rape and imprisonment would appear to be domestic legal issues. What ties them together to render them international crimes against humanity in the ICTY's statute is that they have to be committed in the context of an armed conflict, whether international or internal in character.

The ICTR's statute stretched the boundaries a little more in that the same listed offences are punishable internationally where committed 'as part of a widespread or systematic attack against any civilian population on national, political, ethnic, racial or religious grounds', national, ethnic and racial grounds being new additions to the definition.[140] Unlike previous tribunals, the Rome Statute has severed the link between armed conflict and crimes against humanity.[141] The Rome Statute's definition of crimes against humanity requires an act to be systematic, aimed at a civilian population with the intent and knowledge that that act will further a state or a group's policy.[142] The severing of this link has been described as a groundbreaking normative advance.[143] The severing of this link makes it possible to include certain treaty-based crimes as crimes against humanity. Thus, if classified as crimes against humanity, acts such as slavery, torture and terrorism have universal jurisdiction.[144]

---

[136] *Barbie Case*, p. 140.

[137] Tokyo Charter, *op cit*.

[138] ICTY Statute, Article 5.

[139] ICTY Statute, Article 5(e), (f) and (g) respectively.

[140] ICTR Statute, Article 3. It would have been to see a sexual ground added to this list in order to include rape.

[141] Nuremberg Charter; Art. 6, ICTY Statute; Article 5 and ICTR Statute; Art. 3. There was a required link with armed conflict that is severed in the Rome Statute's Article 7.

[142] Rome Statute, Article 7.

[143] Fife, 'The International Criminal Court Whence it Came, Where it Goes', (2000) *69 NJIL 63, 68*.

[144] See: Cassese, 'Terrorism is Also Disrupting Some Crucial Legal Categories of International Law', *op cit*.

58 *Immunity and International Criminal Law*

Genocide

The Rome Statute includes genocide which, it is interesting to note, is perhaps the most modern of the ICC crimes. We can accredit the creation of the crime of genocide to post-Second World War events. It was only after the Second World War, and the discovery of the enormous crimes committed against the Jewish people by the Nazis, that genocide became an international concern. Prior to that, genocide in various forms had occurred in other places, and even where condemned internationally, those responsible were never held accountable.[145] Prior to the term genocide being coined, genocidal acts were described as crimes against humanity.[146]

The issue of protection of minorities can be traced back as far as the Peace of Westphalia of 1648, which provided some guarantees for minorities. This guarantee seems not to have made a significant impact, as centuries later minorities were still being ill-treated. So much so that in 1915, following the atrocities committed by the Ottoman Empire against the Armenians, the governments of France, Great Britain and Russia felt the need to produce a joint declaration condemning the acts. The declaration stated that in:

> the presence of these new crimes of Turkey against humanity and civilization, the allied Governments publicly inform the Sublime Porte that they will hold personally responsible for the said crimes all members of the Ottoman Government as well as those of its agents who are found to be involved in such massacres.[147]

Not long thereafter, during the Second World War, the world witnessed German minorities being victimized by their own Nazi government. The idea that acts constituting genocide could be international crimes took hold.

The term genocide was coined by Raphael Lemkin in 1944, and was quickly taken up and included in the drafting of the Military Tribunal after the war.[148] It was adopted by the United Nations when they drafted the Genocide Convention. According to this Convention, the crime of genocide occurs when any of the following acts are committed:

> with the intent to destroy, in whole or part, a national, ethnical, racial or religious group, (a) killing members of the group; (b) causing serious bodily or mental harm to the members of the group; (c) deliberately inflicting on the group conditions of life calculated to bring about its physical destruction in whole or in part; (d) imposing measures intended to prevent births within the group; (e) forcibly transferring children of the group to another group.[149]

---

[145] Issue of Armenians massacred by Turkey, discussed below.

[146] Schabas, *Genocide in International Law* (2000), p. 13.

[147] *Ibid*, p. 13, 16.

[148] Lemkin, *Axis Rule in Occupied Europe: Laws of Occupation, Analysis of Government Proposals for Redress* (1944).

[149] Genocide Convention, Article 2. The Rome Statute, Article 6 on genocide is exactly the same. In the *Eichmann Case* the crime of 'crimes against the Jewish people' was not a crime

The punishable act is that of genocide, as is the conspiracy to commit genocide, to direct and publicly incite genocide, attempt genocide, as well as complicity in such an act.[150]

In the Rome Statute the definition given for the crime of genocide is similar to the definition given in the Genocide Convention. The 1994 Draft put genocide on a separate footing and made it possible for state parties who are also members of the Genocide Convention to lodge complaints to the Prosecutor.[151] This mechanism was removed in the final treaty after concerns had been raised during the Diplomatic Conference. The International Committee of the Red Cross (ICRC) was keen to have an international criminal court with jurisdiction over genocide, war crimes and crimes against humanity, rather than just genocide.[152]

Although the crimes described above could be considered as crimes against humanity, they become crimes of genocide where they target a specified group, whether or not in an armed conflict under the Geneva Convention. Unlike crimes against humanity, an armed conflict was not a requirement for genocide, which could be committed during so called peaceful times. Peace is thus relative, as it is only logical to assume that where a group is being targeted to such an extent, peace does not really exist. What may be more appropriate to state is that the situation in the given country is not that of a country undergoing major civil disturbances that affect all parts of society. For example where a *coup d'etat* occurs, a country may not necessarily go through a civil war or major civil disturbances that affect all its citizens. However, certain persons of a particular political persuasion may be tortured and killed whilst life continues for most of society in peace.

The Rules Prohibiting International Crimes: Norms of Superior Status?

Rules are created in international law by treaty and/or custom. In legal disputes involving the application of different rules the status and scope of these norms will come into question. Treaty rules obviously create obligations for states vis-à-vis the other states party to the treaty in question.[153] Customary rules create obligations for states towards each other. Although the issue is that of *locus standi* where there has been a breach of international law, it is closely tied to the question of hierarchy

---

in existence when Eichmann was pursuing his plans to exterminate the Jewish people. However the District Court worked around this issue by establishing that the act criminalized in its crime of crimes against the Jewish people bore a striking similarity to the crime of genocide. *Eichmann (District Court)*, p. 22-3.

[150] Genocide Convention, Article 3(a) (b) (c) (d) and (e).

[151] 1994 Draft, Article 25, *op cit.*

[152] New Zealand conveyed the ICRC's concerns: A/CONF.183/C.1/L.59.

[153] Treaty norms bind states party to them and take precedence as *lex specialis* over customary law between those states. Shaw, *International* Law, *op cit*, p. 96.

of norms.[154] When an international crime is committed the issue of *locus standi* arises in relation to the individual, alongside concerns regarding the prohibition of the crime and proceedings against the individual, which raises the question of state obligation. [155] Are all states obliged vis-à-vis other states or the international community to prohibit international crimes and, where they have a claim of jurisdiction, proceed against individuals? Does this obligation take precedence in all cases irrespective of other norms? The first question demands an analysis of *erga omnes* obligations, the second of *jus cogens* norms. The essence of *erga omnes* is the generality of standing, unlike *jus cogens,* whose fundamental nature is non-derogability.[156]

Erga Omnes Obligations

The ICJ in the *Belgium v Spain (Barcelona, Traction, Light Co. Case)* explored, in *obiter dictum*, the issue of state obligations with regard to international crimes.[157] According to the ICJ, the prohibition of certain international crimes created obligations for states towards the international community as a whole. These prohibitive norms created obligations in whose protection 'all states can be held to have a legal interest' as they are obligations *erga omnes*'[158] *Erga omnes* rules create obligations for which all states have *locus standi* when breached.[159] Once created, *erga omnes* norms generate additional 'rights and obligations which confer standing' 'on *any* of the States subject to that rule' in the 'event of any violation'.[160]

Although working on a different concept, the ILC in its Draft Articles on the Responsibility of States for Internationally Wrongful Acts, noted that with international crimes the injured state includes all states.[161] Thus where genocide has been committed all states have standing to make a claim. Although the ILC

---

[154] *Locus standi*: The right to be heard in court or other proceeding. Bird, *Osborn's Concise Law Dictionary* (1983). Issue of hierarchy of norms is discussed below in Chapter 6.

[155] Individual criminal responsibility under international criminal law is discussed further in the next chapter.

[156] Byers, 'Conceptualising the Relationship between *Jus Cogens* and *Erga Omnes* Rules', (1997*) 66 NJIL 211, 230.*

[157] *Belgium v. Spain (Barcelona, Traction, Light and Power Co. Case)* (1970) ICJ Reps. 3, 3. (Hereinafter *Barcelona Traction Case.)*

[158] *Ibid*, p. 32 paras. 33 and 34.

[159] Byers, 'Conceptualising the Relationship between *Jus Cogens* and *Erga Omnes* Rules', *op cit*, p. 211.

[160] *Ibid,* p. 233.

[161] ILC Draft Articles on the Responsibility of States for Internationally Wrongful Acts (1996) Article 53: An international crime committed by a State entails an obligation for every other State: (a) not to recognize as lawful the situation created by the crime; (b) not to render aid or assistance to the State which has committed the crime in maintaining the situation so created; (c) to cooperate with other States in carrying out the obligations under subparagraphs (a) and (b); and (d) to cooperate with other States in the application of measures designed to eliminate the consequences of the crime. A/LN.4/L.524.

International Crimes 61

was working on state responsibility, their line of thought in this instance can be applied to individual responsibility. As states are obliged to prohibit international crimes and, where possible, proceed against those accused of having committed such crimes, prosecutions by an uninvolved state under universal jurisdiction is evidence of the *erga omnes* character of the crime.

However, the *erga omnes* qualities of state obligations with regard to international crimes is dismissed as the 'product of good-hearted thinking' not capable of functioning 'in the world of affairs'.[162] On the contrary, however, it is suggested that assumptions as to the *erga omnes* qualities of international crimes are based on solid legal principles. Perpetrators of international crimes are enemies of mankind who pose a threat to all states. As such, each and every state has an obligation to proscribe and where possible enforce its laws against individuals. However, it is acknowledged that the difficulty lies in attempting to extend *erga omnes* obligations to crimes other than international crimes. There is a tendency to include within *erga omnes* obligations crimes that are created by treaty. It is illogical to extend this obligation to such crimes as only parties to a treaty have standing. Invoking *erga omnes* for treaty-based crimes is indeed unworkable in international law.

Jus Cogens Norms

There have been many references to *jus cogens* crimes in recent judgments. Lord Hope in *Pinochet (No. 3)* held that the 'careful discussion of the *jus cogens* ...rules in regard to allegations of official torture in *Siderman de Blake v. Argentina*' which he regarded 'as persuasive on this point, shows that there was already widespread agreement that the prohibition against torture had achieved the status of *jus cogens* norm'.[163] In *Siderman de Blake v. Argentina* it was held that 'official acts of torture...constitute a *jus cogens* violation'.[164] The issue of the prohibition of torture as a norm of *jus cogens* was taken up by the European Court of Human Rights (ECHR) in the *Al Adsani Case*.[165] The ECHR referred to the Lords' decision in *Pinochet (No. 3)*[166] and ICTY in *Prosecutor v. Furundzija*[167] and concluded that

---

[162] Rubin, '*Actio Popularis, Jus Cogens*, and Offenses *Erga Omnes*,' (2001) *35 New England L. Rev. 265, 280.*

[163] *Pinochet (No. 3)*, 152. Italics are the author's own.

[164] *Siderman de Blake v. Argentina* (1992) 965 F. 2d 699, 714-8. (Hereinafter the *Siderman de Blake Case*.)

[165] *Al Adsani v. United Kingdom* European Court of Human Rights Application No. 35763/97, 21 November 2001, paras. 51, 59, www.echr.org. (Hereinafter the *Al Adsani Case (ECHR.)*)

[166] *Pinochet (No. 3)*.

[167] *Prosecutor v. Furundzija*, It-95-17/l-T (1999) 38 ILM 317. The ICTY held that the '*jus cogens* nature of the prohibition against torture articulates the notion that the prohibition has now become one of the most fundamental standards of the international community'. Para. 154.

62   *Immunity and International Criminal Law*

the 'prohibition of torture has achieved the status of a peremptory norm in international law'.[168]

It is not only judges who appear keen to use the term *jus cogens*. The ILC, in its work to codify laws on treaties, voiced their opinion that the provisions of the UN Charter prohibiting the use of force constitutes an example of a rule in international law having the character of *jus cogens*.[169] Brownlie is of the opinion that the crime of genocide is a *jus cogens* prohibition.[170] In addition to the prohibition against aggressive use of force, torture and genocide, it is claimed that the prohibition of slavery and apartheid are also *jus cogens* norms.[171] But what exactly are *jus cogens* norms and how do they evolve?

Jus cogens norms are international law rules that cannot be derogated from. They are peremptory norms that are accepted and recognized as such by the international community of nations. The Treaty Convention states that:

> A treaty is void if, at the time of its conclusion, it conflicts with a peremptory norm of general international law. For the purposes of the present Convention, a peremptory norm of general international law is a norm accepted and recognized by the international community of States as a whole as a norm from which no derogation is permitted and which can be modified only by a subsequent norm of general international law having the same character.[172]

Jus cogens norms have been described as rules that define certain key aspects of the international legal system.[173] States are limited when it comes to altering the manner in which they apply them; hence, they can be compared, to a certain extent, to constitutional rules of national legal systems.[174] As constitutional rules they restrict the ability of states to develop, maintain or change other rules and prevent them from violating fundamental rules of international public policy.[175] According to Byers:

> Jus cogens rules, otherwise know as "peremptory rules", are non-derogable rules of international "public policy". They render void other, non-peremptory norms which are in conflict with them.[176]

The peremptory nature of *jus cogens* has roots in natural law sentiments. Unlike their positivist counterparts, adherents to natural law argue that states do

---

[168] *Al Adsani v. United Kingdom*, para. 61.

[169] See: ILC comments in (1966) *2 YBILC 248*.

[170] Brownlie, *Principles of Public International Law, op cit*, p. 514.

[171] Byers, 'Conceptualising the Relationship between *Jus Cogens* and *Erga Omnes* Rules', *op cit*, p. 219.

[172] Treaty Convention, Article 53, *op cit*.

[173] Byers, 'Conceptualising the Relationship between *Jus Cogens* and *Erga Omnes* Rules', *op cit*, p. 219.

[174] *Ibid.*

[175] *Ibid*, p. 220.

[176] Byers, 'Conceptualising the Relationship between *Jus Cogens* and *Erga Omnes* Rules', *op cit*, p. 211.

not have the total freedom to contract with each other to a certain extent as they are bound by certain fundamental principles.[177] In contrast, positivists have argued in the past that as 'international law springs from the relations between autonomous states, what is absolute in it retains the form of ought-to-be, since its actuality depends on different wills'.[178] It is true that the different 'wills' of sovereign independent states may interfere with the development of a cohesive international legal system. However, where all states have accepted that there are certain norms that they cannot derogate from, it would appear that these norms have gone beyond the 'ought-to-be' stage. It is by their very will that these norms have attained the status of *jus cogens* and have become at that moment absolute. Contrary to the belief that states remain superior to the mutual stipulations they make, norms of *jus cogens*, for the time that they are so, are superior to any mutual stipulations that states may make.[179] States can, however, alter the status of these norms, by mutual stipulations that give rise to other *jus cogens* norms.

Notwithstanding all references to *jus cogens*, questions have been posed as to the actual existence of this concept. It has been described as 'a normative myth',[180] as it is clear that although *jus cogens* is often mentioned, there is no complete explanation available as to how norms become *jus cogens*. Nor is there agreement amongst writers as to the current list of rules that are *jus cogens*. D'Amato suggests accurately that, post the Treaty Convention, writers have been drawn to wishful 'inclusion of various norms to lists of jus cogens'.[181] The various human rights norms promulgated as being *jus cogens* are so declared by writers and human rights advocates with a fervour that raises concern. Troubled by such references, Rubin ponders on the possibility of human rights treaties forming part of *jus cogens*.[182] According to him substantive law cannot be found in any treaty binding those who violate human rights.[183] In addition, he questions the peremptory status of these treaty norms where violators fail to perceive their actions as legal wrongs.[184] Persons committed to ethnic-cleansing may fail to see the wrong in killing members of another ethnic group, a wrong based on outsiders' moral perceptions. To Rubin this moral perception makes the act evil but not a legal default.[185] To him the evil act is a moral default not based on a substantive rule of law. Substantive law is a reflection of society's acceptance and recognition of the binding nature of the norms in question. The non-derogable character of *jus*

---

[177] Danilenko, 'International *Jus Cogens*: Issues of Law-Making' (1991) *EJIL 42*.

[178] Hegel, *The Philosophy of Right, op cit*, p. 212 para. 330.

[179] 'The relation between states is a relation between autonomous entities which make mutual stipulations but which at the same time are superior to these stipulations.' Hegel, *The Philosophy of Right (Additions), ibid*, p. 297 para. 191.

[180] Christensen, '*Jus Cogens*: Guarding Interests Fundamental to International Society' *(1988) VJIL 585, 590*.

[181] D'Amato, 'It's A Bird, It's A Plane, It's *Jus Cogens*' (1991) *6 Conn. JIL 1*.

[182] Rubin, '*Actio Popularis, Jus Cogens* and Offenses *Erga Omnes*', *op cit*, p. 275.

[183] *Ibid.*

[184] *Ibid.*

[185] *Ibid.*

cogens is validated through the process creating substantive law, as it is through this means that society recognizes and accepts binding norms. Consequently, without substantive law there cannot be recognition and acceptance, and *jus cogens*.

But even with substantive law in operation, the open-ended nature of the decision as to which norms become *jus cogens* is still a problem.[186] Those who see 'the superiority of the "human rights" components of the moral law, can convert the moral imperatives into legal rules of substance that are different from those whose actions are sought to be affected'.[187] Subsequently, a consensus-based process by which norms of *jus cogens* are created is fundamental.

It is arguable that the probibitory norms of international customary crimes have attained the status of *jus cogens*. Brownlie claims that where two states have an agreement to carry out a joint operation against a racial group, the agreement is void as it conflicts with a rule of *jus cogens*.[188] Achieving such distinction is and must remain a difficult process. The mere insistence by judges, writers and human rights advocates that certain acts have attained the status of *jus cogens* does not make them so. Yet it is understandable why pronouncements on *jus cogens* norms are frequent. If deemed *jus cogens*, norms become non-derogable and thereby superior to other international norms.

But norms only become *jus cogens* when all states believe that it is impossible to 'contract out' of those rules or persistently object to them.[189] *Opinio juris* is, therefore, essential in determining *jus cogens* norms. As these norms cannot be limited by agreement between states, they must be of critical importance to the world community as a whole. Higgins argues that such norms retain their normative quality because the world community consents. She states that:

> norms cannot be artificially protected through classifying them as rules with a higher normativity which will continue to exist even if we fail to make states see the value of giving such prescriptions a normative quality. [190]

Thus, according to Higgins, states must accept and acknowledge the higher standing of a norm to ensure its status as *jus cogens*. She appears to reject the idea that certain norms are hierarchically supreme based on the natural law assumptions of a range of immutable norms that remain constant regardless of attitudes of states.[191] It is arguably the case that states will only see the value of giving prohibitory rules higher normative value when they cease to commit such acts.

---

[186] *Ibid.*

[187] *Ibid.*

[188] Brownlie, *Principles of Public International Law, op cit*, p. 514. The ILC's definition of international crimes is narrower than a rule of *jus cogens*: see: (1985) *YBILC pt. 2, 24*

[189] Higgins, *Problems and Process. International Law and How We Use It, op cit*, p. 22. Byers, 'Conceptualising the Relationship between *Jus Cogens* and *Erga Omnes* Rules', *op cit*, p. 221.

[190] *Ibid*, p. 21-2.

[191] *Ibid.*

International Crimes

Hence, the practice of states is very important in the formation, development and the possible death of *jus cogens* norms. This claim appears at odds with the prohibition of torture. Although it is often cited as being a norm of *jus cogens*, many states still routinely practise torture.

A possible explanation as to how the prohibition of torture is *jus cogens*, irrespective of contrary state practice, is put forward by Garnett:

> It may be argued, therefore, that the absolute nature of the conventional prohibitions, when coupled with the near universal *opinio juris* amongst states as to the illegality of the practice, may be a sufficient basis for concluding that torture is prohibited as a peremptory norm.[192]

Thus for Garnett, it appears that the high normative status of torture is deduced from the treaty itself and *opinio juris*. For him, the prohibition of torture is a norm of *jus cogens*. But Higgins challenges this conclusion. She argues that the

> reason that the prohibition on torture continues to be a requirement of international customary law, even though wholly abused, is not because it has a higher normative status that allows us to ignore the abuse, but because *opinio juris* as to its normative status continues to exist.[193]

For Higgins, the prohibition of torture as a norm of customary law has not attained the status of *jus cogens*. It is, for her, a norm of customary law because of *opinio juris*, even though it is regularly abused. Thus with only acceptance as a criteria, the prohibition of torture is, according to these writers, at least a norm of international customary law.

It is difficult to link the concept of *jus cogens* with notions of peremptory norms or customary law where state practice is for the most part lacking. Although Higgins acknowledges that the prohibition of torture is a customary norm, she fails to clarify how it became so, even though she recognizes that a rule cannot become a customary norm without both practice and *opino juris*. If both practice and *opino juris* are fundamental, how can the prohibition of torture become customary law and then *jus cogens*? It is true that states view acts of torture as violations. But inconsistencies in practice prevent the rule in question from becoming a customary rule, and the main inconsistency with the prohibition of torture would be states not engaging in torture.[194]

It is acknowledged that some human rights violations, of which torture is included, 'occur with distressing frequency and in places far separated.'[195] Amnesty International documents torture in well over half of all states each year.[196] But with full knowledge of this, it is argued that the importance of the values

---

[192] Garnett, 'The Defence of State Immunity for Acts of Torture', *op cit*, at p. 103-4.

[193] Higgins, *Problems and Process. International Law and How We Use It*, *op cit*, p. 22.

[194] Malanczuk, *Akehurst's Modern Introduction to International Law*, op cit, p. 41-2.

[195] Rubin, *'Actio Popularis, Jus Cogens* and Offenses *Erga Omnes'*, *op cit*, p. 275.

[196] www.amnesty.org. See Chart in Appendix.

protected by the prohibition of torture is enough to determine its *jus cogens* status.[197] It is suggested that for both customary and *jus cogens* norms, both *opinio juris* and practice must be evident. Contrary to Shaw's conclusion based on Akehurst's assertion that state practice covers any act or statement by a state,[198] it is suggested that deduction of practice should not rest with any act or statement. More accurately, practice must be the actual cessation of the act in question. Otherwise, human rights norms can never be anything more than mere aspirations.

Consequently, it is suggested that only under international criminal law can human rights become *jus cogens*; thus the prohibitive norms of international crimes are, arguably, *jus cogens*. International criminal law provides the opportunity for tangible legal remedies on moral issues. Without the possibility of legal redress violators can view the law as being in the 'ought-to-be' stage of norm creation. The customary binding nature of international crimes and universal jurisdiction, together with the drive for individual accountability, can help generate the peremptory nature of *jus cogens* norms. State officials, out of fear of prosecution, will cease to violate human rights of their citizens. Thus in both practice and *opinio* they could become international customary crimes, and perhaps norms of *jus cogens*. By targeting the individual, international criminal law can help bring human rights out from its 'ought-to-be' stage.

In conclusion, therefore, it is apt to refer and accept Rubin's warning of the danger to peace and justice in the use of Latin phrases.[199] According to him, there is a distinct lack of thought behind the use of Latin terms and a further absence of analysis as to their implementation in the international order. These deficiencies are, to him, threats to peace and justice. Indeed they create false hopes.

---

[197] *Prosecutor v. Furundzija*. Square brackets as per Lord Browne-Wilkinson in *Pinochet (No. 3)*, *op cit*, p. 108.

[198] Shaw, *International Law*, *op cit*, quotes Akehurst, 'Custom as a Source of International Law'.

[199] Rubin, *'Actio Popularis, Jus Cogens* and Offenses *Erga Omnes'*, *op cit*, p. 280.

Chapter 3

Individual Criminal Responsibility

For the most part, the responsibility for international law violations has rested on states, and such responsibility has been primarily civil in the form of reparations. Although the notion that states could be criminally liable was put forward by the ILC in their 1980 Draft Articles on State Responsibility, it was not warmly received and was removed from the draft.[1] The ILC suggested that crimes of aggression, colonial domination, slavery, genocide and apartheid could give rise to the criminal responsibility of states. However, the effectiveness of international criminal law as a penal system of laws could be called into question when its target ceases to be the individual. International criminal law is best as a deterrent if the individual is its objective.[2] However, it is only recently in the history of inter-state relations that the individual has become a target of international law.

It is now clearly recognized that the individual must bear the responsibility for the commission of international crimes. As outlined in the previous chapter, individuals who commit international crimes are personally responsible. The aim is penal rather than civil.[3] It is for these reasons that international criminal law targets individuals rather than states or groups.

International Law and the Individual

For centuries individuals were not regarded as subjects of international law. They were not afforded rights or duties.[4] States were the only subjects of international law having enforceable rights and duties. Only they had international legal personality.[5] This is the point of view of theorists who adhere to the positivist line of reasoning. Their ideas heavily influenced international law during the 19th century.

---

[1] Article 19 (1980) *2 YBILC 32*. The ILC continued its work in this area. See: Jørgensen, *The Responsibility of States for International Crimes* (2000).

[2] Ratner and Abrahms, *Accountability for Human Rights Atrocities in International Law* (2001), *op cit*, p. 15-7.

[3] Ratner and Abrahms, *Accountability for Human Rights Atrocities in International Law*, *ibid*, p. 15.

[4] Malanczuk, *Akehurst's Modern Introduction to International Law* (1997), p. 100.

[5] *Ibid.*

The Growth and Influence of Positivism

For positivists, states establish or 'will' norms of international law collectively.[6] For them the manner in which a norm is created is very important as laws must be created and laid down by a competent body through proper procedure. Such a body must be discernible as having the capacity to produce legal rules.[7]

By arguing for the creation of law by some distinct source acting through proper procedure, positivists from the 18th century onwards worked towards weakening the idea that certain rules are created from a divine source. Early positivists were able to conceive their theories in a world that was still very much dominated by the Church. Notions of a law natural to man that is unchanging irrespective of human development is a remnant of early Greek philosophy. Classical natural law implied natural functions, ends and duties.[8] It is assumed that in pre-historical times 'so-called primitive mankind shared in the life of nature, was initiated via rituals and ceremonies'.[9] In participating in that structure man came to the belief that nature is sacred and demands respect, hence nature 'became the source of norms for their behaviour'.[10] Guided by such notions, man incorporated nature in his life to bring meaning and order to that life. This led to the perception that nature was of vital importance in norm formation, a perception that influenced the Greeks who sought order in nature as opposed to the variation, chaos, diversity and disorder in the world.[11]

These Greek beliefs influenced Rome, the next great civilization. Thus Cicero incorporated their ideas in his analysis, and created the notion of eternal law.[12] According to him:

> True law is right reason in agreement with nature, diffused among all men; constant and unchanging, it should call men to their duties by its precepts, and deter them from wrongdoing by its prohibitions; and it never commands or forbids upright men in vain, while its rules and restraints are lost upon the wicked. To curtail this law is unholy, to amend it illicit, to repeal it impossible; nor can we be dispensed from it by the order of either senate or of popular assembly;...God, its designer, expounder and enactor, will be as it were the sole and universal ruler and governor of all things.[13]

---

[6] Ago, 'Positive Law and International Law' (1957) *51 AJIL 691, 701*. Hegel refers to the 'will' of states in norm creation. Hegel, *The Philosophy of Right, op cit.*

[7] Ago, 'Positive Law and International Law', *op cit*, p. 697.

[8] Morrison, *Jurisprudence: From the Greeks to Post-Modernism* (1997), p. 26.

[9] *Ibid*, p. 27.

[10] *Ibid.*

[11] *Ibid.*

[12] *Ibid*, p. 54.

[13] Cicero, *De Republica*, 3.22.33, quoted in Morrison, *Jurisprudence: From the Greeks to Post-Modernism, op cit*, p. 54.

Thus was the scene when Christianity took hold over the Western Hemisphere. St Augustine of the early Middle Ages[14] integrated Roman paganism with Christianity and declared the Christian God the author and ultimate ruler of the world.[15] To him natural law was the reason and will of God. Laws created by the state must be in accordance with the principles of that natural law.[16] According to the natural law viewpoint, 'a state's public or political life is under the same set of moral laws as those of the individual. Both spheres ultimately share a single source of truth; entire, inviolate, and not subject to changes in human life. Behind the entities and operations of the world order stands its author and ultimate ruler: God.'[17]

Needless to say, criticisms of divinely superior laws were the starting point in natural law's demise. Although naturalism remained influential, theological origin of law became less persuasive. Indeed, Pufendorf, writing in 1672, based his system on natural law that is binding on all men in an imaginary 'state of nature', of[18]

> nations being composed of men naturally free and independent, and who before the establishment of civil societies lived together in the state of nature; nations or sovereign states must be regarded as so many free persons living together in the state of nature.[19]

Vattel's concept of the equality of states, and Bodin's earlier work on sovereignty,[20] played a part in diminishing the power of natural law's divine premise. As the power of the Church over the political lives of states diminished, it became clear to writers that states were the superior law-making and enforcement bodies. Thus, in elucidating on management of citizens and inter-state relations, writers began to draw less on the centrality of the Church, but more on state-centred perspectives.

Zouche, writing in the 17th century, argued that law is derived from the practice of states.[21] He is credited as being the precursor of positivism,[22] as his assertions appeared to place greater emphasis on state action over and above divine power in the creation of law. Building upon these ideas, other writers adopted the notion of state practice in law creation. In particular, Bynkershoek maintained that

---

[14] St. Augustine (354-430), *ibid.*

[15] Morrison, *Jurisprudence: From the Greeks to Post-Modernism, op cit*, p. 1.

[16] *Ibid*, p. 62.

[17] *Ibid*, p. 61.

[18] Pufendorf, *De Jure naturae et gentium*, from Brierly, *The Law of Nations*, p. 36.

[19] Vattel's equality of states was based on Pufendorf's idea of a 'state of nature'. Vattel, *Les Droit des Gens* (1758), quoted in Brierly, *The Law of Nations, ibid*, p. 37.

[20] Bodin, *Six Livres de la Republic* (1577), referred to by Brierly, *The Law of Nations*, (1963), p. 7-12.

[21] Zouche, *Jus et Judicium jeciale, Sive Jus Intergentes*, (1650), quoted in Brierly, *The Law of Nations, ibid*, p. 35.

[22] *Ibid.*

70   *Immunity and International Criminal Law*

contemporary state practice was the significant indicator of custom: custom being the source of legal rules.[23] These theorists and many of their contemporaries discarded the notion of unchanging law derived from the divine.

This perception dominated the 19th century. Austin, a well-known positivist, recognized as law only those rules created or willed by a politically superior body.[24] As a result, positivists acknowledged states as the only entities capable of creating norms. For that reason, as positivists saw international law as a system of laws that regulates inter-state relations, states are the sole subjects of the international law that they create.

For the most part, contemporary international law remains heavily influenced by positivism. States as subjects are strategically important to international law. As creators of law they are not objects, and thus have rights and duties. Under positivism, individuals, on the other hand, are mere objects of international law and do not have rights and duties under it. This strict positivist interpretation of international law concerning the position of individuals has been, to some extent, tempered in recent decades. It has been difficult to ignore the role of individuals and, indeed, other entities, such as international organizations, in international law. In particular the function that individuals have come to realize in international human rights has been especially important.

The Re-Emergence of Natural Law Influences

Individuals have over the last century acquired rights under international law. Such rights have been defined as human rights, in that they are particular to human beings. By virtue of the fact that one is human, one can assert certain claims 'as of right'.[25] These claims are not based 'upon love, or grace, or brotherhood, or charity: one does not have to earn or deserve them. They are not merely aspirations or moral assertions but, increasingly legal claims under some applicable law.'[26] Whilst restricting government action, human rights also place obligations on society with regards to the individual.[27] Currently the claims that an individual can make regarding his rights are considered inalienable: they cannot be transferred, forfeited or waived.[28]

The notion of rights in law that are predetermined and fixed, irrespective of changes in human society, is consistent with the natural law theory of eternal law. Classical natural law theory emphasized the existence of a law of nature that is

---

[23] Bynkershoek, *Quastiones Juris Publici* (1737), quoted in Brierly, *The Law of Nations, ibid*, p. 36.

[24] Austin, *The Matter of Jurisprudence is Positive Law. From Austin's Lectures on Jurisprudence or the Philosophy of Positive Law* (1920) Part 1, Section 1, Lecture I & VI.

[25] Henkin, *The Rights of Man Today* (1978), p. 1-2.

[26] *Ibid.*

[27] *Ibid*, p. 2.

[28] *Ibid*, p. 3.

independent of laws made by man, or positive law.[29] This law of nature is preordained and constant. Thus the rights of individuals can be said to flow from this natural law position. One has certain rights because one is human, irrespective of man-made positive law.

Natural law's real influence on international law re-emerged after the Second World War. The atmosphere after the Nazi atrocities were uncovered seemed to compel the return of notions of a law that is superior to states. In order to prevent future carnage there was an immediate need to articulate the existence of a system of norms that would bind all states regardless of any laws they create. It was necessary that such norms incorporated certain rights for individuals. Thus according to Henkin, states are bound by international human rights norms 'regardless of their own constitutions or other laws and their official behaviour to the international norms'.[30]

Human rights have evolved from the Universal Declaration of Human Rights of 1948 to a proliferation of treaties granting the individual rights at the international level.[31] States consented to the establishment of these apparently high-ranking laws of human rights treaties. By so consenting they have given the rules their legal basis. According to Henkin the natural law-influenced rules are actually binding positive laws that states have created giving the individual rights under international law.[32]

The Individual in Contemporary International Law

It can now be said with confidence that the individual has rights under contemporary international law. The many rights an individual can claim internationally are directly attributable to the intensified international human rights discourse. But the rights so granted are empty without a sense of duty. Human rights are claimed against states. However, states are abstract entities administered by individuals. It is these individuals who must be made aware that they have a personal duty not to violate international human rights. Without this sense of personal accountability human rights as a system of law is a pretty but empty shell. International criminal law has been vital in ensuring that individuals have that sense of duty. By making individuals personally liable for human rights violations, international criminal law has identified the duties of individuals under international law. Individuals have a responsibility not to commit international crimes. Concurrent with that duty is the knowledge that when they do, they will be held responsible. Individuals have, therefore, rights and duties under international law.

---

[29] Morrison, *Jurisprudence: From the Greeks to Post-Modernism, op cit*, p. 55.
[30] Henkin, *The Rights of Man Today, op cit*, p. 22.
[31] Barker, *International Law and International Relations, op cit*, p. 49.
[32] Henkin, *The Rights of Man Today, op cit*, p. 22.

The duty on individuals in relation to human rights was first spelt out in the Nuremberg Charter, the first international document to do so.[33] Prior to Nuremberg, attempts were made to hold individuals responsible. One example is the Leipzig Trials of 1921. In that situation 12 German individuals appeared before the Criminal Senate of the Imperial Court of Justice of Germany, accused of having committed war crimes during the First World War.[34] These efforts helped establish that a person could be held individually accountable for certain acts at the international level thus making them more than mere objects.

It is acknowledged that some participants in the international sphere may not necessarily constitute international legal persons 'although they may act with some degree of influence upon the international plane'.[35] It is argued that if individuals are regarded as participants the rigid subject/object perception can be avoided.[36] Higgins regards individuals as participants who are not mere objects of international law, like boundaries or rivers. Individuals are, to her, 'part and parcel of the fabric of international law'.[37] She is of the correct assumption that the rigid subject/object dictum has 'no credible reality' nor 'functional purpose'.[38] Certainly, under international criminal law individuals have become more than objects. They are now subjects. It is pointless adhering strictly to the subject/object dichotomy that states and only states are subjects of international law when the effectiveness of international criminal law lies in international law's ability to hold individuals personally liable. The very nature of criminal law makes it impossible to ignore the individual; one needs individuals to apprehend and try. The idea that states should be made criminally liable for international crimes undermines this position. Without an individual's real sense of criminal responsibility, prohibition in itself is futile. In prohibiting certain acts international criminal law must also make individuals aware that they will face charges in a court of law. Hence courts or tribunals are a prerequisite to fulfilling that purpose.

Individuals and International Crimes under National Jurisdictions

As a result of the lack of a single international criminal court, domestic jurisdictions have had to deal with individuals who have committed international crimes. Efforts to establish individual accountability by domestic forums can be traced back to 1268. In perhaps the earliest example, Conradin von Hohenstaufen, Duke of Suabia, was put on trial in Naples for crimes against humankind.[39] Von Hohenstaufen was accused of initiating an unjust war, deemed an offence against

---

[33] Nuremberg Charter, Article 7.

[34] Paust, Bassiouni, et al, *International Criminal Law Cases and Materials*, *op cit*, p. 623.

[35] Shaw, *International Law*, *op cit*, p. 138-9, 183.

[36] Higgins, *Problems & Processes. International Law and How We Use It*, *op cit*, p. 49-50.

[37] *Ibid.*

[38] *Ibid.*

[39] Paust, Bassiouni et al, *International Criminal Law Cases and Materials*, *op cit*, p. 621.

Individual Criminal Responsibility 73

peace and was executed.[40] Another example, perhaps, is the trial of the Duke of Hagenbach who was found guilty of murder, rape, perjury and other crimes that were in violation of the laws of God and man in 1474.[41] These examples occurred prior to the world order we are accustomed to: a world order of sovereign equal states that have defined territories, and final authority for criminal acts within such territories. Von Hohenstaufen and Hagenbach lived in a world in which the Christian Church dominated all aspects of life. Sovereigns were bound by divine laws that superseded any earthly notions of territory.

Jurisdictional Obstacles

With the demise of the Church and its cross-border authority, state power became more centralized. Territorial boundaries became more important as states formed a system based on sovereign equality of states, a process that created complications for individual accountability. Difficulties arose as a result of the scope of a state's authority being limited to its territory. This is an element of a state's sovereignty under the territorial jurisdiction theory. According to this principle an offence has to be committed within a state's territory in order for that state to have jurisdiction over it. A state has subjective territorial jurisdiction where an offence occurs in or its effects are felt within its territory.[42]

This is simple where the entire crime occurred within a particular state's territory. Where part of an offence occurred in one state and its effects were felt in another, both states have a claim to jurisdiction.[43] The objective territorial principle accords jurisdiction where an essential part of the offence is completed in the state's territory, the most common example being the firing of a gun by an individual in one state, into the territory of the neighbouring state, causing the

---

[40] It must be said that the inclusion of this instance as an example of early attempts at accountability at the domestic level is made with some hesitation. The main reason behind the trial of von Hohenstaufen was purely political on the part of Charles of Anjou who was seeking to rid himself of any claims to Naples by the last member of the Hohenstaufen house. Where trials for international crimes are held there should be no doubt in any ones mind that the main purpose of the trial is the crime itself. For a detailed look at events leading up to and including the trial, see: Crawford, *Rulers of the South, Sicily, Calabra, Malta* (1900).

[41] Paust, Bassiouni et al, *International Criminal Law Cases and Materials, op cit*, p. 622.

[42] *Treacey v. DPP* [1971] AC 537.

[43] In the *Lotus Case* Judge Moore held that 'it appears to be now universally admitted that, where a crime is committed in the territorial jurisdiction of one State as the direct result of the act of a person at the time corporeally present in another State, international law, by reason of the principle of constructive presence of the offender at the place where his act took effect, does not forbid the prosecution of the offender at the former State, should he come within its territorial jurisdiction.' *France v. Turkey (Lotus Case)* PICJ Reps. Series A, No. 10. Judge Moore's dissenting decision in which he rejected the protective principle. P. 73.

74   *Immunity and International Criminal Law*

death of an individual in that state's territory.[44] Where attempts have been made to hold individuals accountable for international crimes, the territorial principle has caused difficulties. It has been noted that 'attempts to provide for universal jurisdiction against crimes which are regarded as crimes against humanity have had to overcome the fundamental obstacle of the territorial jurisdiction of the state in which the alleged crime has been committed'.[45]

For example, in the *Habre Case*, the Senegalese courts held that they did not have the jurisdiction to look at offences committed in another state's territory.[46] Hissen Habre was the head of state of Chad between 1982 and 1990. During that time it is alleged that he was responsible for the killings of some 40,000 people and the torture of some 200,000.[47] These acts came to light after he was deposed and his successors established a commission of enquiry.[48] Habre fled to Senegal and lived quietly until 1999. That year, spurred on by the Pinochet case in the UK, Human Rights Watch and a local Chadian human rights group sought to have him tried in Senegal.[49]

The case against Habre was brought before a judge in 1999 and he was placed under house arrest. However, when a new judge took over the case, it was thrown out, based on the judge's decision that Senegal did not have the jurisdiction to look at offences committed in another state's territory. This decision was upheld by Senegal's highest court, the Cour de Cassation on appeal. At that time Senegal had ratified the Torture Convention, and as a monist state, it is assumed that the convention applied directly.[50] However, although torture is a crime in Senegal,[51] the Cour de Cassation, in applying the Torture Convention, was of the opinion that

---

[44] The objective territorial principle is nowadays used to combat violations of anti-trust laws and drugs trafficking. The UK's House of Lords held in *DPP v. Doot* that they had jurisdiction over persons convicted of the conspiracy to import cannabis to the UK. The 'international elements' involved in the case, that of the accused being 'foreigners who had conspired abroad', did not preclude the UK courts from prosecuting them under the objective territorial principle, *DPP v. Doot* [1973] *AC* 807, Lord Wilberforce, p. 817-9.

[45] Barker, *International Law and International Relations, op cit*, p. 143.

[46] The promising start was brought to an abrupt end when the first judge who had indicted Habre, Demba Kandji, was replaced. His replacement followed a change in government. It is alleged that the new government was not keen on the trial and sought to undermine proceedings. The council that oversaw the judge's dismissal from the case was presided over by the President and his minister of justice (Conseil Supérieur de la Magistrature). Post-election turnabouts in policy are not new to African states. Adherence to democracy and human rights by a previous government may turn out to be a thorn in the side of the next.

[47] Information available from Human Rights Watch at www.hrw.com.

[48] Wall Street Journal, 3-4 March 2000 *www.wsj.com*.

[49] Chadian Association for the Promotion and Defence of Human Rights.

[50] Torture Convention, *op cit*. States that are monist tend to treat such obligations, whether arising from treaty or custom, as part of the law of the land to be given direct effect. States that are more dualist in their approach are inclined to draft intervening statutes to give the international rules specific legal effect. Higgins, *Problems & Process. International Law and How We Use It*, (1994), p. 209.

[51] Senegal Penal Code Article 295-1 Law N° 96-15 of 28 August 1996.

Individual Criminal Responsibility   75

as there is no specific statute that could have helped it establish its jurisdiction over acts of torture committed outside Senegal, thus the territorial requirement of the Torture Convention was applied directly.

Jurisdiction under the Torture Convention is primarily limited to the territorial, nationality and passive personality principles. Article 5 of the Torture Convention states that a state shall take necessary steps to establish its jurisdiction over a relevant offence where it occurred in its territory or onboard a ship or aircraft registered to it, or where the offender is its national.[52] The convention also provides for the passive personality principle in that, when appropriate, a state can claim jurisdiction where the victim is its national.[53] By enabling a state to claim jurisdiction simply because the offender is in its territory under the *aut dedere aut judicare* maxim, the convention expands jurisdiction:

> Each State Party shall likewise take such measures as may be necessary to establish its jurisdiction over such offences in cases where the alleged offender is present in any territory under its jurisdiction and it does not extradite him pursuant to article 8 to any of the States mentioned in paragraph 1 of this article.[54]

However, an individual can only be found personally liable for an offence under this maxim with regard to international treaty crime, if the forum state has provided for individual responsibility under municipal law.[55] The *Habre Case* illustrates that where the forum state has not so legislated, the *aut dedere aut judicare* maxim does not expand jurisdiction. Thus the territorial principle of jurisdiction has proved to be inadequate in cases involving international crimes, and in particular international treaty-based crimes.

If the territorial principle were the only jurisdictional principle available, state A would be unable to hold individuals accountable for crimes committed within state B by citizens of state B against their fellow citizens. The boundary of territory in the application of a state's criminal jurisdiction must be flexible. Where international crimes are involved, states must be able to expand the scope of their jurisdiction in order to fulfil their international obligations. Hence states have come to rely on other jurisdictional principles in order to pursue international crimes that may not have occurred within their territory. Other principles that states have relied on in the past include the nationality (active personality),[56] protective[57] and

---

[52] Torture Convention, *op cit*, Article 5(1)(a)(b).

[53] Torture Convention, *op cit*, Article 5(1)(c).

[54] Torture Convention, *op cit*, Article 5(2). Barker acknowledges that this is a form of universality of jurisdiction based on the 'specific consent of the states involved in the regime'. Barker, *International Law and International Relations, op cit*, p. 143.

[55] Barker, *International Law and International Relations, op cit*, p. 144.

[56] The Nationality Principle: States can assume jurisdiction over their nationals who have committed crimes abroad. Common law countries tend to limit the offences that the nationality principle covers. UK law permits jurisdiction over its own nationals who have committed treason, offences under the Official Secrets Act 1989: s.15(1), murder and bigamy, outside UK territory. Countries with civil law systems tend not to limit offences.

76 *Immunity and International Criminal Law*

universal principles. Indeed, in 1935 a group of American lawyers working unofficially produced the Harvard Research Draft Convention on Jurisdiction with Respect to Crime, which adopted these four jurisdictional principles that were considered to be part of international customary law.[58] The Harvard Research Draft also looked at the passive personality principle, but rejected it.[59]

Jurisdictional Solutions

The nationality, protective and universal principles have proved useful to domestic courts in establishing individual criminal responsibility for international crimes. In 1961 Israel relied on the protective and universal principles of jurisdiction to prosecute Adolf Eichmann for crimes against humanity, genocide and crimes against the Jewish people.[60] The District Court, whose decision was later supported by the Supreme Court, did not find any difficulty in utilizing these principles to establish that they had the jurisdiction to hear the case. Although the state of Israel did not exist at the time the acts in question were committed, the District Court and the Supreme Court found that the protective and universal principles were the rules to get round this particular problem. The defence had argued, *inter alia*, attempts by Israel to impose punishment for acts done outside its boundaries before its establishment was contrary to international law.[61]

According to the District Court the Israeli law enacted to punish Nazis was not contrary to international law:

> The abhorrent crimes defined in this Law are not crimes under Israeli law alone. These crimes, which struck at the whole of mankind and shocked the conscience of nations, are grave offences against the laws of nations itself (delicta juris gentium). Therefore, so far from international law negating or limiting jurisdiction of countries with respect to such crimes, international law is, in the absence of an International

---

[57] The Protective Principle: Where a state fears that acts committed by aliens abroad will endanger its national security it may rely on the protective principle to establish jurisdiction over the offence. Although the principle is open to abuse by states, it is relied on primarily because of inadequate domestic legal protection against the security and integrity of foreign states within states. Use of this principle was made in the UK in the case of *Joyce v. DPP* in 1946. The American-born Joyce acquired a British passport fraudulently then left Britain in 1939 to live in Germany. He later claimed to have acquired German citizenship. In deciding if they had jurisdiction over him for charges of treason, the House of Lords held that, although he had fraudulently acquired a British passport, the fact that he had one meant that he owed allegiance to the British Crown. They also found that it did not matter that he had committed the offence of treason outside British territory. *Joyce v. DPP* [1946] *AC* 347.

[58] Harvard Research Draft Convention on Jurisdiction with Respect to Crime (1935) *29 AJIL 519*. (Hereinafter Harvard Research Draft.)

[59] The passive personality principle looks at the nationality of the victim.

[60] *Eichmann Case.*

[61] *Ibid*, para. 8, p.23. Eichmann was charged under the 1950 Nazis and Nazi Collaborators (Punishment) Law 5710.

Individual Criminal Responsibility 77

Court, in need of the judicial and legislative organs of every country to give effect to its criminal interdictions and to bring the criminals to trial.[62]

Consequently, states with custodial enforcement jurisdiction have universal authority over international crimes. Israel's capacity to punish Nazis for crimes against humanity and war crimes is universal, as the crimes in question are part of international customary law. The fact that Israel did not exist at the time the acts in question were committed did not negate its obligation under international customary law once it came into being. International customary law binds all states, even those that may not have contributed to its formation.

The universal jurisdictional principle has been relied upon by several states recently following the conflict in the former Yugoslavia and Rwanda. The Belgians have found it to be of great value. As a monist state universal jurisdiction would have been applicable directly to domestic courts as a matter of customary international law. But the Belgian government has specifically introduced laws that give its court universal jurisdiction for international crimes. By 1999 these included war crimes, crimes against humanity and genocide.[63] Following these advances the Belgian courts have convicted Rwandan citizens – two nuns, a university professor and a former transport minister – for their part in that country's genocide.[64] There was mention thereafter of attempts to bring proceedings against heads of state or government in Belgian courts.[65] Other European countries have also managed to use this principle. Trials have so far produced acquittals and convictions in Germany and Switzerland, amongst other states. Two Bosnian Serbs were convicted in Germany for war crimes committed in the former Yugoslavia: Djajic in May 1997 and Jorgic in September 1997 and in Switzerland: a Rwandan citizen, N, was convicted of war crimes in April 1999.[66]

Universal jurisdiction did not apply in the *Habre Case*. The acts in question fell under the Torture Convention, which gives Senegal limited jurisdiction over offences committed in its territory, or where the offender was or any victims were its nationals.[67] Crucially, the treaty does, however, oblige the state with custodial enforcement jurisdiction to prosecute or extradite. Thus even if the crime did not occur within its territory as a member state to this convention, Senegal should have taken measures to establish its jurisdiction over the offences under the maxim *aut*

---

[62] *Ibid*, para. 12, p. 26.

[63] *Proposition de loi relative à la repression des violations graves du droit international humanitaire,* Belgian Senate, 1 December 1998 1-749/4. www.redress.org.

[64] www.news.bbc.co.uk.

[65] These include Castro of Cuba and Arafat of Palestine. This seems unlikely after the Sharon case was thrown out by the Belgian appeal court in 2002 as the accused was not present in the country. However, the Belgian government is looking to change the law to allow prosecutions irrespective of where they happen to be.

[66] www.redress.org.

[67] Torture Convention, *op cit*, Article 5(1)(a)(b)(c).

dedere aut judicare. It appears that this maxim was not persuasive enough for the Senegalese legal authorities.[68]

If Habre's crimes were considered to be crimes against humanity they would have found it more difficult to conclude that they did not have jurisdiction. The acts that Habre was accused of having committed could be construed as crimes against humanity if perpetrated against a civilian population with the intent to further a government's policy. Now that the link between armed conflicts and crimes against humanity has been severed by the Rome Statute, it is possible to conclude that his crimes were crimes against humanity.

If deemed crimes against humanity, the universal nature of the jurisdiction would have overridden Senegal's presumed need for a territorial link. Indeed if the acts in question had occurred after the Rome Statute, it would have been a perfect case for the ICC.[69]

In order to meet their international obligations states must make use of more adaptable jurisdictional principles. Without this flexible approach individual criminal responsibility will exist in theory only. States can extend their jurisdictional boundaries considerably if use is made of more than one principle. Even though Israel's claim of universal jurisdiction in the *Eichmann Case* was compelling, the District Court defended its jurisdiction further with reference to the protective principle. States use the protective principle when their security is at risk. The risk need not be political, so long as the state in question feels its vital interests are threatened. It is the most likely jurisdictional principle claimed in situations involving espionage, plots for the overthrow of a government or the forging of currency, amongst others.[70]

The situation in the *Eichmann Case* was different, however, as there was no threat per se to the national security of Israel: the acts in question occurred prior to its existence. Thus a contradiction arises between the facts and the District Court's conclusion that the principle is a 'specific or national source' for jurisdiction that 'gives the victim nation the right to try any who assaults its existence'.[71] How can the existence of a state be threatened by acts committed prior to its existence? The defence argued that this international law principle required a connection between the state and the accused.[72] Accordingly, for them, where there is no such link, a state lacks the authority to punish the accused for offences committed abroad.[73] Thus as there was no state of Israel at the time the acts were committed there was no link.

---

[68] It is contended that Senegal could have passed laws to enable the prosecution of Habre if there was political will, as was the case with Germany in the Tadic case mentioned above, p. 21.

[69] Rome Statute, *op cit*, Article 7(1)(f). Torture falls under crimes against humanity, Article 7(2) (a) and (e).

[70] Malanczuk, *Akehurst's Modern Introduction to International Law, op cit*, p. 111-2.

[71] *Eichmann Case*, para. 30, p. 50.

[72] *Ibid*, para. 31, p. 50.

[73] *Ibid*.

The court countered this argument by referring to the 'linking-point' argument. This concept looks at the legal connection linking the punisher and the punished.[74] The protective principle, according to this theory, is not limited to foreign offences that threaten a state's vital interest; rather, states can exert their jurisdiction over a situation that is of a greater concern to them than it is to other states.[75] The importance here is that a state has greater concern. The District Court asserted that the 'linking-point' in the *Eichmann Case* was between the state of Israel and the Jewish people. Their connection is self-explanatory. Accordingly, the linking-point made crimes against the Jewish people a vital interest to the state of Israel over and above the interests of all other states. This in turn gave it a right to punish offenders under the protective principle irrespective of the fact that it did not exist at the time the acts were committed.

> If an effective link (not necessarily an identity) existed between the State of Israel and the Jewish people, then a crime intended to exterminate the Jewish people has an indubitable connection to the State of Israel.[76]

The defence acknowledged that the protective principle safeguards the security and interests of an existing state. However, as the state of Israel did not exist at the time the acts were committed it could not thereafter rely on the protective principle.[77] In rejecting this argument the District Court held that the protective principle safeguarded the interest of the state existing at the time the specific law was enacted.[78] In seeking to protect the special interest it has with Jewish people, the District Court acknowledged that the state of Israel could also rely on the passive personality principle:

> the principle of passive personality which stems from the protective principle, and of which some States have made use through their penal legislation for the protection of their citizens abroad.[79]

The passive personality principle, considered controversial, was left out of the Harvard Research Draft. It has, however, over the years developed into a more acceptable principle. It looks at the nationality of the victim concerned. Under this principle states may assume jurisdiction over offences where their citizens have been affected. Although this rule was referred to as far back as 1886 it faced much opposition from the US.[80] The US did, nonetheless, utilize it when one of its

---

[74] The Court referred to Dahm, *Zur Problematik des Voelkerstrafrechts* (1956) p. 28, taken from *Eichmann Case, ibid*, para. 31.

[75] Dahm, p. 8-39, *ibid*.

[76] *Eichmann Case, ibid*, paras. 33-5.

[77] *Ibid*, para. 37, p. 54.

[78] *Ibid*.

[79] *Ibid*, para. 36, p. 54-5.

[80] The *Cutting Case*. This case dealt with the publications in Texas of defamatory statements illegal under Mexican law. The publications were allegedly made by a US national in the US

80   *Immunity and International Criminal Law*

citizens was killed in the hijacking of an Italian ship, the *Achille Lauro*, in 1985 by a terrorist group in Egyptian waters.[81] The only link the US had to this offence was the death of its citizen, which prompted it to seek the extradition of the leader of the group, Muhammed Abbas Zaiden, from Italy. The US later relied on this principle with regards to the hijacking in 1985 of a Jordanian plane with US nationals onboard. The US authorities were able to apprehend a Lebanese national who was charged and tried in the US for the offences of hostage-taking and piracy.[82] Whatever its initial resistance to the principle, the US saw the advantages of using it in attempting to apprehend those accused of international crimes, particularly for acts of terrorism.[83] Indeed the US was able to make use of this principle in 1999 when it sought the extradition of individuals suspected of having bombed their embassies in Tanzania and Kenya.[84]

States have, therefore, utilized various jurisdictional principles in order to proceed against those accused of international crimes of great interest to them. The *Eichmann Case* shows that where a state is very concerned, it will effectively use the different jurisdictional principles to ensure its position. However, it is unclear just what the situation is where more than one state is determined to exercise its jurisdiction over a case important to it.

Jurisdictional Complexities

The Supreme Court of Israel in the *Eichmann Case* noted the following:

> We have also taken into consideration the possible desire of other countries to try the appellant in so far as the offences contained in the indictment were committed in those countries or their injurious effects extended thereto...and it is reasonable to believe that in face of Israel's exercise of jurisdiction no other State will demand the right to do so itself.[85]

The Supreme Court assumed that other states would not exert pressure on Israel to concede its jurisdiction over the case. Their assumption was accurate, as other states with viable demands did not exhort their claims. Israel relied on the universal

---

against a Mexican national. The Mexican authorities, relying on the passive personality principle, arrested the US citizen when he was in Mexico. The accused was convicted at the trial stage but released on appeal. Letter from Mr Romero to Mr Bayed (1887) *US For. Rel. 766, 957.*

[81] Shaw, *International Law, op cit*, p. 468.

[82] In this case the court accepted that, although controversial, the passive personality principle did provide appropriate jurisdiction. The court also acknowledged that the international community recognized the principle's legitimacy. *US v. Yunis, op cit*, p. 901.

[83] The US has acknowledged that the principle 'is increasingly accepted as applied to terrorist and other organised attacks on a state's nationals by reason of their nationality, or to assassinations of a state's diplomatic representatives or other officials'. *Third Restatement of US Foreign Relations Law. Vol. I p. 240, note 2 para. 402.*

[84] *US v. Usama bin Laden et al* (2000) 92 F. Supp. 2d 189.

[85] *Eichamnn Case* (Supreme Court), p. 303.

and protective principles as the custodial state. However, other states, which included Germany, Romania, Poland, Hungary and the former Czechoslovakia, were also in a position to claim jurisdiction over Eichmann, be it on the basis of the territorial, protective, nationality or universal principles.[86]

With the increased flexibility of a state's jurisdictional boundaries in international criminal cases, the issue of the possibility of multiple viable jurisdictional claims in a given situation arises. A state with custodial jurisdiction will have to decide which jurisdictional basis is most appropriate. Although such state may have the accused in its territory, it may not be able to rely on the territorial basis if the crime did not occur within or have its effects felt within its territory. If the accused or the victims are not its nationals, it cannot rely on the nationality or passive personality principles. Where the acts posed no threat to its security, the protective principle is of no benefit to it. There is, of course, the universal jurisdictional basis if the act in question is an international customary crime.

Concurrent Jurisdiction   In some situations more than one state can make a claim of jurisdiction over a specific act, as occurred in the *Lotus Case*, for example.[87] A Turkish ship and a French ship collided on the Aegean Sea, with the loss of several Turkish lives. *The Lotus*, the French ship, docked in Turkey where the captain was detained and tried. French objections to Turkey exercising its jurisdiction centred on its assumption that as the flag state it had sole jurisdiction over the ship. Turkey on the other hand asserted that, as their ship was a floating piece of Turkish territory, they had the right to try the captain of the French ship. Additional to the territorial basis, Turkey also relied on their Penal Code that gave it the right to exercise its jurisdiction over events in which its nationals are killed.[88] According to the PCIJ there was nothing in international law preventing Turkey from exercising its jurisdiction. If the situation had involved other determined states whose nationals had died, the situation could have been complicated further.

Where a state can lay claim to jurisdiction by use of the universal principle only, a state in whose territory the offence occurred has a feasible jurisdictional claim, as would the state whose national either committed the offence or whose citizens were injured in its commission. All these states have jurisdiction concurrently, and, if each is keen to exercise their authority, the state with custodial enforcement jurisdiction will come under increased pressure to extradite the offender. Although the issue of extradition is raised, it is important only so far as to illustrate the pressure that a state with enforcement jurisdiction will come under

---

[86] Indeed, all states could claim jurisdiction over Eichmann based on the universal jurisdictional principle. However, it is suggested that a state with more than one basis, that is willing to prosecute, be given priority over a state with only universal jurisdiction, no matter how willing.

[87] *France v. Turkey.*

[88] Turkish Penal Code, Article 6. Harris, *Cases and Materials on International Law*, (1998), p. 271.

82   *Immunity and International Criminal Law*

when faced with multiple requests. In that respect, extradition as a legal doctrine will not be examined in any detail.

Where a state with custodial enforcement jurisdiction is faced with claims by other states, it must decide either to yield to their demands or to prosecute. If it decides to yield, a determination must be made as to which state has the better claim. In reaching a decision, it will have to be extremely cautious as the outcome of a prosecution in the state it determines has a better claim can affect future proceedings.

Prioritization of Jurisdictional Claims   Just how states have reached this decision in the past is difficult to determine. Perhaps the best illustrative example is the Ntuyahaga extradition case in Tanzania.[89] Ntuyahaga was a Rwandan army officer during the genocide. He was indicted and detained by the ICTR in 1998. In 1999 the indictment was withdrawn at the request of the prosecutors. Belgium sought his extradition for the murder of the Rwandese Prime Minister who was being guarded at the time by Belgian soldiers, ten of whom died in her defence. The murders were committed as part of a widespread or systematic attack against a civilian population on national or political grounds.[90] Accordingly he was indicted for crimes against humanity by the ICTR.[91] Belgium had already instituted proceedings against him for the murder of its soldiers. Upon his indictment being withdrawn, the ICTR was of the opinion that it could not then 'order the release of a person who is no longer under indictment into the custody of any given State, including the Host state, the United Republic of Tanzania'.[92]

Although the ICTR had not ordered his transfer to Tanzanian custody, he was arrested upon his release by the tribunal on 29 March 1999 by Tanzanian police. He was charged with violating Tanzanian immigration laws.[93] Both Belgium and Rwanda sought his extradition. Rwanda claimed jurisdiction primarily on the territorial principle. The nationality principle is also applicable with regard to Rwanda, as the accused was from Rwanda. The nationality of one of the murder victims also gives Rwanda the right to claim jurisdiction under the passive personality principle. This is a principle that Belgium based its assertion on: the ten soldiers were Belgian. It also had universal jurisdiction for crimes against humanity. Tanzania also had universal jurisdiction over the acts in question, but nothing was ever mentioned about the possibility of trying Ntuyahaga in Tanzania. As the custodial state, Tanzania faced two competing, equally compelling, claims of jurisdiction over a single event. On 6 April 1999 the

---

[89] See: www.bbc.co.uk for information on events leading up to Ntuyahaga's arrest and detention pending extradition from Tanzania.

[90] *Prosecutor v. Ntuyahaga* Decision of 18 March 1999 (ICTR-98-40-T). www.ictr.org.

[91] ICTR Statute, Article 8(1), *op cit*. In requesting the withdrawal of the indictment, the prosecutor was making use of the ICTR's and Belgium's concurrent jurisdiction, although the tribunal has primacy.

[92] *Prosecutor v. Ntuyahaga, op cit.*

[93] Tanzania was prevented from arresting him for the same charges he was indicted by the ICTR under an agreement between the tribunal and the government.

Tanzanian authorities denied Belgium's request because the 'alleged crimes were not committed on Belgian soil'.[94]

In another example, in January 2001, a Mexican judge held that Mexico, as the custodial state, could extradite an Argentine former naval officer to Spain.[95] The officer in question, Cavallo, was charged with genocide, torture and terrorism committed in Argentina, as detailed in the Spanish extradition request, which outlined the torture of its citizens. [96] In February the Mexican Ministry of Foreign Affairs ratified the ruling to enable the extradition to be carried out.[97] Argentina argued for its territorial jurisdiction to be respected, claiming that the suspect should face trial in his country where the events occurred.[98] Argentina, as the territorial state, also had a sound claim based on the nationality and passive personality principles, with Spain having only passive and universal. Mexico could have exercised its jurisdiction over the crime of genocide under the universal jurisdiction principle but chose not to.[99]

In these two examples, states with custodial jurisdiction had other states eager to claim jurisdiction. Both Tanzania and Mexico could have proceeded against the individuals in question, as some of the crimes in both cases were international crimes. In the *Ntuyahaga Case* Tanzania chose to surrender the suspect to the state with territorial jurisdiction. In the *Cavallo Case*, Mexico decided that the state with universal and passive jurisdiction had the better claim. The examples cannot provide a general picture as to which jurisdictional principle will prove more persuasive. It is arguable that politics plays a major role in assisting states in making a choice. Politics appears also to have some influence over the custodial state's apparent lack of will to pursue the case itself. Universal jurisdiction is a sensitive issue as it asks a state to play a part in a crime that it had absolutely no connection with, save for the fact that it is a member of the world community. States appear to want a tangible link between the crime and the state seeking to exercise its jurisdiction.

Whatever a state's sentiment towards the tangibility of a jurisdictional claim, once he is extradited and thereafter prosecuted, the prosecution will have an effect on any future proceedings. For example, Belgium was very keen to

---

[94] Judicial Diplomacy 2001 www.diplomatiejudiciaire.com/UK/Tpiruk/NtuyahagaUK.htm. A District Court judge ruled that extradition to Rwanda was possible before an appeal to the High Court was initiated. Up until submission of this study, Ntuyahaga, is still fighting extradition to Rwanda. See: www.hirondelle.org for news on his extradition trial. I 2004 the Tanzanian High Court ruled that Ntuyahaga could not be extradited to Rwanda because the crimes he was charged with were political in nature and that he would not face a fair trial. *Tanzanian Daily News*, 28 March 2004.

[95] An extradition treaty exists between Spain and Mexico.

[96] *Ibid.*

[97] Amnesty International Press Release. www.amnesty.org.

[98] Maupas, *Judicial Diplomacy 9 September 2000* www.diplomatiejudicaire.com.

[99] In March 2001 a federal judge in Mexico ordered provisional postponement of the proceedings for the extradition of Cavallo as his defence lawyer had filed an action to protect his constitutional rights. www.pdgs.org.ar/platining-gov5.htm.

84   *Immunity and International Criminal Law*

prosecute Ntuyahaga, but had he been extradited to Rwanda, it would have had little chance of prosecution. As the Rwandan case against his extradition from Tanzania has failed, it appears that Belgium is left with no redress. It may be barred from ever proceeding against him for the same facts.

Bar to Future Prosecutions Any state that has custody of an individual takes priority in prosecutions even if its claim is based on an extraterritorial basis. This is simply because the individual is corporeally present on its territory. If it chooses to extradite the individual to another state, that state will then have custodial enforcement jurisdiction, and consequently have priority. Whether a state with custodial enforcement jurisdiction extradites or proceeds, any prosecution that ends in a conviction or acquittal will have an effect over any other states' plans to exercise their jurisdiction.

There are two legal principles that bar proceedings where an individual has already faced trial for the same facts: *double jeopardy* and *non bis in idem*. Although the two terms are taken to represent the same principle, it has been noted that they are in fact rather different.[100] Both terms refer to the theory that no one should be prosecuted twice for the same offence. However, whereas *non bis in idem* protects the individual from 'multiple prosecutions irrespective of the prosecuting authority', double jeopardy is usually applied to 'conflicts within a given legal system'.[101]

The idea that an individual should not be prosecuted twice for the same offence has its origins in Roman law, and became part of English common law during the 13th century.[102] Most states now adhere to this principle, but *non bis in idem* is a term more closely associated with Continental Europe.[103]

As double jeopardy is usually referred to when there is a conflict within a given legal system, it appears not to include prior proceedings in other jurisdictions.[104] Double jeopardy is a phrase utilized predominantly in the US. In that country the courts have consistently ruled that an individual can be prosecuted on the same charge in two different jurisdictions.[105] In *People v. Papaccio*, an Italian national who had committed murder in the US, was convicted and imprisoned in Italy.[106] He was prosecuted under a law that made it a crime for Italian nationals to commit crimes in foreign countries against the laws of those countries on whose territories they live.[107] On his return to the US, he was arrested

---

[100] Lopez, 'Not Twice for the Same: How the Dual Sovereignty Doctrine is Used to Circumvent *Non Bis In Idem*' (2000) *33 Vand. JTL 1263, 1272.*

[101] *Ibid*, p. 1272.

[102] *Ibid*, p. 1267.

[103] Friedland, *Double Jeopardy* (1969), p. 358.

[104] Lopez, 'Not Twice for the Same', *op cit,* p.122.

[105] *US v. Abbate* (1959) 359 U.S. 187, *US v. Mcray* (1980) 616 F.2d 181, *US v. Martin* (1978) 574 F. 2d 1359.

[106] *People v. Papaccio* (1931) 2 N.Y.S. 717.

[107] s.5 Italian Penal Code.

Individual Criminal Responsibility 85

and tried for murder. With reference to the issue of double jeopardy, the New York court held that:

> the conviction in the courts of the Kingdom of Italy, in absence of specific treaty provisions binding our State courts, cannot successfully be pleaded in bar to a prosecution under an indictment in this State when it appears that here is where the crime was committed. The general rule is well stated that conviction of crime against one government cannot be sustained as a bar to prosecution by another government for the same act.[108]

The US has taken the view that prosecutions in other countries will not bar the accused from being tried in the US unless there is a treaty that expressly provides for double jeopardy protection,[109] where the act occurred on territory jointly administered by compact, or where a statute requires.[110]

In contrast, the UK has repeatedly maintained that an acquittal in another country is a bar to proceedings in British courts, 'because a final determination in a court having competent jurisdiction is conclusive in all courts of concurrent jurisdiction'.[111] The UK's common law doctrine of *autrefois convict* or *acquit* are applied to avoid exposing people to double jeopardy. The doctrine is applicable 'whether the previous conviction or acquittal based on the same facts was by an English court or by a foreign court'.[112] In *R v. Thomas (Keith)*, the Court of Appeal held that a conviction or an acquittal could act as a bar to subsequent prosecution on the same facts.[113] However, the defendant in this particular case was tried and convicted in absentia in Italy for aggravated fraud and was subsequently charged in the UK with theft. He had illegally transferred money from his employer's Italian bank to an account in the UK which he had opened using a false name, for his own benefit. As he had not been before the foreign court for charges of theft, he could not rely on the plea of *autrefois convict*.[114] The UK, therefore, appears to follow the principle of *non bis in idem*, as prosecution for theft in Italy would have prevented proceedings against this defendant in the UK for that offence.[115]

There is no uniform applicability of *non bis in idem*. Some states directly apply foreign criminal judgments.[116] Others only apply the rule in cases where the

---

[108] *People v. Papaccio*, p. 720.

[109] *US v. Benitez* (1998) 28 F. Supp. 2d 1361, 1364.

[110] Paust, Bassiouni et al, *International Criminal Law Cases and Materials*, *op cit*, p. 587.

[111] *Rex v. Roche* (1775) 1 Leach 134, 135.

[112] *Treacy v. DPP*, p. 562.

[113] *R v. Thomas (Keith)* [1985] QB 604.

[114] *Ibid*.

[115] The UK Law Commission recently recommended changes to the double jeopardy rules in relation to murder cases. See: Law Commission Double Jeopardy Consultation Paper No. 156 www.lawcom.gov.uk. The new Criminal Justice Act 2003 provides for cases to be retried where there is strong evidence and public interest to do so, thus effectively doing away with double jeopardy in stated cases.

[116] For example: The Netherlands and Peru. Friedland, *Double Jeopardy*, *op cit*, p. 359.

defendant was convicted rather than acquitted.[117] As for extradition, the Chilean Supreme Court held in the *Letelier Case (Chile)* that extradition hearings in which a judgment is passed does not constitute a trial concluding in conviction, acquittal or dismissal for double jeopardy purposes.[118] It is assumed, therefore, that the doctrine's ambit of protection will not include extradition hearings in some states.

Depending on Belgium's approach, if it gives effect to the double jeopardy or *non bis in idem* principles, Ntuyahaga may not have faced charges in Belgium if he were convicted or acquitted in Rwanda, if he had been extradited. Where the accused has faced trial and has been acquitted, the case will not be admissible to the ICC either.[119] A state with jurisdiction, in Ntuyahaga's case, Rwanda, would have the first opportunity to proceed if he had been extradited from Tanzania. If, however, he were acquitted in Rwanda, Belgium and the ICC may feel that justice has not been done.

If Ntuyahaga's case failed in Rwanda, and he walked free, the ICC would not be able to retry him as the ICC adheres to the *non bis in idem* principle. It would appear that the principle is, in some way, also reflected in the complementarity principle, as the ICC will not sit in judgment where an individual has already been investigated and prosecuted by a domestic court with jurisdiction. But specifically, the Rome Statute provides that:

3. No person who has been tried by another court for conduct also proscribed under Article 6, 7, 8 shall be tried by the Court with respect to the same conduct unless the proceedings in the other court:

    (a) Were for the purpose of shielding the person concerned from criminal responsibility for crimes within the jurisdiction of the Court; or

    (b) Otherwise were not conducted independently or impartially in accordance with the norms of due process recognized by international law and were conducted in a manner which, in the circumstances, was inconsistent with an intent to bring the person concerned to justice.[120]

This provision is in keeping with the provisions of the Ad Hoc Tribunal's statute conditions for *non bis in idem*. The ICTY's statute outlines that:

2. A person who has been tried by a national court for acts constituting serious violations of humanitarian international law may be subsequently tried by the International Tribunal only if:

---

[117] Sweden for example, *ibid*.

[118] *Letelier Case (Chile)*. The case in Chile followed on from the case in the USA. Bancroft and Bello, International Decision: Chile – Criminal Jurisdiction – Prosecution of Officials of Secret Service for Assassination of Former Ambassador to the United States (1996) *AJIL* 290, 292.

[119] Obviously this particular case would not be admissible to the ICC as it occurred prior to the Rome Statute coming into force.

[120] Rome Statute, Article 20, *op cit*.

(a) the act for which he or she was tried was characterized as an ordinary crime; or

(b) the national court proceedings were not impartial or independent, were designed to shield the accused from international criminal responsibility, or the case was not diligently prosecuted. [121]

Further, the Rome Statute disallows proceedings in other courts against individuals already prosecuted by the ICC:

No person shall be tried by another court for a crime referred to in Article 5 for which that person has already been convicted or acquitted by the Court. [122]

The Ad Hoc Tribunals have a similar provision:

No person shall be tried before a national court for acts constituting serious violations of international humanitarian law under the present Statute, for which he or she has already been tried by the International Tribunal. [123]

As international tribunals with primacy, the ICTY and the ICTR were intended to have the first opportunity to adjudicate, although jurisdiction is concurrent with national courts. Hence an individual who has been tried and convicted by either one of these tribunals can rely on the principle of *non bis in idem* to shield him from any future prosecutions at the national level. As the ICC does not have primacy, it is arguable that the complementarity principle gives states ample time to proceed. When a case is eventually admissible to the ICC, it is only fair that if it convicts or acquits the individual, he should be free from the threat of future prosecutions by domestic courts. States are given the opportunity to proceed first under the ICC's admissibility procedure, hence it is only reasonable that having failed the first time they should not be given another opportunity where the ICC has already dealt with the case.

However, individuals can still face future proceedings if they happened to be in a state that relies on the double jeopardy principle, as outlined above in the US case: *People v. Papaccio*.[124] Or in states that apply *non bis in idem* only where there is a conviction. For example, if Ntuyahaga was accused of having participated in the killings of US nationals and the case in Rwanda failed, he may face trial in the US at a future date. It is clear that US courts do not preclude trials where an individual has been convicted by a domestic court abroad. What is not so clear is the position of an individual tried and convicted by an international court. Will US courts still proceed against someone who has been tried, convicted or

---

[121] ICTY Statute, Article 10(2), ICTR Statute, Article 9(2), *op cit.*

[122] Rome Statute, Article 20(2).

[123] ICTY Statute, Article 10(1), ICTR Statute, Article 9(1), *op cit.*

[124] *People v. Papaccio, op cit.*

acquitted by an international tribunal like the ICC?[125] It is arguable that the application of double jeopardy, American style, will not protect an individual from dual prosecutions for the same events.

The jurisdictional problems outlined here occur at the domestic level. As jurisdictional boundaries have become more and more flexible, various concerns have cropped up. New situations invariably bring with them new problems. States have found that extending their jurisdiction to hold individuals responsible for international crimes has brought about other complex issues that will have to be addressed. Indeed the very nature of these crimes has created situations where absolute state sovereignty is confronted. The challenge is particular to the weakened position of territory as the primary basis of jurisdiction. As a result, international crimes have undeniably diminished state sovereignty as states seek to apply their prescriptive and enforcement jurisdiction even in situations where there is no direct link between them and the acts constituting international crimes.

Accountability at the International Level

The traditional doctrine of sovereignty precludes states from prescribing or enforcing their laws onto other states. Although states have managed to extend their jurisdiction extraterritorially in limited circumstances, the extent of a domestic court's authority to adjudicate is still limited.[126] Their limitations derive from the need to preserve diplomatic relations. International tribunals, on the other hand, do not have to dwell on inter-state relations as they are established by the world acting together as a community. They are, therefore, the best forums for adjudicating international crimes and the individuals responsible.

Notwithstanding the obvious benefits of international tribunals, international crimes have advanced over the centuries without the help of a single international court that could have acted as a unifying force. The one permanent world court, the ICJ, was not set up to prosecute individuals, but to adjudicate on inter-state issues. This is contrary to international criminal law's emphasis on the individual.

During the war between Bangladesh and Pakistan in the 1970s, the ICJ was provided with the right situation to exercise its jurisdiction over international crimes. India planned to hand over Pakistani troops it had captured during the war to Bangladesh for trial for alleged acts of genocide and crimes against humanity.[127] On 11 May 1973 Pakistan instituted proceedings at the ICJ against India, claiming

---

[125] This is open to question, as the US has been hostile to the ICC. See: Roberts, 'Comment and Analysis' *The Guardian (8 April 2002)*.

[126] It is acknowledged that states, including the UK, do not really want to extend their jurisdiction beyond the territorial basis; however, application of other jurisdictional principles in cases has brought about the broadening of their jurisdiction beyond the territorial principle.

[127] Bangladesh passed a law establishing an international criminal tribunal. Paust, Bassiouni et al, *International Criminal Law Cases and Materials, op cit*, p. 645-653.

that such action by India would be a violation of the Genocide Convention. Pakistan asked for provisional measures of protection to ensure that repatriation of prisoners would continue and that India be prevented from handing its soldiers over to Bangladesh while action was pending at the ICJ.[128] The case was discontinued as negotiations between the parties commenced.[129]

Although the ICJ cannot arbitrate on individual responsibility, it can, however, make determinations on issues involving international crimes. In 1993 it was asked by Bosnia and Herzegovina to adjudicate on the dispute between itself and Yugoslavia over allegations of violations of the Genocide Convention by Yugoslavia during the conflict that followed the break-up of the former Yugoslavia.[130] The Genocide Convention provides for dispute in the interpretation, application or fulfilment of the convention to be submitted to the ICJ.[131] The ICJ was urged to adjudicate and declare that Yugoslavia violated the Genocide Convention.[132]

Recently the ICJ delivered judgment on issues involving international criminal law in the *Arrest Warrant Case*.[133] The case involved an arrest warrant issued by Belgium for a Congolese minister in connection with crimes of an international nature. The case did not seek to apportion responsibility but was based on one state's allegation of the infringement of its sovereignty by another: that in issuing an arrest warrant for a high-ranking minister Belgium had violated Congo's sovereignty. The court had jurisdiction because it was a complaint between states. The ICJ upheld Congo's claim that Belgium had violated its sovereignty in issuing an arrest warrant against an incumbent foreign minister, who, according to the court, is inviolable and immune from the jurisdiction of foreign states.[134]

Without a permanent international criminal court, international tribunals have been established on an ad hoc basis, as and when needed. Any meaningful discussion of individual accountability at the international level must start with the tribunals of Nuremberg and Tokyo, although it is fact that they were in effect the victors' courts. Had the Nazis and their allies won the war they may have created their own tribunals with different mandates. Nonetheless Nuremberg and Tokyo helped establish the principle that individuals who commit international crimes are personally liable, irrespective of their status as state officials. Both Nuremberg and

---

[128] Rosenne, *The World Court What it is and How it Works* (1962), p.204-6. Paust, Bassouni et al, *International Criminal Law Cases and Materials, op cit*, p. 645-50.

[129] UN Press Release 1973 ICJ/339. Ferencz, *An International Criminal Court A Step Toward World Peace (Vol. 2), op cit*, p.65-6.

[130] *Genocide Case.*

[131] Genocide Convention, Article IX, *op cit.*

[132] Preliminary objections from Yugoslavia were dealt with and the case is proceeding. www.icj-cij.org.

[133] *Arrest Warrant Case.*

[134] *Ibid*, p. 26, para. 71. In 2003 the ICJ was once again called upon to adjudicate on a case that touches on international criminal law; *DRC v France (Certain Criminal Proceedings Case)* www.icj-cij.org.

90   *Immunity and International Criminal Law*

Tokyo helped establish that state officials can be held individually responsible and that their immunity will not act as a bar to proceedings in an international tribunal.

International Criminal Tribunals, Individual Accountability and State Sovereignty

It is anticipated that internationally constituted criminal courts have an advantage over their domestic counterparts, in not being hampered by the issue of immunities of state officials. Immunities have and do play a part in restricting individual responsibility at the domestic level. International tribunals can, hopefully, rise above these notions and provide international criminal law with effective mechanisms for individual accountability.

However, it appears that even international criminal tribunals are burdened by the doctrines of sovereignty and immunities. The ICTY in *Blaskic Croatian Subpoena Decisions (Appeal)* held that it did not have the power to order a subpoena against state officials as they are immune from foreign jurisdictions for their official acts.[135] In reaching this decision, the Appeal Chamber relied on, *inter alia*, the assumption that the right of states to demand immunity for their officials from foreign states must be taken into account and respected by international organizations and international courts.[136] The Appeal Chamber paid particular attention to the fact that states rather than individuals have been the primary targets whenever international organizations and courts have made recommendations, decisions, judicial orders or requests.[137] Further the Appeal Chamber was of the opinion that where its prosecutor sought the assistance, of a particular state official, such official was not under any international obligation to provide such assistance as the obligation is on the state.[138]

This point of view seems somewhat defeatist and contrary to the spirit of international criminal law. The Ad Hoc Tribunals were established to hold individuals accountable. It is the individual who is the 'star', for want of a better phrase. Granted, other international organizations and courts have always addressed states and their authorities rather than individual officials, but they were not established to deal with the individual as the primary target. Indeed, the ICJ was set up to resolve inter-state disputes. The Ad Hoc Tribunals and other international criminal courts are set up to look at individuals; thus to turn round and put the state in the forefront is an affront to international criminal law. It is acknowledged that the penal nature of subpoenas under common law systems would make it difficult for the Ad Hocs as they lack enforcement measures, a point not lost on the Appeal Chamber.[139]

---

[135] *Blaskic Croatian Subpoena Decisions (Appeal)*.

[136] *Ibid*, para. 41.

[137] *Ibid*.

[138] *Ibid*.

[139] *Ibid*, para. 25: Under the French system, for example, subpoena as 'assignation' does not 'necessarily imply any imposition of a penalty'.

Nonetheless, it is suggested that as penal judicial bodies, international criminal tribunals and courts must be able to address subpoenas to individual state officials. The fact that they are established to try individuals puts them in a class separate from other international organizations and courts. In this distinct category, they must not be tied to issues of state sovereignty, a doctrine that is part of the notion of immunities. Where states collectively agree to an international criminal court, or indeed where one is established by the Security Council by use of its delegated powers under Chapter VII, states give up some of their sovereignty. With regard to prosecuting individuals for international crimes they accept that the international court or tribunal is at the pinnacle in a 'vertical' relationship between them and the tribunal, rather than 'horizontal' as between themselves.[140] In recognizing this vertical relationship, states are in fact subjugating their sovereignty to the tribunal or court. Thus the acceptance of the Appeal Chamber that it must take into account state sovereignty in carrying out its duties is superfluous. Indeed the ICJ in the *Reparations Case* held that 'the rights and duties of an entity...must depend upon its purpose and functions as specified or implied in its constituent documents and developed in practice'.[141] The purpose of international criminal courts is to address individual accountability and it is individuals, irrespective of official status, who are their primary targets, be it by indictment or subpoena. Immunities must not be allowed to defeat the purpose and function of such courts.

---

[140] The Appeal Chamber makes this distinction in para. 47.

[141] *Reparations Case, op cit*, p. 180.

Chapter 4

Immunities

The ICC as a mechanism under international criminal law for holding individuals personally responsible for international crimes, has been made possible by the introduction of rights and duties of the individual at the international level. The ICC, like other international criminal tribunals, does not acknowledge immunity for heads of state or those in government.[1] A person's immunity will not act as a bar to its jurisdiction. However, to get suspects, the ICC will have to issue surrender requests,[2] and a state party receiving such a request is obliged to take steps to apprehend the person in question.[3] The person apprehended must appear before a competent judicial authority in that custodian state in order to establish that the apprehension was properly executed and was in compliance with local laws.[4]

Paust, writing in 2000, claims that international law does not permit immunity of a person accused of a international customary crime.[5] He refers to the ICTR case of *Prosecutor v. Kambanda* where a former Prime Minister of Rwanda was charged with genocide.[6] It is quite correct to say that, before the ICTR, Kambanda was unable to rely on his status as a government official to avoid prosecution. Indeed the tribunal did not spend much of its time looking at the issue of the accused's status barring its jurisdiction.

International tribunals may not permit immunity for international customary crimes, but domestic courts do. As mentioned in the previous chapter, domestic jurisdictions are bound by the doctrine of jurisdiction. In holding an individual accountable for international crimes, a state will have to determine if it has jurisdiction. If the individual in question is a person of certain status, such as a diplomat, the state in question may be barred from detaining the accused. As part of its sovereign power, a state has jurisdiction over all persons and things within its territorial limits for both civil and criminal cases.[7] As a sovereign and independent entity, it has the power to lay down rules (prescriptive jurisdiction) and the power

---

[1] Rome Statute, Article 27.

[2] Rome Statute, Article 58.

[3] Rome Statute, Article 59(1).

[4] Rome Statute, Article 59(2)(b).

[5] Paust, 'The Reach of ICC Jurisdiction over Non-Signatory Nationals' (2000) *33 Vand JTL* 14.

[6] *Prosecutor v. Kambanda* IT-97-23-S, www.ictr.org.

[7] *Compania Noviera Vassongada v. S.S. Christina* [1938] A.C 485. (Hereinafter The Christina.)

Immunities 93

to enforce such rules (enforcement jurisdiction) through its courts (adjudicative jurisdiction).[8] Yet, within its territory a state has to concede jurisdiction to certain individuals who have immunity in accordance with customary law that has developed through time.[9]

Historical Development

Sovereignty and the Dominion of Kings

Sovereignty became a relevant principle when autonomous secular states started to emerge after 1324, when the idea that kings were sovereign within their territories evolved. Nevertheless, God's law was still the standard within which governments could operate legitimately, as God was above the king. The king was, however, the highest authority in the kingdom. This was the accepted wisdom at the time the term sovereignty was coined in 1576.[10] The principal point of sovereign majesty and absolute power consisted of the giving of laws to subjects without consent on their part.[11] Just how the sovereign got such power is open to debate. It has been suggested that it comes from the people: that they consented to the sovereign having such powers.[12] How a sovereign attains power is a topic beyond the scope of this book. It is sufficient to note that, having attained power, a sovereign became immune within his territory and without.

The immunity of kings was expressed in the maxim *par in parem non habet imperium*, that is: equals cannot exercise authority over each other. According to Schwarzenberger, in a situation where 'entities base their relations on the principles of equality...sovereignty is transformed from an absolute into a relative'.[13] Thus, according to this line of thought, relative sovereignty is a negative sovereignty where there is 'non-recognition of any superior authority'.[14]

State immunity grew from this personal immunity of the sovereign. Although it has historical links to the person in charge of the state, later developments saw the establishment of the state as an entity deserving of immunity in itself. The law relating to immunities of states, once referred to as involving sovereign immunity, is now generally referred to as state immunity.[15] The

---

[8] Malanczuk, *'Akehurst's Modern Introduction to International Law'*, *op cit*, p. 109.

[9] States accord each other's representatives immunity on a reciprocal basis, as will be shown in the historical analysis of immunity.

[10] The term was coined by Bodin, *Six Livres de la Republic* from Brierly, *The Law of Nations, op cit*, p. 7-12.

[11] Majestie or Soveraignte is the most high, absolute, and perpetual power over the citizens and subjects in a commonweale. Bodin, *Six Livres de la Republic, ibid*.

[12] Hobbes, *Leviathan* (1996, ed R. Tuck), p. 121.

[13] Schwarzenberger, *International Law and Order* (1971), p. 61-2.

[14] *Ibid*, p. 62.

[15] It is arguable that reference to a head of state's immunity as state immunity is a misconception. Only a state as an abstract entity has state immunity. A head of state can

94 *Immunity and International Criminal Law*

immunity accorded to its head has developed separately acquiring its own rules and customs without the aid of an international convention. It is more a matter of customary international law evolving around state practice making it rather 'unsettled'.[16]

Developments based on custom enabled the evolution of the doctrine of sovereign immunity (precursor to state immunity) that was influenced by other doctrines, such as equality of states and in particular, sovereignty which, during the 19th century, was also considered to be absolute. The unqualified application of the concept of sovereignty coincided with the rapid growth in positivism. The development of the theory that states were the sole creators of law enabled the sovereign to gain complete freedom of action within his state and in international relations.

The King's Envoys

A sitting head of state, as the holder of the highest office and the representative of his state, is immune from legal suit in a foreign court.[17] In earlier times, a sovereign was exempt from the jurisdiction of each other sovereign's legal authority as befitting the sovereign's regal dignity and his absolute independence from any superior authority. The sovereign's regal dignity was upheld by receiving states granting his diplomatic representatives immunity.

Immunity of envoys is a concept that has existed for millennia.[18] Thousands of years ago it was decided that bearers of messages from one leader to another were sacrosanct. This idea eventually grew to the practice we now know as diplomatic inviolability and immunity.[19] Development of this immunity has taken

---

only be accorded immunity emanating from his state's immunity, that being head of state immunity. Head of state immunity can be looked at as an aspect of state immunity. Perhaps it is better described as a by-product of state immunity rather than another form of state immunity. Lord Slynn, in *Pinochet (No. 3)*, held that head of state immunity is a derivative of the principle of state immunity. *Pinochet (No. 3)*, p. 1464. The difference is essential, and becomes clearly so when one tries to balance on the one hand sovereignty and on the other apportionment of responsibility for crimes of an international nature.

[16] Watts, 'The Legal Position in International Law of Heads of State, Heads of Government and Foreign Ministers', *op cit*, p. 35-6.

[17] Heads of state can be heads of government as well, as is the case in the US.

[18] The immunity of an ambassador can be traced back to pre-history, to a time when it is assumed that primitive societies decided that hearing the message was perhaps more important than eating the bearer of the message. Hamilton and Langhorne, *The Practice of Diplomacy* (1998), p. 7.

[19] Nicolson, *Diplomacy* (1988), p.6. Being regarded as sacrosanct meant that the messengers had personal immunity. In ancient times diplomats were mostly assigned on ad hoc missions. Such missions, described as "an institution as old as human civilization", eventually lost prominence in the 15th century. Nahlik, 'Development of Diplomatic Law Selected Problems' (1990) *222 Hague Recueil des Cours' 188, 205*. The foundations for modern diplomatic immunity developed once permanent missions were established and became commonplace. The permanent ambassador, his property and staff remained immune

Immunities 95

many centuries and was, to a considerable extent, based on the representative role played by the ambassador.[20] The envoy represented his sovereign. A sovereign being the equal of another sovereign, a representative of one could not be detained and charged for any criminal offence by the other.[21] Another basis was that of exterritoriality, which emphasized the nature of the diplomatic premises as being the territory of the sending state. The receiving state could not exercise its jurisdiction within the premises. This basis was found to be a 'fiction' having no 'foundation in either law or in fact' by the Special Rapporteur to the League of Nations in 1926.[22]

---

from the jurisdiction of the receiving state. The envoy remained inviolable during his residency in the receiving state. Inviolability and immunity from jurisdiction were, at this stage in the development of diplomatic law, considered to be one and the same thing; criminal proceedings depended on the arrest and detention of the person in question. Denza, *Diplomatic Law A Commentary on the Vienna Convention on Diplomatic Relations* (1998), p. 229.

[20] By the 5th century the Greeks developed a complicated system of constant diplomatic relations between their city-states. Ambassadors sent to keep alliances going and promote peace between states were regarded as being under Zeus' protection and were accorded immunity. McClanahan, *Diplomatic Immunity Principles, Practices, Problems* (1989), p. 21. The Romans extended immunity to visiting ambassadors and their staff, but not to diplomatic correspondence, residence or servants. Diplomatic agents found to have committed offences against Roman law were escorted out of Rome and back to their sending countries. Nicolson, *Evolution of Diplomatic Method* (1954). The Italian city-states developed the resident ambassador in the 15th century. Although suspicion and mistrust overshadowed diplomatic activity in the 16th century as ambassadors employed devious methods in acquiring information, immunity from the jurisdiction of the receiving state remained. Denza, *Diplomatic Law A Commentary on the Vienna Convention on Diplomatic Relations, op cit*, p. 229-31.

[21] The representative basis for immunity was the prevailing basis in the earlier centuries of the law's development. However the 'halcyon days of the "representative character theory"...have long gone.' Barker, 'The Theory and Practice of Diplomatic Law in the Renaissance and Classical Periods', (1995) *Diplomacy & Statecraft 593, 609*. In the 20th century the necessity of diplomatic function became a more popular basis promoted for diplomatic immunity. This basis looks to the delicate functions that diplomats perform and their need to perform such functions with the knowledge that they can carry out such functions in peace and security. The Vienna Diplomatic Convention also places greater stress on the functional basis, but does mention the representative basis in paragraph 4 of the Preamble. It states: 'Realizing that the purpose of such privileges and immunities is not to benefit individuals but to ensure the efficient performance of the functions of diplomatic missions as representing States'. It is noted that the functional necessity basis had been advocated prior to the 20th century by the likes of Grouts, Bynkershoek and Wicquefort. Barker, 'The Theory and Practice of Diplomatic Law in the Renaissance and Classical Periods', *op* cit, p.604-5 In *Radwan v. Radwan* (1972) 55 ILR 579, the UK's High Court held that diplomatic premises were not to be regarded as forming part of the sending state's territory.

[22] Special Rapporteur Diena, 'Report to the Sub-Committee on Diplomatic Immunities of the Committee of Experts for the Progressive Codification of International Law', (1926) *20 AJIL No. 153 supplementary.*

96   *Immunity and International Criminal Law*

During this period, sovereigns had the right to make and repeal laws that did not bind them.[23] For laws to become part of the law of the land they needed to be sanctioned by the sovereign, even if the laws in question were natural laws from all eternity.[24] However, elements of natural law persisted, with some writers arguing that although the sovereign was supreme within his territory, he could not breach divine law.[25]

Establishing Limitations on the Absolute Nature of Immunities

During the 19th century, when sovereignty was of such dominance, it was generally understood that a sovereign had absolute immunity outside his state under both civil and criminal jurisdictions.[26] His diplomats also had immunity but only in their receiving states.[27] The strength of sovereignty reinforced the absoluteness of immunities. The absolute nature of immunity for states covered all state organs,

---

[23] Hobbes, *Leviathan, ibid*, p. 126.

[24] *Ibid*, p. 185.

[25] *Ibid*, p. 224.

[26] In *The Schooner Exchange v. McFaddon* in 1812, the US Lord Chief Justice Marshall held that: a '...sovereign in no respect amenable to another; and being bound by obligations of the highest character not to degrade the dignity of his nation, by placing himself or its sovereign rights within the jurisdiction of another, can be supposed to enter a foreign territory only under an express licence, or in the confidence that the immunities belonging to his independent sovereign station, though not expressly stipulated, are reserved by implication, and will be extended to him'. And that 'the perfect equality and absolute independence of sovereigns...have given rise to a class of cases in which every sovereign is understood to waive the exercise of a part of that complete exclusive territorial jurisdiction, which has been stated to be the attribute of every nation'. *The Schooner Exchange v. McFaddon* (1812) 7 Cranch 116, 137. In *Duke of Brunswick v. King of Hanover*, (1848) 2 HLC 1, 17, it was held that the courts of the UK could not sit in judgment upon an act of a sovereign effected by virtue of his sovereign authority abroad, an act not done as a British subject, but supposed to have been done in the exercise of his authority vested in him as sovereign. Immunity was granted in this case even though it was alleged that property had been illegally retained under a guardianship document. In *De Haber v. Queen of Portugal* (1879) 17 Q.B.171, 20, Lord Campbell C.J. held that to 'cite a foreign potentate in a municipal court, for any complaint against him in his public capacity, is contrary to the law of nations and an insult'. In *Mighell v. Sultan of Johore* [1874] 1 Q.B. 149, immunity was granted to a ruler of a Malayan state when he was accused of breaching a promise to marry, a promise made whilst he was on a private visit to the UK. In the *Cristina Case*, Lord Atkin supported the absolute stance. Although the other judges in this case differed in their opinion as to the nature of a sovereign's immunity, they did agree that the requisition of the ship by Spanish authorities showed Spanish government interest in the case sufficient to have it dismissed.

[27] Diplomats also had and continue to have immunity in third states if passing through en route to their duty stations. See Denza, *Diplomatic Law A Commentary on the Vienna Convention on Diplomatic Relations, op cit*, p. 366-72. Diplomats and third states is discussed below.

Immunities 97

even those set up for purely commercial purposes.[28] However, the shift towards a more restrictive position vis-à-vis states occurred during the early 20th century in civil cases.

Civil Jurisdiction

In the 18th and 19th centuries states tended to stay away from private acts of trade and commerce so the boundary between the acts of a state and that of private citizens in commerce was clear. As a result immunity was absolute irrespective of the circumstances. But states started to became more and more involved in trade. They established state organs and enterprises that operated commercially, and in some cases they nationalized industries.[29] These were acts that belonged to the private sphere, yet they were now being attributed to the state. Absolute immunity became, therefore, increasingly inappropriate as the requirements of the contemporary commercial world changed. Absoluteness seemed in such situations contrary to the notions of stability, fairness, and equity in the market place.[30] If the absolute theory persisted, governmental organizations engaged in trade would have been in an extremely unfair position. Consequently countries started to develop ways to ensure that commercial governmental agencies and private citizens were placed on an equal footing. They did so under the restrictive doctrine by looking to the acts in question and determining whether they were public (acts *jure imperii*) or private acts (acts *jure gestionis*). Acts *jure imperii* attract immunity, but those that are *jure gestionis* do not.

The Restrictive State Immunity Doctrine This restrictive position was not new to the 20th century development. It was evident as early as 1878 in the case of *Rau van den Abeele et Cie v. Duruty* where immunity for the Peruvian Government was denied in a Belgian court in a contract case.[31] In 1903 the Belgian Cour de Cassation in *S.A. des Chemins de Fer Liégeois-Luxembourgeois v. L'Etat Néelandais* held that where a state acquires or possesses goods, enters into contracts or engages in commerce, it acts as a private individual.[32] In such circumstances it can be sued in a Belgian court without sovereign immunity becoming an issue, as the proceedings will only be looking at private law rights.[33]

However, it was during the 20th century that the concept of restrictive immunity really took hold. By the middle of this century the restrictive state

---

[28] Agencies clearly forming a ministry or department were granted immunity. *Krajina v. Tass Agency* [1949] 2 All ER 274, the Russian news agency was held to be a USSR state organ, hence entitled to immunity in the UK.

[29] Nationalizing industries is a public act; however, when such industries carry on their businesses they engage in private acts.

[30] Higgins, 'Certain Aspects of the Law of State Immunity' (1982) *29 NILR 265.*

[31] Sinclair, 'The Law of Sovereign Immunity. Recent Developments.' (1980) *167 Hague Recueil des Cours 112, 132.*

[32] *Ibid,* p. 133.

[33] *Ibid.*

98   *Immunity and International Criminal Law*

immunity doctrine was more or less fully in use in Western Europe in civil cases, apart from the UK. In 1950 the Austrian Supreme Court exhaustively surveyed state practice on state immunity in the case of *Dralle v. Republic of Czechoslovakia.*[34] The court concluded that the absolute doctrine had so lost its force due to states' increased commercial activities that it could no longer be an international law rule.[35] Within two years of this decision the USA decided to grant immunity to states only for acts deemed public and produced legislation to regulate this position in 1976, the Foreign Sovereign Immunities Act (FSIA).[36] The UK followed suit with the first acknowledged use of the restrictive position in a case in 1977[37] with Parliament passing legislation to this effect in 1978, the UK State Immunity Act (SIA).[38] The UK's highest court, the House of Lords, then endorsed the use of the restrictive doctrine in 1981.[39] Other countries followed these examples and many produced statutes clarifying this position.[40] Statutes that restrict immunity do so with reference to public and private acts, more often in a commercial setting.[41] Indeed the UK's SIA specifically excludes criminal proceedings.[42] At the international level, state immunity is also restricted in civil cases under the European Convention on State Immunity 1972.[43] The ILC produced the Draft Articles on Jurisdictional Immunities of States and Their Property in 1991, which it adopted after years of debate in 2001.[44]

---

[34] *Dralle v. Republic of Czechoslovakia* 17 ILR 155.

[35] *Ibid*, p. 163.

[36] The Tate letter issued by the State Department put forward this position. The Tate Letter (1952) 26 Department of State Bulletin 984. The US courts affirmed this restrictive approach in *Alfred Dunhill of London v. Republic of Cuba* (1976) 15 ILM 735. The USA Foreign Sovereigns Immunities Act 1976 28 U.S.C. §§1330.

[37] *Trendex Trading Corporation Ltd. v. Central Bank of Nigeria* [1977] 2 WLR 356, [1981] 2 All ER 1064.

[38] The UK State Immunity Act 1978.

[39] *I° Congreso del Partido* (1983) 1 AC 244. Applied to facts prior to 1978.

[40] Singapore's State Immunity Act 1979, South Africa's Foreign States Immunities Act 1981, Pakistan's State Immunity Ordinance, Canada's State Immunity Act 1982, and Australia's Foreign States Immunities Act 1985. States that adhere to the restrictive doctrine without legislation include Austria, France, Germany, Italy, Spain and Switzerland. Higgins explains that the process from absolute to restrictive doctrine is still being revised in the states of the former USSR, Eastern European countries. Some Latin American countries and members of the Commonwealth are opposed to the restrictive doctrine. Higgins, *Problems and Processes. International Law and How We Use It, op cit*, p. 81.

[41] As organs of states, heads of state government's immunity experienced restrictions in line with the limitations placed on the immunity of states. As organs of states that are abstract entities run by individuals, they have immunity for acts deemed public acts of state. See Chapter 4 below for further details.

[42] SIA s16(4).

[43] European Convention on State Immunity (1972) 11 ILM 470

[44] (1991) Vol. II(2) YBILC. www.un.org/law/ilc/texts/jimmm.htm. See: Caron, 'The ILC Articles on State Responsibility: The Paradoxical Relationship between Form and Authority' (2002) *96 AJIL 85.* The Ad Hoc Committee on Jurisdictional Immunities of

Immunities 99

Limits on Diplomatic Immunity

Civil Jurisdiction Immunity for civil cases is now also limited for diplomats. Historically, those who supported diplomatic immunity for civil jurisdiction argued that being sued in civil proceedings would leave the envoy without the time and freedom of mind to carry out his duties.[45] Indeed, when the British codified the international customary rules regulating diplomats in 1708 they made civil procedures against foreign envoys criminal offences.[46] Nevertheless, some states did attempt to place limits on the immunity of ambassadors in civil proceedings. In 1772 the French government sent out a memorandum to all diplomats accredited to the French court telling them that it would not tolerate envoys leaving France with unsettled debts.[47] Notwithstanding continental strides to limit diplomatic immunity from civil jurisdiction, Britain continued to maintain the absolute position, and was not alone.[48] In 1928 the Pan-American Union produced the Havana Convention on Diplomatic Officers. Under this Convention diplomatic officers were considered:

> exempt from all the civil or criminal jurisdiction of the state to which they are accredited; they may not, except in the case when duly authorised by their governments, waive immunity, be prosecuted or tried unless it be the courts of their own country.[49]

The Havana Convention did not differentiate between civil and criminal jurisdiction and thus seemed to take the absolute stance. The differences in approach did not dissipate until, arguably, the Vienna Diplomatic Convention in 1961.[50] By placing clear limitations on diplomatic immunity for civil proceedings, this Convention appears to have standardized the global approach to immunities for civil proceedings. Under this convention immunity from civil jurisdiction is limited and excludes: actions relating to private immovable property; action relating to succession in which the agent is involved as executor, heir or legatee as

---

States and their Property acknowledged that the Draft Articles do not refer to criminal proceedings. A/AC.262/L.4 (February 2002). See: Fox, *The Law of State Immunity* (2002), p.216-54.

[45] Vattel, *Le Droit des Gens*, from Barker 'The Theory and Practice of Diplomatic Law in the Renaissance and Classical Periods', *op cit*, p. 605-6. For an historical analysis of diplomatic immunity see: Young, 'The Development of the Law of Diplomatic Relations' (1964) *BYIL 141*.

[46] Diplomatic Privileges Act 1709. This Act was not comprehensive in its detail on criminal jurisdiction nor did it cover the issue of inviolability of mission premises. It was later replaced by the Diplomatic Privileges Act 1964.

[47] Nahlik, 'Development of Diplomatic Law Selected Problems', *op cit.*

[48] Denza, *Diplomatic Law A Commentary on the Vienna Convention on Diplomatic Relations*, *op cit*, p. 231.

[49] Havana Convention on Diplomatic Officers, Article 19. The Havana Convention on Diplomatic Officers was adopted at the Sixth International American Conference Havana, 20 February 1928 (hereinafter the Havana Convention).

[50] Vienna Diplomatic Convention, *op cit.*

Immunity and International Criminal Law

a private person; and action relating to any professional or commercial activity exercised by the agent in the receiving state outside official functions.[51] Thus, a:

> diplomatic agent shall enjoy immunity from the criminal jurisdiction of the receiving state. He shall also enjoy immunity from its civil and administrative jurisdiction, except in the case of:
>
> (a)   a real action relating to private immovable property situated in the territory of the receiving State, unless he holds it on behalf of the sending State for the purposes of the mission;
>
> (b)   an action relating to succession in which the diplomatic agent is involved as executor, administrator, heir or legatee as a private person and not on behalf of the sending State;
>
> (c)   an action relating to the professional or commercial activities exercised by the diplomatic agent in the receiving State outside his official functions.[52]

Criminal Jurisdiction   Visits abroad by heads of states were, until recently, somewhat rare.[53] Envoys played a great role in representing their monarchs and leaders in foreign states. Envoys were initially inviolable and immune from the criminal jurisdiction of their receiving states on the basis of their representative status. However, it is argued that contemporary international law favours a more functional approach.[54] Nonetheless, in fulfilling their role as representatives of their sovereigns, 'no ambassador was ever put to death, nor even subjected to any prolonged period of imprisonment for crimes committed in the 16th and 17th centuries'.[55] When the Spanish and French ambassadors accredited to the English court of Elizabeth I were found to be assisting in the conspiracy to overthrow her, they retained their inviolability and were not arrested and detained.[56] Denza notes that irrespective of the suspicions surrounding envoys in the 17th century, there appears to have been no arrest and prosecution, emphasizing that, thereafter 'the rule of immunity from criminal jurisdiction continued virtually unchallenged until its incorporation into the Vienna Diplomatic Convention'.[57]

According to Denza inviolability of diplomats was firmly established as a rule of international customary law by the end of the 16th century.[58] The earliest

---

[51]   Vienna Diplomatic Convention, Article 31(a)(b)(c), *ibid*. For Articles 31(a) and (b) actions are non-immune only if the agent was not acting on behalf of his state.

[52]   Vienna Diplomatic Convention, Article 31, *ibid*.

[53]   Deák 'Organs of State in their Extraterritorial Relation: Immunity and Privileges of Organs of the State' *Manual of Public International Law* (1968), *op cit*, p. 387.

[54]   Barker, *The Abuse of Diplomatic Privileges and Immunities. A Necessary Evil?* (1996), p. 75.

[55]   Adair, *The Extraterritoriality of Ambassadors in the Sixteenth and Seventeenth Centuries* (1929).

[56]   Denza, *Diplomatic Law A Commentary on the Vienna Convention on Diplomatic Relations*, *op cit*, p. 229-20.

[57]   *Ibid*, p. 230.

[58]   *Ibid*, p. 210.

Immunities 101

legislative account of diplomatic inviolability is said to be in a Dutch statute of 1651. According to this legislation it was an offence to offend, damage, or injure:

> by word, act or manner, the ambassadors, residents, agents, or other ministers of the kings, princes, republics, or others having the quality of public ministers; or to do them injury or insult directly or indirectly, in any fashion or manner whatever, in their own persons, gentlemen of their suite, their domestic servants, dwellings, carriages, etc., under penalty of being corporeally punished as violators of the laws of nations and disturbers of the public peace.

In 1928 inviolability appeared in an international convention, the Havana Convention:

> Diplomatic officers shall be inviolate as to their persons.[59]

Up until that time, although inviolability was acknowledged in various drafts and conventions, it was relatively undefined.[60] The Vienna Diplomatic Convention affirmed the 1928 definition of inviolability maintaining that:

> The person of the diplomatic agent shall be inviolable.

But extended the definition to include:

> He shall not be liable to any form of arrest and detention.[61]

Thus codified the Vienna Diplomatic Convention's inviolability provision is reflected and given force in domestic jurisdictions. The USA's Diplomatic Relations Act 1978 established the Vienna Diplomatic Convention as the primary source of law in the US on the subject of diplomatic immunity.[62] Consequently, the Third Restatement of the Foreign Relations Law states that:

> A diplomatic agent of a state, accredited to and accepted by another state, is immune…from arrest, detention, criminal process.[63]

---

[59] Havana Convention, Article 14.

[60] For example the Harvard Research Draft in International Law: Diplomatic Privileges and Immunities (1932) *26 AJIL Supplement 15, 98.*

[61] Vienna Diplomatic Convention, Article 29, *op cit.* The second part of this article obliges receiving states to take appropriate steps to prevent attacks on a diplomat's person, freedom or dignity.

[62] Diplomatic Relations Act 1978 22 U.S.C. § 254a-254e.

[63] Third Restatement of the Law, Foreign Relations Law of the United States (1987), American Law Institute, §464.

102 *Immunity and International Criminal Law*

The Second Schedule of the Tanzanian Diplomatic and Consular Immunities and Privileges Act 1986 gives Article 29 of the Vienna Diplomatic Convention effect of law in Tanzania.[64]

Civil Limitations for Criminal Acts Limitations on states and their agents have not been restricted to commercial activities. Victims or their families can pursue remedies through compensatory proceedings in civil courts for tortious acts committed by state agents. In keeping with the restrictive doctrine, individuals could seek civil compensation for acts deemed *gestionis*. Such acts are thereby deemed private and cannot be immune. Most statutes on immunity specifically restrict immunity in civil compensatory cases for tortious acts or omissions that have caused death or personal injury, damage to or loss of tangible property, where committed by foreign states' officials during the course of their employment.[65]

This statutory exception was successfully used in 1980 in the case of *Letelier v. Republic of Chile*.[66] The family of a former Chilean ambassador, Letelier, was able to gain compensation from the Chilean government through the US courts for the death of the ex-ambassador who was killed by a car bomb, planted by Chilean agents in his car.[67] The incident happened in Washington D.C.; for this reason, it fell clearly within the exception outlined in the FSIA.

The FSIA governs all actions brought against a state or its agents according to the Supreme Court in *Argentine Republic v. Amerada Hess Shipping Corp.*[68] The Supreme Court held in *Amerada Hess* that the FSIA was the 'sole basis for obtaining jurisdiction over a foreign state' in US courts, and that 'immunity is granted in those cases involving alleged violations of international law that do not

---

[64] Dualist states will mostly have statutes that give effect to the Convention. See: Shaw, *International Law, op* cit, p. 104-5.

[65] Section 5 of the UK SIA: A State is not immune as respects proceedings relating to (a) death or personal injury; or (b) damage to or loss of tangible property, caused by an act or omission in the United Kingdom. UK SIA, *op* cit. The US FSIA section 1605(a) (5) denies immunity where 'money damages are sought against a foreign state for personal injury or death, or damage to or loss of property, occurring in the United States and caused by the tortiuous act or omission of that foreign state or of any official or employee of that foreign state while acting within the scope of his office or employment', FSIA, *op cit*. European Convention, Article 11 allows 'redress for injury to the person or damage to tangible property, if the facts which occasioned the injury or damage occurred in the territory of the state of the forum, and if the author of the injury or damage was present in that territory at the time when those facts occurred European Convention, *op cit*.

[66] *Letelier v. Republic of Chile* (1980) 488 F. Supp. 665, (1980) 502 F. Supp. 259. Hereinafter *Letelier Case*.

[67] The court in this case rejected Chile's argument that the act in question was not a private act, stating that 'Nowhere is there an indication that the tortious acts to which the Act makes reference are to only be those formerly classified as 'private'. *Letelier Case*, p. 671.

[68] *Argentine Republic v. Amerada Hess Shipping Corp.* (1988) 488 U.S. 428, 434,436. The plaintiff sought compensation for the loss of a ship, which he alleged the Argentine Air Force had damaged in violation of international law during the Falklands war. (Hereinafter the *Amerada Hess*).

Immunities 103

come within one of the FSIA's exceptions'.[69] Under this statute the incident in question must occur within US territory. The *Letelier Case* is an exception, as it is very rare that a state will commit criminal acts within the territory of another state. In contrast, in *Siderman de Blake*, the Court of Appeal held that it was bound by the Supreme Court ruling in *Amerada Hess* as to the limits imposed by the FSIA.[70] The court in *Siderman de Blake* believed that torture was a violation of international *jus cogens*.[71] But, since the violation of the *jus cogens* in question occurred outside the US it did not fall under that statute's exception to state immunity.[72] The court had no choice but to grant the state immunity. Similarly, in the UK, in the case of *Al Adsani v. Government of Kuwait*,[73] the Court of Appeal held that the act must have been committed in the UK in order for the tort exception to apply under the UK's SIA.[74] The ECHR appeared to agree with this position when the case came before it.[75] In reaching its decision that the SIA did not unjustly restrict the applicant's access to court, the court held that it could not establish that there is acceptance in international law that states are not entitled to immunity in respect of civil claims, even though there is a growing recognition of the overriding importance of the prohibition of torture.[76] Accordingly the court maintained that the '1978 Act, which grants immunity to States in respect of personal injury claims unless the damage was caused within the United Kingdom, is not inconsistent with those limitations generally accepted by the community of nations as part of the doctrine of State immunity'.[77]

The statutes on immunity grant a domestic court jurisdiction based on the territorial principle, as only those cases that occur within the territory are justiciable. Jurisdiction could be sought by forum states through the use of the nationality, protective, passive personality or the universal principles. However as the immunity statutes work on the territorial basis they fall outside the ambit of the exception to state immunity in most of these statutes.[78] This territorial connection is the most 'limiting factor in the application of the torts exception'.[79] Not only is it limiting in the application of the tort exception, but looking at the broader picture,

---

[69] *Ibid.*

[70] *Siderman de Blake, op cit.*

[71] *Ibid*, p. 717.

[72] *Ibid.*

[73] *Al Adsani v. Government of Kuwait* (hereinafter the *Al Adsani* Case), unreported. Lexis at www.butterworths.co.uk.

[74] *Ibid.*

[75] *Al Adsani Case (ECHR).*

[76] *Ibid*, p.21 para. 66 and 67. The applicant had claimed that the SIA restricted his access to the courts unjustly under Article 6 of the European Convention on Human Rights and Fundamental Freedoms 1950.

[77] *Ibid*, p.21 para. 66.

[78] Under other statutes: South Africa – s.6 Foreign States Immunities Act 1981, the Australian Act, s13.

[79] Schreuer, *State Immunity: Some Recent Developments*, p. 51.

104 *Immunity and International Criminal Law*

it prevents victims of international crimes from claiming compensation from states and their agents through civil procedures.

Nonetheless, in the USA certain statutes give its courts jurisdiction to hear cases involving foreign victims of some international crimes that occur outside the US: the Alien Tort Claims Act 1789 (ATC) and the Torture Victim Protection Act 1992 (TVPA).[80] The ATC gives US courts original jurisdiction in any civil action by an alien for a tort committed in violation of the laws of nations or a treaty of the United States. The act was used in 1980 by Paraguayan citizens seeking compensation for torture by their state's police in *Filartiga v. Peña-Irala*.[81] These two statutes could effectively be used to render a form of justice for victims of international crimes committed by states through payment of compensation, and have been utilized in various cases, for example: *Alvarez-Machain v. US,*[82] *US v. Ramzi Ahmed Yousef, Eyad Ismoil et al*[83] and *Simpson v. Socialist People's Libyan Arab Jamahiriya.*[84] Paradoxically, these statutes can only be used against states and their agents through the FSIA as per *Amerada Hess*. It is therefore a matter of fitting the act in question within this statute's exceptions, which is difficult because of the territorial-link requirement. Although the statutes appear in theory to erode absolute immunity, in reality immunity is still conclusive, as *Amerada Hess* demands that the FSIA is the only route to claim compensation from states and their agents. As the FSIA's exceptions are few, and jurisdiction under the statute is tied to territory, there has not been the expected erosion into immunities that the ATC and TVPA could have delivered.

Criminal Jurisdiction and the Absolute Nature of Immunities

Civil jurisdiction limitations on immunities have eroded the once absolute sovereignty states had in their international commercial dealing. The use of tort exceptions in state immunity statutes to hold those accused of international crimes accountable is limited by the territorial principle. If action is through the criminal jurisdiction, domestic courts could use the other more flexible jurisdictional principles in order to pursue those with immunities. Due to the penal nature of international criminal law it is not practical to pursue criminal proceedings against states.[85] Thus the option is to pursue the individuals in government who have the

---

[80] The Alien Tort Claims Act 1789 (28 USC § 1350), Torture Victim Protection Act 1992, (28 USC s. 1350).

[81] *Filartiga v. Peña-Irala* (1980) 630 F.2d 876 (2ⁿᵈ Cir.) This case was heard prior to *Amerada Hess*.

[82] *Alvarez-Machain v. US* (2003) US Appl Lexis 10949.

[83] *US v. Ramzi Ahmed Yousef, Eyad Ismoil et al* (2003) US Appl. Lexis 6437.

[84] *Simpson v. Socialist People's Libyan Arab Jamahiriya* (2003) US App. Lexis 7492.

[85] The ILC considered the possibility of states being criminally responsible in its Draft Articles on State Responsibility as stated above, Chapter 3.

Immunities

power to commit international crimes. Immunities under criminal jurisdiction have not developed as comparably as immunities under civil jurisdiction.

Kings and Absolutism: The Capacity to Act with Impunity

As outlined above, sovereign immunity developed from the notion that a king is the supreme legal authority not under the control of his state nor other kings. In Western Europe this doctrine was absolute during feudal times.[86] It was believed that the king received his power to rule from God, rather than the people, under the maxim *rex gratia dei*. His power to rule being derived from God, he was not open to rebuke or complaint as that would entail a challenge to God.[87] Sovereign immunity implied, therefore,that 'the king can do no (temporal) wrong and cannot be held accountable or tried in any temporal tribunal'.[88] No earthly being was superior to the king, and he could not be a defendant in his own court.[89] The worldly authority of kings was unqualified. The king could commit crimes and not be held accountable.

It is argued that during the 13th and 14th centuries 'the fortress of absolute power' was besieged by 'juridical norms, natural law, reason, custom, privilege, obligation' which in effect outlined the 'constitution of the realm'.[90] In other words legal jurists during that period in time always qualified a king's powers with references to notions of, *inter alia*, custom and natural law, hence, absolute power never was absolute.[91] According to Meron, the UK's Magna Carta of 1295 limited the power of English medieval kings thereafter.[92] Even before the Magna Carta, he is of the opinion that 'feudal systems of relationships between vassals and sovereign also gave the vassal rights'.[93] Even so, rights vassals may have had vis-à-vis their sovereign did not empower them to hold a king personally accountable for crimes. Irrespective of what theologians, jurists and academics wrote, it was evident that kings considered themselves above temporal law. Put simply, a king during feudal times was not likely to face murder charges in a court in his own

---

[86] During these times society was based on a pyramidical structure with serfs at the bottom, followed by lords of the manor and dukes with the king at the apex. Hurwitz, *The State as Defendant: Governmental Accountability and the Redress of Individual Grievances* (1981), p. 10.

[87] *Ibid.*

[88] *Ibid.*

[89] The feudal system involved courts at each level of the pyramid. Serfs were judged by lords of the manor who in turn were judged by dukes, who were judged by the king. The king, of course, judged all but himself. Hurwitz, *The State as Defendant, op cit*, p. 11.

[90] Pennington, *The Prince and the Law, 1200-1600: Sovereignty and Rights in Western Legal Traditions* (1993), p. 8.

[91] *Ibid.*

[92] Meron, 'Crimes and Accountability in Shakespeare' (1998) *92 AJIL 1, 4.*

[93] *Ibid.*

106 *Immunity and International Criminal Law*

country.[94] This feudal conception of kingly power remained unmodified in Western Europe until the 16th century.[95]

Head of State Immunity: Limitations on Monocracy?

Through the centuries the king was perceived to rule his subjects by the grace of God, as stated in the maxim: *rex gratia dei*. Various theorists challenged this divine source of authority in the 16th century. The maxim was slowly eroded and taken over by another: *rex gratia populi*: king by the grace of the people.[96] In the 16th century Bodin wrote:

> For if we define freed from all laws [as absolute power] no prince anywhere possesses sovereignty (iura maiestatis), since divine law, the law of nature, and the common law of all the people, which is established separately from divine and natural law, binds all princes.[97]

Although divine natural law might bind the king, it was only when the divine right to rule theory was challenged did the possibility of a king being held criminally liable tentatively emerge. Sovereigns began to be restricted in their actions by notions of 'multitudes of men' agreeing to be represented by a single person.[98]

During the 17th century theorists advanced notions that a king derived his right to rule from his subjects, rather than God. Thus the opportunity to hold him personally responsible for crimes became a possibility.

Hobbes, writing in 1651, two years after a British king, Charles I, was beheaded, challenged the divine right to rule theory:

> A *Common-wealth* is said to be *Instituted*, when a *Multitude* of men do Agree, and *Covenant*, *every one*, *with every one*, that to whatsoever *Man*, or *Assembly of Men*, shall be given by the major part, the *Right* to *Present* the Person of them all, (that is to say, to be their *Representative*;) every one, as well he that *Voted for it*, as he that *Voted against it*, shall *Authorise* all the Actions and Judgements, of that Man, or Assembly of men, in the same manner, as if they were his own, to the end, to live peaceably amongst themselves, and to be protected against other men.

---

[94] Individual kings could have been held accountable for certain acts by another ruler deemed superior. For example during the 12th century the Emperor of the Romans was an elected prince from one of the various Christian kingdoms in Western Europe. As emperor of the seat of Christian power, he was the de facto ruler over all Christians, and was thus, theoretically, superior to all other kings. However, there existed continuous tensions between the Emperor of the Romans and other kings; consequently it is doubtful whether he exercised actual jurisdiction over all Christian kingdoms. Pennington, *The Prince and the Law*, *op cit*, p. 165-201.

[95] Hurwitz, *The State as Defendant*, p. 12.

[96] *Ibid*, p. 13.

[97] Bodin, *De republica libri sex* (3rd ed. Frankfurt: 1594) 132, from Pennington, *The Prince and the Law*, *op cit*, p. 8.

[98] Hobbes, *Leviathan*, *op cit*, p. 121.

Immunities 107

> From this institution of a Common-wealth are derived all the *Rights*, and *Facultyes* of him, or them, on whom the Soveraigne Power is conferred by the consent of the People assembled.[99]

Thus for Hobbes the sovereign derived his authority from a social contract between himself and his subjects. However, although Hobbes challenged a king's divine right to rule, he vehemently defended sovereign immunity, stating that:

> whatsoever he doth, it can be no injury to any of his Subject; nor ought he to be by any of them accused of Injustice. For he that doth any thing by authority from another, doth therein no injury to him by whose authority he acteth:[100]

> no man that hath Soveraigne power can justly be put to death, or otherwise in any manner by his Subjects be punished.[101]

Even though he failed to challenge sovereign immunity, his attack on the *rex gratia dei* enabled other writers to do so.

Writing some years after Hobbes, Locke accepted the social contract between the king and his subjects. However, unlike Hobbes his contract was more in line with a trust arrangement: the king existed only to carry out the will of the people.[102] Accordingly, the king was not the source of the law and could therefore do wrong.[103]

Combining Hobbes' efforts to differentiate between the divine right to rule and a sovereign's immunity and Locke's attempt to establish that a sovereign could act contrary to his duties as trustee, the notion that a king could err emerged. These two theorists influenced attitudes in the United Kingdom. Since the 14th century individuals with a complaint against the sovereign could be granted a *petition of right* and have their cases heard. This procedure was largely abandoned between the 15th and 18th century, but saw a revival during the 19th century.[104] Although not totally attributable to Hobbes and Locke's theories, the revival of an individual's right of petition certainly augmented the notion that a sovereign could do wrong.[105] Theoretically, a British sovereign could make mistakes; however he or she could not be arrested.[106] Consequently if such sovereign were to commit a crime, the action would be acknowledged as criminal, but any court in his or her realm would

---

[99] *Ibid*, p. 121.

[100] *Ibid*, 124.

[101] *Ibid*.

[102] Hurwitz, *The State as Defendant, op cit*, p. 17.

[103] *Ibid*, p. 18-19.

[104] *Ibid*, p. 18.

[105] Industrialization and the development of the modern state system helped the revival. *Ibid*.

[106] Berriedale-Keith, *The King and the Imperial Crown: The Powers and Duties of His Majesty* (1936), p. 328-9.

not try him or her for it, nor indeed could a foreign court.[107] Accordingly, he or she carried that absolute immunity from penal measure with them when they travelled abroad.

This absolute immunity prevailed during the 19th and 20th centuries, becoming part of custom. The inviolability of a monarch travelled with him abroad and is considered absolute. So much so that writing in 1968, Deák failed to find a single instance where a state sought to exercise its criminal jurisdiction over a visiting head of state.[108] Thus their inviolability and immunity from suit in a criminal court of a foreign state has become part of international customary law. As modern state systems developed, many states adopted a parliamentary style of government with the sovereign taking a more ceremonial position. Thus the heads of such governments, in their representative roles abroad, were also considered inviolable and immune. When heads of state ventured abroad, they were deemed inviolable and free from criminal proceedings. Although exceptions were granted in civil cases, their immunity from criminal cases remains absolute.

The question is, therefore: Is there a legitimate way around the immunity which persons of such status are accorded in order to facilitate ICC surrender requests? If such a way does not exist then Article 27 of the Rome Statute was dead before it was conceived, as those with immunity will evade arrest and detention for transfer to the ICC. In attempting to answer this question, immunity of heads of state, government and diplomats must be analysed in greater detail.

---

[107] *Ibid.*

[108] Deák, 'Organs of States in their External Relations: Immunities and Privileges of State Organs and of the State', *op cit*, p. 388.

Chapter 5

High-Ranking State Officials and Crime

With regard to criminal proceedings in a foreign court, a serving head of state's immunity is generally accepted as absolute.[1] Diplomats are also afforded absolute immunity from criminal jurisdictions under the Vienna Diplomatic Convention in their receiving states.[2] For both heads of state and diplomats there are two branches (for want of a better word) of immunities: immunity *ratione personae* and *ratione materiae*. Immunity *ratione personae* relates to the individual and *materiae* to the acts. Lord Millett in *Pinochet (No. 3)* appeared to make the distinction between individual immunity as being immunity *ratione personae* and state immunity for civil jurisdiction as immunity *ratione materiae*.[3] In reliance on this distinction the ECHR in *Al Adsani* noted that:

> The House of Lords (and in particular Lord Millett at p. 178) made clear that their findings as to immunity *ratione materiae* from criminal jurisdiction did not affect the immunity *ratione personae* of foreign sovereign States from civil jurisdiction in respect of acts of torture.[4]

According to Barker, 'this analysis betrays a fundamental misunderstanding of the distinction between immunity *ratione materiae* and immunity *ratione personae*.'[5] Barker maintains, correctly, that the immunity *ratione materiae* of a diplomat or head of state is in fact state immunity and that a state cannot possess immunity *ratione personae*.[6]

Immunity *ratione materiae* relates to acts of the state. Conduct that is directly attributable to state action is considered an act of state. As the person in question does not commit such acts for his own personal benefit, foreign domestic courts have to grant such acts immunity. Although the person in question commits the act, he is considered to be immune from prosecution for such conduct because

---

[1] Watts, 'The Legal Position in International Law of Heads of State, Heads of Government and Foreign Ministers', *op cit*, p. 54.

[2] Vienna Diplomatic Convention, Article 31. Under the Vienna Diplomatic Convention members of the diplomat's family also enjoy the same immunity as the diplomat; Article 37(1) Official correspondence, archives and documents are also immune, Articles 27(2) and 24.

[3] *Pinochet (No. 3)*, p. 179.

[4] *Al Adsani Case (ECHR)*, para 34.

[5] Barker, '*Immunity Ratione Personae and Jus Cogens Norms – Approach with Caution* April 2002 Conference Paper ILA (British Branch) Spring Conference p. 4.

[6] *Ibid.*

110 *Immunity and International Criminal Law*

it is his state that has acted. The act itself is non-justiciable in a foreign court for an indefinite period. It has been described as 'permanent though partial immunity'.[7]

Dinstein argues that both immunity *ratione materiae* and *personae* are exemptions from local process.[8] He claims that one ends upon the termination of a diplomat's duties, the other lingers on, but that 'there is no distinction in their relation to local law'.[9] Immunity *ratione personae* prevents domestic authorities, be they judicial or not, from enforcing local laws (criminal or civil) on internationally protected individuals. Immunity *ratione materiae* prevents local judicial authorities from adjudicating cases based on the non-justiciability of the internationally sensitive subject matter. With immunity *ratione materiae*, individuals need not appear before a court.

Personal Immunity: Immunity *Ratione Personae*

Immunity *ratione personae* covers the person concerned whilst he holds that office, and thus draws no distinction between what he does in his official capacity (i.e. what he does as head of state or diplomat for state purposes) and what he does in his private capacity.[10] This is because it is his person that is immune from the enforcement jurisdiction of a state. He is inviolable. Inviolability denotes freedom from arrest. This immunity attaches to the person in question by virtue of their office. Hence, once the individual's term in office ends, he ceases to enjoy immunity *ratione personae*, and he can therefore be arrested and detained.

Speaking in 2001 in relation to the proposed case against Sharon in Belgium, Philippe Mahoux, a Belgian senator, stated that the issue of immunities 'needs reflection' and that there was a need for a 'formula that allows serving heads of state not impunity but something like temporary immunity while they're serving as head of state' that would permit them to be 'prosecuted when their mandate has expired'.[11] It is suggested that this temporary immunity the senator was referring to already exists in the form of immunity *ratione personae*.

It is acknowledged and accepted that initially inviolability was 'the basis from which all other privileges and immunities derived'.[12] A person is inviolable because he has immunity *ratione personae*, and he has immunity *ratione personae* because he is inviolable. It has been submitted that 'inviolability demands as a prerequisite immunity from jurisdiction'.[13] This is perhaps true with regard to immunity *ratione materiae*, as certain acts render the person immune. In other words, where the acts in question are those of his state he cannot be held

---

[7] *Ibid.*

[8] Dinstein, 'Diplomatic Immunity from Jurisdiction *Ratione Materiae*' (1966) *ICLQ 76, 81*.

[9] *Ibid.*

[10] Lord Saville, *Pinochet Case (No. 3)*, p. 168.

[11] Belgium's Legal Trap for World Leader, 23 January 2002, CNN, www.cnn.com.

[12] Do Nascimento e Silva, *Diplomacy in International Law* (1972), p. 89.

[13] Barker, *The Abuse of Diplomatic Privileges and Immunities, op cit*, p. 77.

High-Ranking State Officials and Crime 111

accountable for them in a foreign court, which in turn denotes that he cannot be charged for those acts. However, there is no distinction between immunity *ratione personae* and inviolability as immunity *ratione personae* is inviolability.

Inviolability and Heads of State and Government and High-Ranking State Officials

Heads of state or government are inviolable and cannot be arrested in any foreign state.[14] The inviolability of a head of state is confirmed by the provisions of the Convention on Special Missions, whereby a head of state as part of a special mission has personal inviolability, which includes non-liability to any form of arrest and detention when he travels abroad on mission.[15]

> When a head of state or government comes on an official visit to another country, he is generally given the same personal inviolability...as are accorded to members of special missions.[16]

A visiting head of state is inviolable for that particular visit as a non-resident representative of his state.[17] Although head of state inviolability is connected to diplomatic inviolability when they are abroad,[18] this inviolability does not fall under the Vienna Diplomatic Convention as this convention only covers accredited diplomats in the receiving states. The inviolability of heads of state or government is applicable *erga omnes*, that is, at all times, everywhere. *Erga omnes* obligations are obligations that all states have an interest in protecting. [19]

The inviolability of heads of state and government would appear to include freedom from service. However, in a recent US case, it was held that they could be served in certain circumstances. In 1994 several Zimbabwean citizens filed a civil law suit against Robert Mugabe in his capacity as president of the ruling party,

---

[14] Watts, 'The Legal Position in International Law of Heads of State, Heads of Government and Foreign Ministers', *op cit*, p. 100-113.

[15] Convention on Special Missions 1969 Gen. Ass. Res. (1970) XXIV 2530. Article 29. Watts, 'The Legal Position in International Law of Heads of State, Heads of Government and Foreign Ministers', *op cit*, p. 52.

[16] Third Restatement of the Law, Foreign Relations Law of the United States, *op cit*, §464, para. 14.

[17] Foreign ministers as non-resident representatives of their states are also considered inviolable when abroad. US case of *Kim v. Kim Yong Shik* (1964) 58 AJIL 186. The ICJ in its decision on 14 January 2002 regarding the arrest warrant issued by Belgium against a minister of foreign affairs of Congo reaffirmed the absolute position. The ICJ took the view that whilst in office, such official is absolutely immune from the jurisdiction of other states even for international crimes, discussed below.

[18] Bröhmer, *State Immunity and the Violation of Human Rights* (1997), p. 30.

[19] *Erga omnes* obligations are obligations that all states are all held to have a legal interest in protecting, *Barcelona Traction Case*, *op cit*, p.32. The case outlined these obligations as derived from the 'outlawing of acts of aggression, and genocide'. and 'from the principles and rules concerning basic rights of the human person including the protection from slavery and racial discrimination'.

Zanu-PF.[20] He was served notice whilst in the US for a meeting at the UN, but the US government filed a 'suggestion' of his immunity with the court, stating, *inter alia*, that as a head of state Mugabe had personal inviolability and could not be served in any capacity.[21] Although the court acknowledged that as a sitting head of state he was immune from the jurisdiction of the US courts, it was of the opinion that service to Zanu PF, as a non-immune entity, could be effected through Mugabe, an inviolable individual.[22] The court based this decision on its interpretation of customary norms of inviolability applicable to heads of state. According to the court, service to effect jurisdiction over matters collateral to the head of state's official status is possible as the head of state will not have to appear in court, nor be subject to the court's compulsory powers 'in a manner that could be deemed an assertion of territorial authority over the foreign dignitary'.[23] The court held that service could be effected where 'a head-of-state or diplomat would not be subjected to a foreign court's jurisdiction nor exposed to liability in that court'.[24] The US government rigorously challenged this decision to effect service through an inviolable individual.[25] The government was of the opinion that the ruling 'will give rise to vexatious and embarrassing assaults on the dignity of foreign leaders and diplomats, as individuals who wish to protest or humiliate such officials will be able through simple artifice to plead a complaint against a nongovernmental entity with which an official allegedly is affiliated, and then to publicise and stage a highly-visible service of process on the visiting dignitary'.[26]

The *Tachiona Case* appears to be at odds with the ICJ's recent judgment in the *Arrest Warrant Case*.[27] Although dealing with a foreign minister, the ICJ concluded that their functions vis-à-vis their states are similar to heads of state:

> a Minister for Foreign Affairs, responsible for the conduct of his or her State's relations with all other States, occupies a position such that, like the Head of State

---

[20] *Tachiona et al v. Mugabe, Zanu PF, Mudenge et al* (2001) 169 F. Supp. 259. The plaintiffs were awarded damages on 11 December 2002. Lexis 23830 at www.butterworths.co.uk.

[21] *Ibid*. Although restrictions exist under civil jurisdiction for compensation, a sitting head of state is inviolable to service of notice.

[22] *Tachiona Case, ibid*, p. 296. The FSIA does not deal with head of state immunity as a separate issue. The Second Restatement of Foreign Relations Law of 1965 extended sovereign immunity to include heads of state. However, the Third Restatement does not.

[23] *Ibid*, p. 309.

[24] *Ibid*, p. 308.

[25] Memoradum of Law in Support of the United States' Motion for Reconsideration, 16 November 2001, *Tachiona Case*.

[26] *Ibid*, p.10. The government's action was denied by the court on 14th February 2002. *Tachiona v. Mugabe, Zanu PF, Mudenge et al* (hereinafter *Tachiona Case (No. 2)* (2002) 186 F. Supp. 2d. 383.

[27] *Arrest Warrant Case*.

or the Head of Government, he or she is recognized under international law as representative of the State solely by virtue of his or her office.[28]

Thus the court was able to conclude that:

> the functions of a Minister for Foreign Affairs are such that, throughout the duration of his or her office, he or she would enjoy full immunity from criminal jurisdiction and inviolability. That immunity and that inviolability protect the individual concerned against any act of authority of another State which would hinder him or her in the performance of his or her duties.[29]

The jurisdiction in question in the *Arrest Warrant Case* was criminal, unlike Tachiona, where it was civil; however, the ICJ's ruling is applicable to the *Tachiona Case*. First, according to the ICJ, the position of a head of state and foreign minister vis-à-vis foreign jurisdictions is analogous, hence their decision is applicable to Mugabe as head of state of Zimbabwe. Second, the ICJ was clear that an incumbent foreign minister is inviolable against any act of authority of another state. Service is without doubt an act of authority of a state, in fact an act of legal authority. Third, the act must be such as to hinder the individual from performing his duties. It is possible to imagine that service to Mugabe, the party president, will affect Mugabe the head of state. The person is one and the same, irrespective of the fact that service was pertaining to collateral matters.[30]

It is true that persons of certain status in government need to be able to operate in an international capacity on behalf of their states without the fear of arrest. They must be able to travel freely. Where there is fear of arrest they may not be able to fully fulfil their official functions and this will most definitely be detrimental to international relations. International law cannot operate in a vacuum as it regulates international relations. And where international law upsets the delicate equilibrium achieved by a system of sovereign equal states, inter-state relations will be jeopardized. Hence the lack of distinction between private and public acts for immunity *ratione personae*.

Immunity Ratione Personae and the International Law Doctrine of Recognition[31]

Immunity *ratione personae* may not apply where the state official in question comes from a country whose government is not recognized by the state conferring

---

[28] *Ibid*, p. 19, para. 53.

[29] *Ibid*, p. 20, para. 54.

[30] The US government's action against Tachiona and in support of absolute inviolability for Mugabe was denied in *Tachiona (No. 2)*. It would have been interesting to see if the US court would have adhered to the ICJ's position if *Tachiona (No. 2)* occurred after the ICJ's ruling. Both judgments were given around the same time.

[31] The doctrine of recognition will not be discussed in much detail and in-depth, as that would detract from the emphasis of this book. However, it is perhaps useful as an illustrative tool in clarifying immunity *ratione personae* and the scope of its applicability.

immunity. Heads of state and government's immunity *ratione personae* from criminal jurisdiction was developed by, and is currently still, based on custom. It became part of custom for states to accord immunity to governments and heads of state that they recognized, thus the international law doctrine of recognition evolved. This doctrine is applicable to both states and their governments. When a new state comes into existence other countries have to decide whether to recognize it or not.[32] The doctrine of recognition also arises where there has been a change in government, and, as governments have progressively become the agencies of the sovereign, the recognition of new governments is essentially a question of the recognition of the agency that exercises the sovereignty of a nation.[33] Consequently:

> A government which has supreme control, without opposition, within the territory of the nation, exercises the sovereignty of the nation and represents the nation. It speaks and acts for the nation and, therefore, it has the power in most respects to bind the nation internationally.[34]

Thus where there has been an illegitimate change in government, the head of state, as the representative of the nation, and/or the head of government are subject to the doctrine of recognition as instrumentalities of the government.[35]

A government and its organs so recognized are immune from the domestic legal enforcement jurisdiction of states that recognize it as exercising such sovereignty. A non-recognized government and its organs will usually be denied

---

[32] The recognition of states is beyond the scope of this book. However, it must be borne in mind that some issues pertaining to the recognition of governments are also applicable to the recognition of states, in so far as the existence of an effective and independent government is the essence of statehood whereby the recognition of states may take the form of recognition of a government. Brownlie, *Principles of Public International Law, op cit*, p. 92-3. A change in government does not effect the status of a state already recognized.

[33] Woolsey, 'Editoral Comment: The Non-Recognition of the Chammorro Government in Nicaragua' (1926) *20 AJIL 543*, 545. It has been noted that the principle of recognition is simply the acknowledgement that a new government 'exercises the sovereignty of the nation and speaks and acts for it with authority. Thus according to this point of view the legitimacy of a government's "origin or the means by which it came to possession of sovereignty" are of secondary importance.' Woolsey 'Editoral Comment', *ibid*, p. 546.

[34] *Ibid.*

[35] It is indeed true that an 'independent state has the power and right to choose and establish whatever kind of government it please, by whatever means it may nominate'. However, a situation may arise where a government has effective control over a state without legal authority to realize such control. In other words it has *de facto* control but lacks *de jure* control. Where a government has control only in fact, *de facto*, it does not mean that it does not have legal control, only that its legal basis for control is questionable. A government that has legal basis to control a state is defined as a *de jure* government.

inviolability.[36] In the US case of *Lafontant v. Aristide* the issue of recognition was central to the determination that an exiled head of state was entitled to head of state immunity *ratione personae*.[37] According to the complaint, after a thwarted coup d'etat to prevent Haitian president-elect Aristide from taking office, Lafontant was arrested and sentenced to life imprisonment for his involvement in the attempted coup. Aristide, it is alleged, ordered the killing of Lafontant in jail two days prior to his exile from Haiti following a successful military coup. During his exile he was consistently recognized by US government as being the lawful head of state of Haiti. Accordingly the court held that:

> A head-of-state recognized by the United States government is absolutely immune from personal jurisdiction in United States courts unless that immunity has been waived by statute or by the foreign government recognized by the United States...The United States government does not recognize the de facto military rulers of Haiti. It has repeatedly condemned their regime. Because the United States does not recognize the de facto government, that government does not have the power to waive President Aristide's immunity.[38]

Concluding that:

> This court has subject matter jurisdiction, but it cannot exercise in personam jurisdiction over defendant because of his head-of-state immunity.[39]

Thus the court could look at the subject matter but Aristide could not be arrested. Another example would be Panama in the late 1980s. General Noriega of Panama annulled elections and took control of the country as head of the military, and was, thereafter, the *de facto* ruler of the country. However, the US government refused to recognize this new government and its supposed new head, recognizing instead Guillermo Endara, as the legitimate winner of the election, but continuing to recognize the previous head, Eric Delvalle.[40]

---

[36] This is true in particular with the USA and the UK, and is assumed applicable to the Commonwealth countries.

[37] *Lafontant v. Aristide* (1994) 844 F. Supp. 128.

[38] *Ibid*, p. 132, 134.

[39] *Ibid*, p. 140.

[40] The US executive tended to withhold recognition in demonstration of its political disapproval of new non-democratically elected governments. Although it was decided at the beginning of the 20th century that non-recognition did not have any effect on the foreign governments' right to claim sovereign immunity in US courts, the general trend thereafter established that non-recognition leads to denial of immunity. *US v. Noriega, 746 F. Supp. 1506. Wulfsohn v. Russian Socialist Federated Soviet Republic* (1923) 234 N.Y. 327. The case also looked at the issue of a state's continuing immunity irrespective of a change in its government by non-democratic means. In 1977 the US position with regards to recognition centred on the need to de-emphasize and avoid the use of recognition in cases of changes of governments, but to ascertain whether it wished to have diplomatic relations with the new governments. Shearer, *International Law, op cit*, p. 127.

116   *Immunity and International Criminal Law*

The US government's refusal to recognize Noreiga, a political act, had legal consequences in the form of the denial of head of state immunity *ratione personae* in US municipal court proceedings. Noriega was arrested and forcibly transferred to US territory by US military personnel in Panama. He was tried and convicted for, *inter alia*, drugs trafficking in the US. The US district court in *US v. Noriega* held that:

> In order to assert head of state immunity, a government official must be recognized as a head of state. Noriega has never been recognized as Panama's Head of State either under the Panamanian Constitution or by the United States.[41]

According to the court, as the US continued to recognize Delvalle as the legitimate head of state, Noriega was never accorded the status of head of state by the US executive so as to render him immune from US jurisdiction.[42] The court was bound by the executive's decision and applied previous case law that dictated that 'recognition of foreign governments and their leaders is a discretionary foreign policy decision committed to the Executive Branch and thus conclusive upon the courts'.[43]

Noriega's argument that as *de facto* ruler he had a right to immunity was denied in this instance, although the court accepted his status as *de facto* ruler of Panama in a previous sitting.[44] In this instance the court was of the opinion that running a country does not entitle an individual to immunity from US courts. This is especially true where a 'claim to a "right" of immunity [is] against the express wishes of the Government' and 'is wholly without merit'.[45] US courts, it appears, do not have the capacity to review executive decisions as to a foreign government's status as recognized or unrecognized.[46]

---

[41] *US v. Noriega*, p. 1519.

[42] *Ibid.*

[43] *Ibid*, p. 1519. Reference made to *Republic of Panama v. Air Panama* (1988) 745 F. Supp. 669.

[44] Earlier case: *US v. Noriega* (1988) 683 F. Supp. 1373, p. 1374.

[45] *US v. Noriega.*

[46] Presidential decisions to recognize a government are binding on the courts, and the courts must give them legal effect: *Lafontant v. Aristide*, p. 133. The UK position is different. In the Court of Appeal in *Republic of Somalia v. Woodhouse* [1993] QB 54, Hobhouse formulated a test to determine if a particular entity is a government. This position is tied to the UK government's policy of not according recognition but assessing effective control. Policy Statement of UK's Foreign Secretary Lord Carrington 1980. HL Deb, Vol. 408, cols 1121-22; HC DE, Vol. 983, cols. 277-9.

Diplomats and Immunity Ratione Personae

In ancient times envoys were considered sacrosanct rather than being immune from the territorial jurisdiction of a nation state.[47] With the introduction of the concept of territorial jurisdiction, notions of personal immunity from that jurisdiction were assimilated into the concept of inviolability.

Diplomats are obliged to obey the laws of their receiving states, but where they break the law they 'cannot be arrested or detained by the executive authorities of the receiving' state.[48]

> Diplomatic agents are not, in virtue of their privileges as such, immune from legal liability for any wrongful acts. The accurate statement is that they are not liable to be sued in the English Courts unless they submit to the jurisdiction. Diplomatic privilege does not import immunity from legal liability, but only exemption from local jurisdiction.[49]

Being inviolable they are not liable to any form of arrest and detention in their receiving states and thus cannot come before the penal system.[50]

Inviolability is considered as the most fundamental rule of diplomatic law.[51] It is the cornerstone of diplomatic privileges and immunities.[52] According to the ICJ there is:

> no more fundamental prerequisite for the conduct of relations between States than the inviolability of diplomatic envoys and embassies, so that throughout history nations of all creeds and cultures have observed reciprocal obligations for that purpose.[53]

Inviolability of diplomatic agents is unqualified only within the territory of the receiving state, whose legal officers cannot enter diplomatic premises to arrest or search for evidence or documents irrespective of the circumstances. Express permission from the head of the mission is required.[54] Thus diplomatic persons and premises are inviolable.

---

[47] Denza, *Diplomatic Law. A Commentary on the Vienna Convention on Diplomatic Relations*, *op cit*. Immunity being the exemption from local jurisdiction has been well established since the Middle Ages.

[48] Satow, *A Guide to Diplomatic Practice* (1922), *op cit*, p. 120.

[49] *Dickinson v. Del Solar* (1930) 1 KB 376, Lord Hewart C.J.

[50] Vienna Diplomatic Convention, Article 29. This article maintains the ancient position of an envoy being sacrosanct.

[51] Shaw, *International Law*, *op cit*, p. 533.

[52] Barker, *The Abuse of Diplomatic Privileges and Immunities*, *op cit*, p. 71.

[53] *US v. Iran (Provisional Measures)* (1979) ICJ Rep. 7, 19, para. 8.

[54] Vienna Diplomatic Convention, Articles 22 and 30: Mission premises and the diplomat's private residence and property are inviolable.

118 *Immunity and International Criminal Law*

The ILC unanimously adopted the inviolability provision, even though attempts to erode the absolute nature of the inviolability of premises were made during the drafting of the Vienna Diplomatic Convention. There was mention during the debate that, under certain emergency situations, entry by a receiving state should be obligatory.[55] This suggestion was not accepted, as the Vienna Diplomatic Convention gives mission and residential premises absolute inviolability, even in emergency situations.

The US Restatement acknowledges that a 'diplomatic agent's immunity from arrest or detention is absolute unless it is waived by the sending state'.[56] Their inviolability is a privilege that is of 'the Sovereign by whom the diplomatic agent is accredited, and it may be waived with the sanction of the Sovereign or of the official superior of the agent'.[57] A waiver from the sending state must authorize action against a diplomat in a receiving state. Waiver must always be express.[58]

Without a waiver the receiving state is powerless to arrest a diplomat and to enter premises, as was seen in the UK in 1984. After the shooting of a policewoman by persons within the premises of the Libyan People's Bureau in 1984, the British authorities did not enter the premises nor did they arrest the suspects. Reciprocity is an important factor behind diplomatic inviolability, and in that respect, diplomatic inviolability is absolute. The event in 1984 in the UK exposed the absolute nature of the inviolability of diplomats and their premises. In response to this criminal incident the British authorities terminated diplomatic relations with Libya, with the request that the Bureau be evacuated by a given time, whereupon the premises was sealed. The British authorities entered only in the presence of a representative of the Saudi Arabian Embassy. Nobody was ever arrested for the murder.[59]

In its report following the incident the Foreign Affairs Committee concluded that there was no support within the European Community or elsewhere for the idea of bilateral or limited mutual agreements to waive immunity either generally or in specific cases.[60] The Committee also noted that were they to apply restrictions on immunity to diplomats within the UK they would expect reciprocal behaviour from other countries, which may use such restriction for political or simply retaliatory purposes.[61] Consequently the only option available to a receiving state

---

[55] Mexican delegate, UN Doc A/Conf.20/C.1/L.129, p. 20.

[56] US Third Restatement of Foreign Relations, *op cit.*

[57] *Dickinson v. Del Solar*, Lord Hewart C.J, p. 376.

[58] Vienna Diplomatic Convention, Article 32(1)(2).

[59] In 2004 Libya and the UK entered into talks that could pave the way to someone being held accountable for the incident.

[60] Diplomatic Immunities and Privileges Government Report on Review of the Vienna Convention on Diplomatic Relations and Reply to "Abuses of Diplomatic Immunities and Privileges". The First Report from the Foreign Affairs Committee in the Session 1984-1985, Cmnd. 9497. p. 24 para. 66. (Hereinafter the UK Government Diplomatic Report).

[61] *Ibid*, p.24, para. 66.

High-Ranking State Officials and Crime

in such situation is the declaration of the individuals in question as *persona non grata*.[62]

Following the incident in 1984 there was a general public outcry in the UK. Notions of inviolability and reciprocal behaviour did not impress the British public. They were infuriated that nobody could be arrested for the murder of the policewoman. Although faced with public outrage, the UK government were prevented from taking action because of the strength of the personal immunity granted to accredited diplomats. It is difficult for lay people to imagine that there are more important issues at stake. A diplomat needs to know that he or she will not face harassment from the authorities of the receiving state through criminal procedures taken for political motives.[63] That he or she will be able to carry out their delicate diplomatic functions freely is vital to inter-state relations.

There are other examples where diplomatic inviolability was maintained even though the crime in question was of a very serious nature. A particularly interesting one is that of *Regina v. Palacios*. In 1983 a Nicaraguan diplomatic agent formerly accredited to Canada was granted immunity after being arrested for drugs and weapon charges.[64] The diplomat's duties ended on 12 July and he was arrested on 23 July and his residence searched on 28 July. It was held that he was entitled to immunity even after his duties ended as he was to be given reasonable time to leave the country permanently. Another example of interest occurred in 1988, when a commercial attaché at the Cuban Embassy was expelled from the UK without being charged, after having fired a gun into a street in London.[65]

It would, therefore, be correct to say, and it can be regarded as a settled principle of law, that a serving diplomatic agent cannot be prosecuted under any circumstance in the receiving state for any criminal offence that he may commit unless immunity is waived.[66]

Are There Limitations on the Absolute Nature of Diplomatic Criminal Inviolability?

Nonetheless, there have been attempts in the past to restrict or place limits on the absolute nature of inviolability historically. Some writers promoted the idea of restrictions on inviolability where an envoy was engaged in acts amounting to conspiracy to overthrow a receiving sovereign.[67] In such situations, writers such as Grotius argued that an arrest would not be an infringement of the envoys right to

---

[62] Vienna Diplomatic Convention, Article 9.

[63] See: Higgins, *Problems and Processes. International Law and How We Use It, op cit*, p. 89.

[64] *Regina v. Palacios* (1984) 45 O.R. (2d) 269, 274-80.

[65] The Times, 14 September 1988.

[66] Sen, *A Diplomat's Handbook of International Law and Practice* (1979), p. 108.

[67] Grotius, *The Rights of War and Peace* (1901); Hurst, *International Law: Collected Papers* (1950*)*; Satow, *A Guide to Diplomatic Practice, op cit*.

inviolability. According to Grotius the arrest and detention of an envoy for reasons of self-defence was possible.[68]

> But if an ambassador excites and heads any violent insurrection, he may be killed, not by way of punishment, but upon the natural principle of self-defence.[69]

In 1895 the International Law Institute passed a resolution limiting inviolability of a diplomatic agent in three instances. Article 6 of this resolution states:

> Inviolability may not be invoked:
>
> 1. In case of lawful defence on the part of individuals against acts committed by persons who enjoy the privilege;
> 2. In case of risks run by the said persons, voluntarily or unnecessarily;
> 3. In case of reprehensible acts committed by them, compelling the State to which the minister is accredited to take defensive or precautionary measures.[70]

Self-defence States have the right to defend themselves if attacked. This right is limited to instances where it is shown that there is a 'necessity of self-defence, instant, overwhelming, leaving no choice of means and no moment of deliberation'.[71] Although these conditions were articulated many years after Grotius, they are considered to represent classical prerequisites for justifiable self-defence as expounded by him.[72] However it is acknowledged that during the 16th and 17th centuries, when the abuse of diplomatic immunity was considered a serious problem, no receiving sovereign relied on self-defence as a reason to take measures stronger than expulsion.[73]

In keeping with writers in the past, Sandström of the ILC included in the draft of Article 29 of the Vienna Diplomatic Convention the following:

> Being inviolable, the diplomatic agent is exempted from certain measures that would amount to direct coercion. This principle does not exclude either self-defence or, in exceptional circumstances, measures to prevent the diplomatic agent from committing crimes or offences.[74]

This provision was not, however, included in the final draft.

---

[68] Grotius, *The Rights of War and Peace*, Chapter XVII, IV p. 209.

[69] *Ibid.*

[70] Resolution of the International Law Institute, Cambridge (1895).

[71] *The Caroline Case* (1837) 29 BPFSP 1137.

[72] Malanczuk, *Akehurst's Modern Introduction to International Law, op cit*, p. 314.

[73] Denza, *Diplomatic Law. A Commentary on the Vienna Convention on Diplomatic Relations, op cit*, p. 211.

[74] (1957) *1 YBILC p.209-210*; (1958) *2 YBILC p. 97.*

High-Ranking State Officials and Crime

-It has been suggested that exceptions to the inviolability of the diplomat can occur when a diplomat commits a violent act that disturbs the internal order of the state, or when an agent causes damage to property or injures individuals.[75] In these situations the diplomat can be temporary detained.

Temporary Detention It is noted that states have only on rare occasion taken forcible action against diplomats. Some states have proposed that they can detain diplomats, albeit temporarily to prevent them from committing offences. Canada has stated that:

> If the police should arrest a diplomat for the purpose of disarming him, the Department [of External Affairs] would have a defensible position under international law. It is recognized that even though the person of a diplomat is inviolable such inviolability is not as absolute as to prevent the receiving State taking measures of self-protection or measures to protect the diplomat against himself.[76]

Indeed, other states have taken the same view. Swedish police disarmed and confiscated a pistol from a Yugoslavian ambassador in 1988.[77] A Brazilian ambassador was tied down in order to prevent him damaging hotel property in Moscow in 1947. Brazil understandably argued that that action was 'unjustified'.[78] It appears, therefore, that where a diplomatic agent commits acts of violence liable to disturb the internal order of the receiving state, such state is entitled to temporarily restrain him in order to prevent him from committing or recommitting the acts in question.[79]

In *US v. Iran* (*The Hostages Case*),[80] the ICJ held that although inviolability must be respected even during armed conflict or in the case of a breach of diplomatic relations, a diplomat caught 'in the act of committing an assault or other offence may' be 'briefly arrested by the police of the receiving State in order to prevent the commission of the particular crime'.[81]

But the international community has made it clear that forcible long-term detention of diplomats is a direct violation of international law. The ICJ condemned the Iranian government's tacit approval of the imprisonment of American diplomats by militant students in 1980. The ICJ interpreted the government's inaction as a 'clear and serious violation' of a diplomat's inviolability under Article 29 of the Vienna Diplomatic Convention.[82] Thus it can be said with certainty that this immunity is absolute, even in the face of international crimes.

---

[75] Wilson, *Diplomatic Privileges and Immunities* (1967), p. 83.

[76] (1983) *Canadian YIL 309, 310*.

[77] The Times, 17 May 1988.

[78] Do Nascimento e Silva, *Diplomacy in International Law, op cit*, p. 93.

[79] *Ibid*, p. 93-4.

[80] *US v. Iran* (*Hostages Case*) (1980) ICJ Reps. 3.

[81] *Ibid*, p. 41, para. 86.

[82] *Ibid*, paras. 67, 74, 76-8.

It must be noted, therefore, that the US court in *Tachiona (No. 2)* erred in their decision that an inviolable individual can be served notice if he will not have to face court charges.[83] The *Arrest Warrant Case* demonstrates that a serving officer cannot be pursued by legal processes of domestic courts, irrespective of the subject matter. That Mugabe the person was not to answer the charges against Zanu PF does not justify service.

Diplomatic Immunity Ratione Personae and Third States

The Vienna Diplomatic Convention does not seek to cover third states; its primary function is to regulate bilateral diplomatic relations. Under this Convention third states have a duty to grant a diplomat passage through their territory en route to his duty station or back to his country, and immunities as may be required to ensure his transit or return.[84] The Vienna Diplomatic Convention does not give a diplomat the right of transit. Diplomats travelling or stopping in third states en route to their duty stations or back home normally obtain diplomatic visas from that third state before entering its territory. Diplomats holding such visas are usually immune from the jurisdiction of the third state for as long as the visa is valid.

In 1998 diplomatic immunity and third states was the issue in a German case. In *S. v. Berlin Court of Appeal and District Court of Appeal of Berlin-Tiergarten* the German District Court issued a warrant for the arrest of the former ambassador of Syria accredited to the German Democratic Republic (GDR, East Germany).[85] The charges included assisting in the commission of murder and helping in the terrorist bombing of property in West Berlin in 1983. The ambassador received orders from his government to do everything possible to assist a terrorist organization called 'Carlos'. He refused to allow the use of a diplomatic car to ferry a bag containing explosives over the border into West Berlin, but failed, however, to prevent the person concerned from removing the bag from the embassy. He was charged with assisting in the commission of the bombing later in West Germany by not preventing the bag from being taken out of the embassy premises. The Constitutional Court, which heard the case on appeal, held that diplomatic immunity is only effective in the receiving state, in this case the GDR.[86] The court also held that the Vienna Diplomatic Convention provides immunity for diplomats in third states only if they are passing through the third state's territory while proceeding to the take up of or return from their posts, returning home, or where their presence in a third state is due to *force majeure*.[87]

---

[83] *Tachiona Case (No. 2), op cit.*

[84] Vienna Diplomatic Convention, Article 40(1)(2) & (3). This duty covers members of the diplomat's family, correspondence and other diplomatic communications.

[85] *S. v. Berlin Court of Appeal and District Court of Appeal of Berlin-Tiergarten* 24 Europäische Grundrechte-Zeitschrift 436. See: Fassenbender (1998) *92 AJIL 74.*

[86] *Ibid.*

[87] Vienna Diplomatic Convention, Article 40 (1). Fassenbender, *op cit*, p. 92.

High-Ranking State Officials and Crime 123

The court further stated that the law on diplomatic immunity is a 'self-contained regime' whose rules are not directed at the relationship between a diplomat and a third state, and that as receiving states are able to fall back on conventional protections against abuse, such as declaration of *persona non grata* and termination of diplomatic relations, they have an incentive to grant immunity. Incentives a third state may not have.[88] As the ambassador was accredited to the GDR when the act in question occurred, his immunity did not cover him in West Germany. As the ambassador was not accredited to West Germany it had the right to apprehend him and try him for his part in the offence.

Diplomats in transit, however, are ordinarily accorded immunity *ratione personae* in third states. For example in *Bergman v. De Sieyes*, a French minister accredited to Bolivia was served with process in New York whilst en route to Bolivia. The court of appeal held that a diplomat *in transitu* is entitled to the same immunity *ratione personae* as a diplomat *in situ*.[89] In another example, in 1972, an Algerian diplomat en route to Brazil from Damascus was granted immunity *ratione personae* even though he was found to be carrying grenades and different types of weapons and explosives in his baggage at a Netherlands airport. Although his baggage was confiscated, he was allowed to continue his journey as the Netherlands applied the relevant provisions of the Vienna Diplomatic Convention.[90]

A diplomat entering the third state without a diplomatic visa may not be granted immunity *ratione personae*, nor will it be accorded to a diplomat on holiday, for example, as the Vienna Diplomatic Convention does not cover such situations.

Immunity for Acts: Immunity *Ratione Materiae*

When a person of status ceases to hold office, his immunity *ratione personae* ends, and it is at this point in time that his immunity *ratione materiae* comes to the fore.[91] Although this immunity covers acts, it also covers the person, as individuals with immunity *ratione materiae* cannot be held personally accountable for such acts. Protection is, therefore, two pronged: Personal immunity for the person committing the act, and *non-justiciability* for the act itself under the act of state doctrine.

---

[88] Fassenbender, *ibid*, p. 76.

[89] *Bergman v. De Sieyes* 170 F.2d (2nd Cir 11/04/1948). www.versuslaw.com.

[90] Denza, *Diplomatic Law A Commentary on the Vienna Convention on Diplomatic Relations, op cit*, p. 369.

[91] Dinstein, 'Diplomatic Immunity from Jurisdiction *Ratione Materiae*', *op cit*, p. 76, 78

The Act of State Doctrine

Act of state is a doctrine that prevents the domestic courts from adjudicating upon the transactions of foreign sovereign states.[92] It comes into effect where it is felt that an examination of the issues in a case will involve the court looking at the acts of another state and perhaps passing judgment as to its adherence to international law. Domestic courts cannot sit in judgment on issues pertaining to another state's sovereign power.

The doctrine was first outlined in the USA in the case of *Underhill v. Hernadez* in 1897:

> Every sovereign State is bound to respect the independence of every other sovereign State, and the courts of one country will not sit in judgment on the acts of the government of another within its territory. Redress of grievances by reason of such acts must be obtained through the means open to be availed of by sovereign powers themselves. [93]

Thereafter, the doctrine was affirmed in *Banco Nacional de Cuba v. Sabbatino*.[94] The case arose from a dispute between a Cuban-owned subsidiary of a Cuban company whose capital stock was mostly owned by US citizens and the National Bank of Cuba, a government organ. The dispute was centred on who was entitled to the proceeds of sale of a shipload of sugar. The Cuban subsidiary was the original owner. The expropriation of industries in Cuba created confusion and controversy between that subsidiary's receivers and the bank. The US Supreme Court held that as a rule of judicial restraint the court in the USA could not determine the validity of a foreign sovereign state's act of expropriation within its territory even if such act was contrary to international law.

When faced with acts of state the judiciary should show 'restraint or abstention' in such cases.[95] It is now accepted that 'municipal courts have not and cannot have the competence to adjudicate upon or enforce rights arising out of transactions entered into by independent sovereign states between themselves on the plane of international law'.[96]

Immunity *ratione materiae* is therefore only concerned with preventing domestic courts from looking at issues pertaining to foreign state action. State officials, including diplomats acting in their official capacity, are considered to be committing acts of state that are protected by the act of state doctrine. In recognition of the need to protect foreign envoys for their official acts the Harvard Diplomatic Research Draft included the following provision:

---

[92] *Buttes Gas and Oil Co. v. Hammer* [1982] 3 AC 888.

[93] *Underhill v. Hernadez* (1897) 168 U.S. 250, 252.

[94] *Banco Nacional de Cuba v. Sabbatino* (1964) 376 U.S. 398, 427-8.

[95] *Buttes Gas and Oil Co*, Lord Wilberforce, p. 931.

[96] *Maclaine Watson v. Department of Trade and Industry* [1988] 3 WLR 1033, 1169, Lord Oliver.

A receiving state shall not impose liability on a person for an act done by him in performance of his functions as a member of a mission. [97]

The act of state doctrine has been used to question the existence of immunity *ratione materiae*. Kelsen considers it as part of the general doctrine of acts of state.[98] He limits the scope of this immunity, vis-à-vis diplomats, to private acts.[99] Kunz concurs:

> It must be emphasised that the exemption from local jurisdiction of diplomatic agents pertains exclusively to the private acts of the diplomatic agents. Their exemption from local jurisdiction for their official acts has nothing to do with diplomatic privileges and immunities; their official acts are "acts of State" and are legally imputed not to them but to the sending State.[100]

Accordingly Kunz and Kelsen would do away with the notion of immunity *ratione materiae*, leaving just *ratione personae* and the acts of state doctrine. This conclusion is far from ideal. Although immunity *ratione materiae* covers acts, it also covers the individual as it prevents his arrest and detention.

In support of immunity *ratione materiae*, Dinstein argues that international law does not acknowledge all acts in any circumstance as acts of state:

> International theory and practice are in unison in their rejection of the doctrine [of act of state] in its all embracing from, covering every act of State in any circumstance.[101]

Consequently an independent and separate immunity is essential.[102]

Although his conclusion is accurate, Dinstein appears to focus this separate immunity solely on diplomats. He compares the immunities accorded a diplomat in his receiving state and a state official visiting the same state as a tourist, arguing that the diplomat is accorded immunity with the consent of the receiving state.[103] In accrediting the diplomatic agent, the receiving state 'assents by implication to his functioning in its territory as a diplomatic agent and performing official acts there'.[104] However, a state official, other than a head of state, in a foreign state for tourist purposes is not entitled to any form of immunity, as he is accorded immunity by a host state only if he is in its territory for official purposes. Thus the

---

[97] Harvard Diplomatic Research Draft, Article 18, *op cit.*

[98] Kelsen, *Principles of International Law* (1966), p. 230.

[99] *Ibid*, p. 229-31.

[100] Kunz, 'Privileges and Immunities of International Organizations' (1947) *41 AJIL 828, 838*

[101] Dinstein, 'Diplomatic Immunity from Jurisdiction *Ratione Materiae*', *op cit*, p. 87.

[102] *Ibid*, p. 87-8.

[103] *Ibid*.

[104] *Ibid*, p. 88-9. Dinstein acknowledges that employees of governments in exile have the host state's consent.

host state consents to him performing official acts in its territory. Immunity *ratione materiae* is applicable to all state officials on state visits abroad and to diplomats in their receiving state.

Because international law does not recognize all acts in any situation as acts of state, an independent and separate immunity is available in the form of immunity *ratione personae*. For those acts not deemed acts of state the individual is inviolable for as long as he holds office. Once he ceases to hold office, he can be held accountable for such acts, as they are private acts, irrespective of his status at the time he committed them. However, where the acts are acts of state, he cannot be held accountable for them even after he ceases to hold office, and in a sense, he is inviolable vis-à-vis those acts for life.

Kunz and Kelsen's position does not appear to acknowledge the fact that this immunity also attaches to the person as it makes him inviolable. By making immunity *ratione materiae* a part of the act of state doctrine the inviolability of an individual for acts of state is neglected. It is suggested that the act of state doctrine in relation to individual responsibility is part of immunity *ratione materiae* and not the other way around. This supposition is based on the need to protect an individual from arrest and detention where the act in question is of a criminal nature. In assuming that immunity *ratione materiae* is a part of the act of state doctrine one concentrates on state accountability, in particular under civil jurisdiction. Under criminal jurisdiction it is the individual who is key, rather than an abstract entity. The act of state doctrine on its own does not have the inviolability factor relevant to immunity *ratione materiae*.

Immunity Ratione Materiae for Heads of State and Government: Criminal Acts as Acts of State

Only state organs competent to represent the state in relation to other states can perform acts of state.[105] The government and its head are considered to be competent to engage other states.

According to Hegel, states are sovereign because particular acts and powers of a state do not exist in isolation.[106] Nor do such acts or powers subsist because of an individual state agent's will; rather, these activities and powers have their roots in a unified single self that is a state.[107] States as political entities must have unity between power and action, and individuals having the power to carry out activities have such office not because of their personality, but based on an external and objective manner. Thus the functions of a state cannot be private property.[108] It is for these reasons that sovereign immunity is best regarded as being composed of state and head of state immunity. Separating head of state immunity from that of state immunity makes it possible to look at certain acts which an individual

---

[105] Kelsen, *General Theory of Law and State* (1945), p. 359.

[106] Hegel, *The Philosophy of Right, op cit*, p. 179-180, para. 278.

[107] *Ibid.*

[108] *Ibid*, p. 179, paras. 276, 277,

commits as being his own. If head of state immunity is state immunity, all acts committed as a head of state must be attributed to his state. However, when dealing with issues of penal law it is the individual who is important; hence divisibility of head of state immunity from that of state immunity is absolutely essential.

Although it is usual to refer to an illegal act of government officials as being exercised 'in his official function', Kelsen rejects this phraseology. In his opinion an individual performing an illegal act 'cannot be considered to be an organ of the State'.[109] According to him, it is 'more correct to speak of illegal acts performed by an individual in connection with his official function as a State organ'.[110] He does not, however, consider this analysis relevant to international law, as any

> act performed by a member of the Government directly or through a lower organ commanded or authorized by it, whether in conformity with the national legal order or not, but performed in connection with the official function of the acting individual as a State organ, has to be considered, from the viewpoint of international law, as an act of state.[111]

This line of reasoning must be qualified. State officials, including heads of state or government, can commit crimes whilst in office. However, it is arguable that the commission of certain acts should exclude an individual from being classified as a state organ for international law purposes. If an individual commits an international crime he cannot be seen to be acting as a state organ under either domestic or international law. The fact that individuals are criminally responsible under international criminal law for their actions irrespective of status, demonstrates that under international law an individual performing an illegal act cannot be considered to be an organ of the state. In committing international crimes, individuals of status do not do so in their official function but in connection with their official function as state organs. Even though the crimes are committed in connection with their official function, they are strictly private acts.

As a result, in perpetrating international crimes the individual does not act as a state organ. He will be unable to subsequently claim immunity for those acts in a foreign domestic court. Lord Bingham C.J. in the Divisional Court in the *Pinochet Case* stated that:

> a former head of state is clearly entitled to immunity in relation to criminal acts performed in the course of exercising public functions. One cannot therefore hold that any deviation from good democratic practice is outside the pale of immunity. If the former sovereign is immune from process in respect of some crimes, where does one draw the line? [112]

---

[109] Kelsen, *General Theory of Law and State, op cit*, p. 359.

[110] *Ibid.*

[111] *Ibid*, p. 360. Kelsen's analysis did not look at individual responsibility of state officials for violations of international law, hence his analysis is somewhat limited in scope.

[112] Quoted by Lord Goff, *Pinochet (No. 3)*, p. 126. For the High Court's Decision: [1998] All ER (D) 629.

Immunity and International Criminal Law

It is suggested that one draws the line in respect of international crimes. By making a distinction between state and head of state immunity it is then possible to say that international crimes cannot be attributed to the state, as the individual is personally accountable. The idea that an act constituting an international crime can be an act of state was rejected in the Nuremberg Tribunals[113] and in the *Eichmann Case*.[114]

Judge Vandermeersch in *Pinochet (Belgium)* was of the opinion that immunity for a head of state appears not to apply to crimes against humanity, although he failed to clarify which immunity.[115] Lord Browne-Wilkinson in *Pinochet (No. 3)* questions, 'how can it be for international law purposes an official act to do something which international law itself prohibits and criminalizes?'[116] The French Supreme Court in 2001 in the *Qaddafi Case* held that the Libyan head of state is immune from suit for charges that included murder and destruction of an aircraft.[117] These are serious acts that are international treaty crimes. The Cour de Cassation tacitly acknowledged that there are certain crimes for which a sitting head of state will not be accorded immunity, in their accurate conclusion that the crime of terrorism is not one for which immunity can be excluded for a sitting head of state.[118]

Thus it has been acknowledged that a head of state may be personally liable for acts of such seriousness that they constitute not merely international wrongs but international crimes that offend against the international community's public order.[119] Watts confirmed that:

> It can no longer be doubted that as a matter of general international customary law a Head of State will be personally liable to be called to account if there is sufficient evidence that he authorised or perpetrated such serious international crimes.[120]

In order to act as state organs in their official function, heads of state and government must act in line with their state's position in a given subject matter, or act within that state's given boundaries for action. Then and only then can their acts be deemed official. For example, where international customary law prohibits

---

[113] *Goering at al* (1946) 13 An. Dig. 203, 221.

[114] *Op cit*, p. 44-8, para. 28.

[115] Judge Vandermeersch, Belgian investigating judge in *Pinochet Belgium* 1998, Tribunal de Premierè Instance de Bruxelle. Decision of Investigating Magistrate (18 November 1998). www.redress.org/annex.html.

[116] *Pinochet (No.3)*, Lord Browne-Wilkinson, p. 114.

[117] Zappalà 'Do Heads of State in Office Enjoy Immunity from the Jurisdiction for International Crimes? The Ghaddafi Case before the French Cour de Cassation' (2001) *12 EJIL 595*.

[118] *Ibid*. Terrorism as explained in Chapter 2 is a broad-based category of various crimes rather than a distinct international crime.

[119] Watts, 'The Legal Position in International Law of Heads of State, Heads of Government and Foreign Ministers', *op cit*, p. 81.

[120] *Ibid*, p. 84.

the doing of a certain act, a head of state committing such acts cannot then claim that such acts are acts of his state. In that situation he has not acted as a state organ. The consensus nature required for the formation of international customary norms implies that his state acquiesced to the creation of the rule in question.

Where a state, as a result of ratification of an international treaty, prohibits the doing of certain acts, it is arguable that a head of state cannot claim immunity *ratione materiae* for such acts thereafter. Lord Hope in *Pinochet (No. 3)* held that immunity *ratione materiae* for the former head of state was lost on the date that Chile's ratification of the Torture Convention took effect.[121] As he derives his immunity from his status, not his person, by acting contrary to his state's position he can only be acting in his private capacity. As the functions of a state cannot be private property, an official must act within certain boundaries; exceeding those boundaries turns the act into a private one.[122] Denza notes that if the conduct in question is imputable or attributable to the state, immunity *ratione materiae* should subsist even if the state did not expressly order or sanction the act.[123] When dealing with international criminal law, states as abstract entities cannot order or sanction conduct punishable under criminal jurisdiction, nor indeed can a state carry out such acts itself. Hence the notion of imputability under international criminal law is impossible and individual responsibility feasible. Further, in a situation where customary norms prohibit certain acts or there exists a treaty that the state in question has ratified, imputabiliy is impossible.

There are crimes, therefore, that are not acts of state even where committed by a state official. For that reason, the question arises: is the nature or purpose of the act the decisive factor in the classification of acts as acts of state?

The Nature or Purpose of Acts Debate It is now generally accepted that a head of state or government will not have immunity *ratione materiae* for certain international crimes. The act being an international crime is the decisive factor. There are those who acknowledge that the nature of the act in question is indicative of its status as an act of state.[124]

Immunity *ratione materiae* can only attach to the office of the head of state or government as the highest offices in the land. Such offices must abide by the state's existing international law obligations. The head of state, to put it in metaphoric terms, wears the cloak of his office which provides him with immunity; upon removing that cloak he is only immune for those acts that were permissible by the state for one wearing such a cloak. If an act not befitting the office brings about a result that such office is established to effect, the fact that it brought about such a result is not enough to justify the conduct itself as being governmental.

---

[121] *Pinochet (No. 3)*, p. 152, Lord Hope.

[122] Hegel, *The Philosophy of Right*, *op cit*, p. 179, paras. 276, 277.

[123] Denza bases the imputability test on the Vienna Diplomatic Convention's Article 39(4) with reference to Pinochet's immunity *ratione materiae* as a head of state. Denza, '*Ex Parte Pinochet*: Lacuna or Leap? (1999) *48 ICLQ 941*.

[124] Barker, 'The Future of Head of State Immunity after *ex Parte Pinochet*' (1999) *48 ICLQ 937, 941*.

130   *Immunity and International Criminal Law*

Panama ratified the Single Convention on Narcotics Drugs 1961 on 4 December 1963.[125] Consequently it is arguable that for all heads of that state thereafter, immunity *ratione materiae* for acts involving drugs trafficking cannot be claimed. If General Noriega, disregarding his country's ratification of the Drugs Convention, involved himself in drugs trafficking to obtain funds for public works, for example building hospitals and roads, would his actions then be considered official, thereby attracting immunity *ratione materiae*?[126] Barker is of the opinion that if one asserts that the nature of an act in question is more decisive than the purpose of that act, one misunderstands the basis of immunity *ratione materiae*, primarily because immunity *ratione materiae* 'although relating to official acts is nevertheless individual immunity attaching to the head of state'.[127]

It was proposed above that immunity *ratione materiae's* protection is two pronged: the non-justiciability of the act and freedom from accountability for the act for the individual. That this immunity is also a personal one is not disputed, but how it affects the nature or purpose debate is unclear. Irrespective of whether the immunity attaches to the person or not, the nature of the act is the decisive factor in making an act an act of state.

Torture has been described as an official act, as it is more likely to be committed by a state official. The Torture Convention describes torture as being 'inflicted by or at the instigation of or with the consent or acquiescence of a public official or other person in an official capacity'.[128] The House of Lords in *Pinochet (No. 3)* were of the opinion that in torturing citizens a head of state can be acting in his official capacity.[129] It has been argued that to deny torture's official character is 'to fly in the face of reality'.[130] Torture's official treaty definition is descriptive; the act is carried out by someone in office 'in connection with his official functions' not 'in his official function'.[131] Thus although the individual is an office holder, he does not in that particular instance act as a state organ. The 'official capacity' requirement of the Torture Convention does not denote the act as an act of state. It refers to the person committing the act. Irrespective of his purpose ,by its very nature the act itself will still be private, as it cannot be attributed to the state.

Barker points out that the denial of official status for torture, and indeed other offences, may remove any liability that a state would have under

---

[125] Single Convention on Narcotics Drugs 1961 (520 UNTS 204). (Hereinafter the Drugs Convention).

[126] *US v. Noriega* 746 F. Supp. 1506, 1519. US District Court Judge held that: 'Criminal activities such as narcotics trafficking…can hardly be considered official acts or governmental duties which promote a sovereign state's interest, especially where….the activity was allegedly undertaken for the sole personal benefit of the foreign leader.'

[127] Barker, 'The Future of Head of State Immunity after *ex Parte Pinochet*', *op cit.*

[128] Torture Convention, Article 1, *op cit.*

[129] *Pinochet (No. 3)*, Lords: Millett, p.179, Saville, p. 169-70, Hope, p. 147, Goff, p. 125-6.

[130] Barker, *International Law and International Relations*, *op cit*, p. 153.

[131] Kelsen, *General Theory of Law and State*, *op cit.*

international law for the acts of its individuals.[132] This is true, as victims of torture or their families may not then be in a position to seek compensation from states. If the acts are not official the state will not be responsible. However, as torture is a crime, it is suggested that the best compensation is the arrest and detention of the accused, notwithstanding civil reparations from the accused as well. If individuals are to be personally accountable for international crimes, the nature of the act must be the deciding factor as to acts of state. Only then can their immunity *ratione materiae* be restricted. If state officials knew that compensatory claims could be made against them personally or their estates rather than their states, torture could be eradicated.

Immunity *ratione materiae* for criminal acts can be and is restricted. It may be an individual immunity, in that it covers a person who happens to be head of state in respect of the acts they commit. Nevertheless, as pointed out above, it derives from the state. It is arguable that giving significance to purpose rather than nature when an act is prohibited by customary rules or by a ratified treaty imports immunity to the head rather than the state.

As part of international customary law, all states are obliged to prohibit international customary crimes. If a head of state commits genocide in order to bring stability to his country he is acting for his state's benefit. Having achieved stability by killing thousands of people belonging to a certain ethnic group his country achieves peace. He has attained what is part of his official function: to preserve stability in his state. But his state could not have sanctioned action that is totally contrary to international customary law. The very nature of the act disqualifies him from having acted as a state organ in this particular instance; hence his acts are not acts of state.

Diplomatic Immunity Ratione Materiae

Diplomatic immunity covers the person and his acts. The Harvard Research Draft of 1932 on Diplomatic Immunities and Privileges identified that a diplomatic agent is exempted from the jurisdiction of his receiving state and is not liable for acts deemed official.[133] The Vienna Diplomatic Convention's Article 39(2) outlines that immunity for acts performed in the exercise of the agent's function at the mission survive after the agent's duties comes to an end.[134]

When a criminal act is committed, the fact that the courts of a receiving state cannot adjudicate does not make that act less criminal. Immunity *ratione materiae* does not alter the character of an act. Dinstein correctly acknowledges that it is implausible that 'when a foreign diplomat violates local criminal law in his official capacity, no crime is committed'.[135] Thus a diplomat can commit crimes, but where

---

[132] Barker, *International Law and International Relations, op cit*, p. 153.

[133] Harvard Diplomatic Research Draft, p.98. (Hereinafter: Harvard Diplomatic Research Draft).

[134] Vienna Diplomatic Convention, *op cit.*

[135] Dinstein, 'Diplomatic Immunity from Jurisdiction *Ratione Materiae*', *op cit*, p. 80.

132 *Immunity and International Criminal Law*

such crimes are acts of state, he is inviolable and the acts cannot be the subject matter of court proceedings. Are such crimes capable of being acts of state so as to attract immunity *ratione materiae*?

It has been argued previously that where a diplomat 'performs in the territory' of his receiving state 'an act of State which is not connected with his diplomatic functions', he is not entitled to immunity *ratione materiae*.[136] It is possible that a diplomat may be asked by his state to commit a crime that may jeopardize relations between his state and the receiving state. It is arguable that such acts cannot form part of his diplomatic function and cannot therefore be considered as acts of state.

Panhuys is of the opinion that official acts of a diplomat are those that are 'closely connected with the fulfilment of the diplomatic function'.[137] By infusing the act of state doctrine into immunity *ratione materiae* for purposes of individual accountability, it is possible to state that immunity *ratione materiae* must be confined to acts of state that form part of the individual's functions as a state official, for the purpose of furthering the objectives of his state. If the act of state doctrine is given precedence, criminal acts committed by an individual could be acts of state. Thus where a diplomatic agent is instructed by his government to commit a criminal act in his receiving state the act of state doctrine will render the acts non-justiciable and the individual immune for those acts. However, if immunity *ratione materiae* is the dominant doctrine, certain criminal acts may not form part of his diplomatic function, as the individual is considered to know or ought to know which orders he should follow to prevent future court action.[138]

Diplomats and the Restricted Immunity Ratione Materiae   Under the Vienna Diplomatic Convention acts performed by the diplomat in the exercise of his functions shall continue to subsist.[139] Where abuses of diplomatic immunity occur there may be justification for receiving states to take measures to try and curb such abuses by limiting diplomatic immunity *ratione materiae* in particular cases. When dealing with international crimes there may be greater emphasis for such measures. In its 1985 report, the UK's Foreign Affairs Committee noted that the main abuse lies in the 'reliance on immunity to protect individuals for offences without obvious connection to the efficient performance of the function of a diplomatic mission'.[140]

---

[136] *Ibid*, p. 89.

[137] Panhuys, 'In the Borderlands Between the Act of State Doctrine and Questions of Jurisdictional Immunities' (1964) *13 ICLQ 1193, 1209.*

[138] Defence of superior orders can be used to support this point of view.

[139] Vienna Diplomatic Convention, Article 39(2).

[140] The UK Government Diplomatic Report, *op cit,* p. 23, para. 24. The Committee also notes that the number of alleged offences is small. In para. 60 p. 22 the Committee presented statistics of serious offences committed by persons entitled to diplomatic immunity from 1974 to 1984, as supplied by the Home Office. In para. 61, on the same page the Committee states that the alleged cases of serious offences 'are comparatively small in percentage terms'.

Where a diplomat is accused of having committed a crime, a determination must be made as to that act being an act of state if immunity *ratione materiae* is to be granted. It has been suggested that driving negligently en route to a formal event is not official and is not therefore an act of state.[141] Dinstein argues that immunity *ratione personae* covers the act at that time so that the diplomat can carry on his functions without hindrance devoid of the need to give the act official status so as to attract immunity *ratione materiae*. For Dinstein applying immunity *ratione materiae* to this act is not justified, as only official diplomatic acts can be imputed to the state.[142]

If by implication the receiving state acknowledges that a diplomat will be performing official acts in its territory, it is also by implication that in engaging in his functions all his acts will be those of his state. Granted a diplomat making his way to an official reception is en route to pursuing his official duties; as he drives to the venue, he is not in fact actually engaging in his official functions, which he will do once he enters the building. Thus Dinstein's contention that negligent driving may not form part of a diplomat's functions is plausible.

It is thus possible to place restrictions on diplomatic immunity *ratione materiae* by placing limits on acts of state. No such restrictions are possible for immunity *ratione personae*. In 1984 the USA started a policy whereby diplomats deported for criminal violations would upon returning to the USA thereafter face charges. This is possible if the acts in question are deemed unconnected to their diplomatic function.[143] This position arose after many years of diplomatic traffic and other criminal violations going unpunished as a result of immunity *ratione personae*. Events culminated in the shooting and wounding of a US citizen by the son of the Brazilian ambassador.[144] In another case involving two US citizens injured in a road traffic accident caused by the apparently drunk Papua New Guinean ambassador, Absinito,[145] the State Department was of the opinion that the ambassador was not acting officially as a member of the mission when the accident occurred and rejected the Papua New Guinean argument that later prosecution would be contrary to international law. Although the diplomats could not be arrested because of the absolute nature of immunity *ratione personae*, their immunity *ratione materiae* could be denied in such circumstances. Hence the US authorities can prepare a criminal case against the diplomat in question, then simply wait for his foolhardy return as a normal civilian.

---

[141] Dinstein, 'Diplomatic Immunity from Jurisdiction *Ratione Materiae*', *op cit*, p. 82.

[142] *Ibid*, 82-3.

[143] This position was outlined by the State Department in a Circular Note to the Chiefs of Mission in Washington. See: Leich 'Contemporary Practice of the United States Relating to International Law' (1984) *78 AJIL 658*.

[144] McClanahan, *Diplomatic Immunity, op cit,* p. 14-15. *Skeen v. Federative Republic of Brazil* (1983) 566 F. Supp. 1414.

[145] Absinito affair. See: Barker, *The Abuse of Diplomatic Privileges and Immunities, op cit,* p. 6-8.

134 *Immunity and International Criminal Law*

It has been argued by some that this restrictive theory has existed for many years. Pecoraro relies on the English civil case of *Empson v. Smith*.[146] It was held in that case that loss of immunity, be it by waiver or termination of diplomatic appointment, opened the way to proceedings that had been stayed as a result of inviolability.[147] In another case involving the Chinese Legation in Japan, the defendants were not granted immunity although at the time that they violated local firearms laws, they were with the Chinese Legation. The Japanese Supreme Court denied them diplomatic immunity as their employment had been terminated prior to the prosecution. The Court was of the opinion that although they could not be tried whilst employed by the Chinese Legation, having lost such employment they had also lost their immunity.[148] In other words, having lost their immunity *ratione personae* upon termination of employment and their acts not being covered by immunity *ratione materiae* as they were not acts of state, the individuals could be tried.

This restrictive theory considers unofficial acts as not being immune. Problems arise as to which acts are official and which are not. It is arguable that international crimes can never form part of a mission's functions. In deciding that international crimes do not form part of any mission's function, reliance could be placed on the purpose for which diplomatic missions are established. The functions of the mission, to enable bilateral diplomatic relations, would hardly include the commission of international crimes within or without the receiving state. In fact such actions can destabilize international relations and should not be protected by immunities that are there to afford the diplomatic agent with a safe, secure and trouble-free working environment. Foreign domestic courts faced with a surrender request from the ICC for a former accredited diplomat will not find it a problem arresting and surrendering a diplomat who has returned on unofficial business.

A case against a state official may be admissible to the ICC once the individual's immunity *ratione materiae* is deemed inapplicable for international crimes, thus when his inviolability for those acts under this immunity will not apply. At this stage Article 27 will seem functional; status has not barred the individual from the jurisdiction of the ICC. However, as a sitting head of state or government, or accredited diplomat, his immunity *ratione personae* will remain operational within the domestic jurisdictions of states.

As Article 98 requires consent or waiver, the individual may never be apprehended during his term in office, as his immunity *ratione personae* will be absolute until his term in office ends. The challenge is, therefore, narrowed down to finding ways around immunity *ratione personae* if current state officials are to be surrendered to the ICC.

---

[146] *Empson v. Smith* [1965] 2 All ER 881.

[147] Pecoraro, 'Diplomatic Immunity: Application of the Restrictive Theory of Diplomatic Immunity. The Absinito Affair' (1988) *29 Houston ILJ 53.3*.

[148] *The Empire v. Chang et al* AD 1919-22. See: Deák, 'Organs of State in their Extraterritorial Relations: Immunity and Privileges of Organs of State', *op cit.*

Chapter 6

The Need for Balance: The Pursuit of International Justice Versus Stable Inter-State Relations

Finding measures to legitimately circumvent immunity *ratione personae* so as to evade the use of Article 98 is not an easy task. What makes this endeavour particularly arduous is the fact that states are the key players in international law. Indeed it has been argued that absolute 'power in the world is consolidated in the state, which is independent of all other states' and where 'states disagree in their inability to harmonize their wills, war occurs'.[1] Hegel's words ring true if one imagines the destabilizing effect on international relations if the incumbent leader of a sovereign state was arrested and tried in another state.

Although states can no longer claim to have absolute power, as contemporary international law and the UN have eroded their supremacy, a state that feels threatened in any way may resort to armed force. Knowing that the use of force may not always be legitimate, states have in the past relied on the notion of self-defence to justify armed force in situations that may not readily give rise to a claim of self-defence. The US has over the years in various situations used self-defence as a reason for the use of armed force. For example, it bombed Libya in 1986 as a result of alleged Libyan involvement in an attack on its servicemen in West Berlin.[2] It is suggested that the arrest and trial of a leader in a foreign domestic court may be reason enough for a state, such as the USA, to use armed force.

The fear of armed hostilities must not, however, on the one hand, hinder the pursuit for individual accountability in international criminal law. On the other hand, international criminal law cannot operate outside the existing international framework. It cannot work in a vacuum and must acknowledge the important role that the doctrine of immunity, especially immunity *ratione personae*, plays in maintaining international peace and security.

As much as there is a need to hold officials accountable for international crimes, there is an equally valid need to preserve immunity *ratione personae* accorded to sitting heads of state or government and accredited diplomats. For

---

[1] Hegel, *The Philosophy of Right, op cit*, p. 214

[2] Shaw, *International Law, op cit*, p. 793. It is arguable that war in Iraq in 2003 is evidence that states will act where they feel that their security is at risk, even where that risk may not be thought pressing by other states.

these reasons, a balance must be struck between the needs of international criminal law and the necessity for immunities. If Article 27 of the Rome Statute is to be effective, this balance must be realized.

A foreign domestic court will be unable to detain and surrender an individual who is inviolable. It must be taken into account that the inter-state discourse could cease if sitting heads of state and government as well as diplomats were denied immunity *ratione personae*. The lack of mobility for such persons, due to fear of arrest, would seriously infringe the smooth running of their states. This would be particularly disastrous where the person in question is a democratically elected leader. The detrimental effects this will have on democracy are insurmountable and far beyond the scope of this book. The importance of Article 98 of the Rome Statute is, therefore, not underestimated. Nonetheless, it will have a negative effect on Article 27.

Possible solutions can be adopted in attempting to minimize any negative effects of Article 98. One solution looks at the theory of implied waivers. Arguably, at the heart of this notion lies the issue of a hierarchy of norms. In a hierarchy, norms deemed superior take precedence over and above those deemed inferior. Consequently if the norms prohibiting international crimes are considered supreme they will take precedence over and above the norms regulating immunities, thus negating the need for waivers. Another solution may lie with the establishment of an international constabulary.

Implied Waiver Theory

The issue of waivers is applicable to all who ordinarily enjoy immunity in foreign jurisdictions. A waiver is the permission given by the state of the individual concerned, authorizing the state with custodial enforcement jurisdiction to proceed with investigation, arrest and trial of the individual concerned. Waivers have, in most cases, been the subject of much debate with regard to diplomats and less so with heads of state and governments. This is, perhaps, the case because waivers have been clearly provided for in the Vienna Diplomatic Convention.

Waivers and Diplomatic Immunity

There is a tendency amongst states not to waive the immunity of their officials, especially diplomats, as will be discussed below. Where a diplomat has committed crimes, the receiving state can request the waiver of his immunity from his state.[3] Waivers must be express and come from the government recognized by the receiving state at the time when the waiver is given.[4] Under the current system, without a waiver from the sending state, the receiving state can only hope that a diplomat alleged to have committed an international crime is prosecuted by his

---

[3] Vienna Diplomatic Convention, Article 32.

[4] *Ibid*, 32(2).

The Need for Balance 137

state upon his return. Where waiver is denied, and being unable to arrest an accredited diplomat, a receiving state can declare him *persona non grata* and effectively deport him.[5]

Waivers have proved to be unpopular with regard to diplomats and sending states. In one of a very few examples of its kind, immunity was waived in 1985 by the President of Zambia to allow British authorities to pursue a case against the third secretary of the Zambian Embassy in London who was apprehended with heroin in his possession.[6] Prior to the waiver, the British authorities halted all action once his identity was confirmed, and had written a letter of apology to the mission. The head of mission was approached for permission by British authorities to pursue the case. After consulting his President, immunity was waived. In his letter, which was made public, the President of Zambia stated that diplomatic immunity was 'not intended to prevent the investigation of serious crimes'. He felt that although his action was unprecedented, in the fight against addictive drugs, a 'terrifying menace', waiver of immunity was the right action to take.[7] In another rare example, immunity was also waived by Georgia, to enable the prosecution of one of its diplomat involved in a fatal traffic accident in the US in 1998.[8]

With waivers proving so unpopular, some states have chosen to dismiss their diplomats rather than waive their immunity. Zaire (DRC) did just that in January 1997, after its ambassador to France, Ramazani Baya, killed two teenagers in a car crash in November 1996. The incident caused friction between the two countries as France sought the waiver of his immunity from the then President Mobutu Sese Seko.[9] The ambassador was recalled to Zaire, whereupon it was announced that he had been fired and would be returning to France to face prosecution. The decision to dismiss him ended the dispute between France and Zaire over the waiver of immunity.[10]

---

[5] Vienna Diplomatic Convention, Article 9 states that the 'receiving State may at any time and without having to explain its decision, notify the sending State that the head of the mission or any member of the diplomatic staff of the mission is persona non grata or that any other member of the staff mission is not acceptable'.

[6] McClanahan, *Diplomatic Immunity* (1989), p. 156-7.

[7] In 1987 the USA refused to waive immunity for the spouse of their diplomat accredited to the UK, who was to be charged with gross indecency with a minor girl, a crime carrying a prison term of up to five years. The American Embassy refused to waive immunity taking into consideration their government's policy on such issues. McClanahan notes that the 'practice of the State Department in this incidence indicated that even when there is little question of the fact of a serious crime having been committed, of the probable fairness of the courts, or of the treatment that would be accorded the accused if detained, other considerations may be of sufficient weight to cause refusal of a waiver of immunity'. McClanahan, *Diplomatic Immunity, op cit,* p. 138.

[8] *John A. Knab v. Republic of Georgia et al.* (1998) U.S. District Lexis 8820. www.butterworths.co.uk.

[9] www.cnn.com/WORLD/9612/01/briefs/france.ambassador.

[10] At that particular time, France was one of Zaire's main political allies in its bid to recover territory from ADFL rebels. Hence the decision to return the ambassador to France was political. *Ibid.*

The rarity of waiver cases allows one to presume that sending states are loath to waive immunity in criminal cases. Thus it is possible to conclude that where a state with custody is the receiving state, declaring a diplomat *persona non grata* is the only option, with the hope that the diplomat will face charges in their own country, as outlined in the Vienna Diplomatic Convention:

> The immunity of a diplomatic agent from the jurisdiction of the receiving State does not exempt him from the jurisdiction of the sending state.[11]

Although unusual, there are cases of diplomats facing charges in their home state once declared *persona non grata*. In one such case, a Russian diplomat in the embassy in Ottawa, Canada, killed a woman in a car crash and was recalled to Russia.[12] He was charged and convicted in a Moscow court and received a five-year sentence and a driving ban for three years. However, in general states have proved as unwilling to prosecute their deported diplomats as they have been to waive their immunity.

With waivers being unpopular, and prosecution at home highly unlikely, another solution must be found. Reference can be made to the restrictive theory favoured by the USA. This theory, outlined in the previous chapter, considers unofficial acts as not being immune and that the commission of certain acts cannot form part of a mission's functions. It is possible to integrate the restrictive theory into the implied waiver concept. In so doing, one may argue that as international crimes cannot form part of a diplomat's and indeed any state official's function, the commission of such acts is an automatic waiver of immunity.

Waiving the Immunity of State Officials by Implication

The implied waiver theory has its advocates in the USA.[13] It has been raised in various cases dealing with *jus cogens* and sovereign immunity, in which the plaintiffs sought to exclude immunity under the FSIA in order to claim compensation for acts of torture committed by foreign states.[14] In *Siderman de Blake*, the claimants argued that a foreign state that breaches *jus cogens* norms is not entitled to sovereign immunity with respect to the breaching act.[15] According to the plaintiffs the higher-ranking norm trumps the inferior rule, thus the state

---

[11] Vienna Diplomatic Convention, Article 31(4).

[12] www.bbc.co.uk/1/low/world/europe/1881488.stm.

[13] Belsk, Merva and Roht-Arriaza, 'Implied Waiver under the FSIA: A Proposed Exception to Immunity for Violations of Peremptory Norms of International Law' (1989) *77 Calif. L. Rev. 365*.

[14] *Siderman de Blake, op cit*; *Hugo Princz v. Federal Republic of Germany* (1994) 26 F 3d 116.

[15] *Siderman de Blake, op cit*, p. 717-718.

The Need for Balance

committing the act automatically waives its immunity in a domestic court.[16] Their argument is based on the implied waiver theory, which in turn is based on the hierarchy of norms concept.

Hierarchy of Norms Within domestic legal systems there exists a hierarchy of norms with the constitution, for most states, at the apex.[17] All other laws are subordinate to the constitution, and any laws created contrary to its rules are invalid. For example, the Tanzanian Constitution declares that individuals shall not be put to torture, treated in a cruel and degrading manner nor unusually punished.[18] Any rules passed thereafter, that purport to permit an individual to be so treated, are invalid. According to Kelsen, a legal norm is created and validated by other norms, and the 'norm determining the creation of another norm is the superior norm'.[19] In this respect, constitutional norms, being the determining rules, are supreme.

On the international stage, however, there is no single constitution that binds all states. There is no centralized mechanism that can create a constitution when all states are sovereign and equal. Therefore, the task of determining the existence of a hierarchy of norms based on the domestic model is difficult. Nonetheless, international law is a system of norms, and as a system of law, there must be some manner of hierarchy. But determining if superior rules exist at all is a complex process that can be approached by analysing the sources of international norms, as rules are not established in a vacuum.

The Statute of the ICJ provides the court with the various sources of laws it can refer to in its adjudication.[20] It provides for: international conventions, custom, and general principles of law as primary sources of public international law.[21] These are mechanisms of rule creation. A rule created by one of these mechanisms incorporates the importance given to the vehicle used in its creation. Hence, if the mechanism of international treaty between states is given precedence over custom, it is assumed that the rules created by treaty will take priority in a dispute.[22] It is acknowledged that treaty rules between states as *lex specialis* take priority as against general customary norms between them.[23] Shaw notes that where a conflict

---

[16] Although the courts in the USA have found these arguments persuasive, they have failed to give them in effect because of the FSIA. 'The fact that there has been a violation of *jus cogens* does not confer jurisdiction under the FSIA.' *Siderman de Blake, ibid*, p. 719.

[17] The concept of supremacy of the constitution denotes the lower ranking of other statutes, and indeed the legislator. Limbach, 'The Concept of the Supremacy of the Constitution' (2001) *64 MLR 1*.

[18] The Constitution 1977 Part 3: Sehemu ya Tatu, Haki na Wajibu Muhimu Haki ya Usawa 13(6) (e) ni marufuku kwa mtu kuteswa, kuadhibiwa kinyama au kupewa adhabu zinazomtweza au kumdhalilisha. (Translated by author.)

[19] Kelsen, *General Theory of Law and State, op cit*, p. 124.

[20] Statute of the ICJ, UN Charter, *op cit.*

[21] ICJ Statute, Article 38(1).

[22] Shaw, *International Law, op cit*, p. 96.

[23] *Nicaragua v. US (Merits) Case*, p. 137.

arises as to a treaty or custom, the 'later in time will have priority' as treaties are 'usually formulated to replace or codify existing custom'.[24] Conversely, new custom can evolve from a treaty. According to Akehurst 'treaties and custom are normally of equal authority as sources of international law, and override other sources'.[25] Thus international law appears not to give custom priority over treaty.[26] Attempts to prioritize treaty as against custom, or custom over treaty can prove inconclusive, because treaty and custom as sources are given equal importance. It cannot be said with certainty, therefore, that the manner in which a norm is established decides its hierarchical status.

However, in a dispute between two states, norms of *jus cogens* take priority over and above treaty and customary laws.

The Superior Status of Jus Cogens Norms The doctrine of *jus cogens* under the Treaty Convention creates obligations on states not to produce treaties that will contradict norms of *jus cogens*.[27] The fact that the ICJ has not had to utilize the relevant section of the Treaty Convention on *jus cogens* is to Tomuschat perhaps an indication that states have adhered to their moral obligation not to produce treaties that are contrary to the international community's core norms.[28] States, have, therefore, accepted the binding nature of *jus cogens*. But its obligatory nature does not automatically give rise to superiority. Thus it is questionable whether it places obligations on states, or its norms are superior and negate those contrary to it.

It is possible to state that the only function of *jus cogens* is to place obligations on states, and it is equally valid to claim that the importance of *jus cogens* lies in its ability to create norms that are superior and therefore of fundamental nature. Both approaches are correct and viable. Norms of *jus cogens* cannot be limited or derogated from by agreement between states because the world community as a whole regards them as of critical importance. Hence, they cannot 'contract out' of them.[29] Because *jus cogens* norms are fundamental and superior they place an obligation on states not to contract or act contrary to them. In adhering to their obligations states create norms of superior status.

Being superior and placing obligations on states, *jus cogens* norms take precedence over other international norms. However, it is open to question whether *jus cogens* norms can supplant inconsistent domestic statutes. Some writers have

---

[24] Shaw, *International Law, op cit*, p. 96.

[25] Akehurst, 'The Hierarchy of the Sources of International Law' (1974-1975) *47 BYIL 273, 283*.

[26] *Ibid.*

[27] Vienna Treaty Convention, Article 53, *op cit.*

[28] Tomuschat, 'International Law: Ensuring the Survival on the Eve of a New Century' (1999) *281 Hague Recueil des Cours 13, 81-82*.

[29] Higgins, *Problems and Processes. International Law and How We Use It, op cit*, p. 22.

The Need for Balance

concluded international *jus cogens* norms supersede domestic legislation.[30] They argue that national sovereignty is incompatible with *jus cogens* as it is for the benefit of the world community and at its behest that norms attain such status.[31] However, on various occasions US courts have rejected arguments that would have in effect given international *jus cogens* priority over domestic statutes. In cases involving torture, where it was put forward that the prohibition of torture is *jus cogens*, the courts have consistently maintained that the provisions in the FSIA take priority.[32] This specific issue remains unclear, but what is clear is that *jus cogens* norms are superior to other international norms.

In attempting to provide a solution to the problem presented in this thesis that is based on the implied waiver theory, a paradigm of the hierarchy of norms will now be put forward. It is suggested that the norms governing immunity *ratione personae* and the norms prohibiting international customary crimes have the potential to be rules of *jus cogens*; hence in this hierarchical model they are given such status.

The Hierarchical Status of International Crimes, Universal Jurisdiction and Immunities Under this supposed model, the situation is thus:

1.   The norms prohibiting international customary crimes are rules of *jus cogens*.
2.   Universal jurisdiction for these crimes is part of international customary law.
3.   Immunity *ratione personae* for heads of state/government, foreign ministers and accredited diplomats, is part of international *jus cogens*.
4.   Immunity *ratione materiae* for both heads of state or government and accredited diplomats is a international customary norm.

With reference to this model, immunity *ratione personae* as a rule of *jus cogens* will surpass any contrary customary and treaty international norm. However, it was asserted in *Pinochet (Belgium)* that as a 'matter of international customary law, or even stronger as a matter of *jus cogens*, universal jurisdiction over crimes against humanity exists, authorising national authorities to prosecute and punish the perpetrators in all circumstances'.[33] This is partly correct. Universal jurisdiction for crimes against humanity is part of international customary law, but

---

[30] Haffke, 'The Torture Victim Protection Act: More Symbol than Substance' (1994) *43 Emory LJ 1469, 1502*. Turpil and Sands, 'Peremptory International Law and Sovereignty: Some Questions' (1988) *3 Conn. JIL 364, 369*.

[31] *Ibid.*

[32] *Siderman de Blake*; *Hugo Princz*. Perhaps the use of torture to support arguments in this section is not so appropriate, as the international treaty crime of torture is not a norm of *jus cogens*. Indeed, jurisdiction under which the plaintiff sought to make their claims is tied to the Torture Convention rather than international customary law with regard to universal jurisdiction.

[33] *Pinochet (Belgium)*, Judge Vandermeersch.

it cannot be said that it has attained the status of *jus cogens*. Arguably as an international norm of a customary nature, universal jurisdiction could certainly develop into a *jus cogens* norm, but at present it is not.

Nevertheless, the contention that immunity *ratione materiae* and *personae* may be norms of jus cogens can be challenged. Indeed, the possibility of a functional-based principle such as diplomatic immunities being *jus cogens* has already been questioned.[34] According to Ben-Asher the problem lies in attempting to merge the natural law undertones of *jus cogens* with a reciprocal-based doctrine such as diplomatic immunity.[35] Notions of higher laws that bind all states seem, according to this viewpoint, out of place with state-centred reciprocity, in that states only obey the laws in question because it is in their interests to do so. In addition, Ben-Asher questions how natural law can justify a doctrine '...destined to prevent justice from being done by allowing murderers, rapists, child abusers, and drug smugglers to retreat behind the sanctuary of their privileged utility-based status'.[36] Understandably, the emotive stance taken is a reflection of the material relied upon to document diplomatic abuse. However, one must not lose sight of the fact that norms of *jus cogens* are, if translated literally, 'compelling law'.[37] Many rules considered *jus cogens* are 'quite clearly in the interests of most States, as those states see and manifest those interests to be'.[38] Although the natural law origins of *jus cogens* are founded on the notion of higher or divine law, contemporary notions must rest on the idea of compelling law. This position removes the divine and mystic connotations surrounding *jus cogens* by a simple claim of obligatory law. Obligation brought about by reciprocity and state interest.

The immunity of diplomats and heads of state or government, and in particular immunity *ratione personae* is a persuasive and forceful doctrine. With their own interests in mind, states adhere to the absolute inviolability of diplomats and heads of state or governments for the sake of continued international discourse. When Belgium failed to honour the immunity *ratione personae* of the incumbent Congolese foreign minister, it was reminded of its duty to do so by the ICJ.[39] Because of a lack of a centralized system of law creation, there is a great need for state interest in norm creation. States will accept and adhere to laws that are of interest to them and their citizens. Denial of this situation is unrealistic. Without state interest there is no international customary law, treaty law and indeed *jus cogens*. The suggestion that states will create and obey laws that are totally at odds with their interests is unsustainable. Rather, where states strongly adhere to compelling law, '...the weighing of supporting, ambivalent and opposing State

---

[34] Ben-Asher, 'Human Rights Meets Diplomatic Immunities: Problems and Possible Solutions', *www.law.harvard.edu*. Functionality is referred to here in terms of the basis upon which immunity is granted.

[35] *Ibid*, p. 24.

[36] *Ibid*.

[37] Byers, 'Conceptualising the Relationship between *Jus Cogens* and *Erga Omnes* Rules', *op cit*, 222.

[38] *Ibid*.

[39] *Arrest Warrant Case*.

The Need for Balance

practice may be a facilitative, and not an always necessary exercise' in the determination of *jus cogens*.[40] Thus keen state interest in a given norm can create *jus cogens*.

Arguably, therefore, by virtue of its crucial and vital characteristics, coupled with ardent state interest, immunity *ratione personae* has the potential to be a norm of *jus cogens*. States adhere to this doctrine absolutely. Conversely, it can be said that due to its qualified position, immunity *ratione materiae* has not attained the status of *jus cogens*. Although part of international customary law, states and their courts are far more willing to analyse immunity *ratione materiae* and at times deny it, if deemed appropriate and in their interests. States, through their civil jurisdiction, have managed to place limits on the scope of the immunity *ratione materiae*. It is in their interest to do so. In so doing they have shown that as an international norm it can, to a certain extent, be abrogated. Immunity *ratione materiae* is not, therefore, a norm of *jus cogens*.

Immunity *ratione personae* is not only compelling, but also *erga omnes* for visiting heads of state or government. All have an obligation to accord inviolability. But not so for diplomats, whose inviolability is confined to their receiving state. It has been put forward that diplomatic inviolability is an *erga omnes* norm but not *jus cogens*.[41] This point of view seems somewhat tenuous if one equates *erga omnes* norms with the capacity of all states to have the right of standing to make claims if inviolability is violated.[42] The obligation to accord inviolability is tied between the sending and receiving states. It does not follow, therefore, that in this situation a third state, that is not a transit state,[43] will have *locus standi* to make a claim. Diplomatic immunity is dependent upon bilateral diplomatic relations between states. Although a single unifying treaty that incorporated some customary rules applicable to all states exists, the bilateralism of the relationship the norms were created to govern would appear to nullify any attempts to designate diplomatic immunity as *erga omnes*. Even if it were considered to involve 'a series of identical bilateral relationships between every possible pair of States', 'a violation of the bilateral relationship between two States would not give other States any right to make a legal claim'.[44] The violating state has not breached its obligations with those other states. Diplomatic immunity *ratione personae* is a *jus cogens* norm, vis-à-vis receiving and sending states only, but is not *erga omnes*. On the other hand, immunity *ratione personae* of heads of state and government is both *jus cogens* and *erga omnes*.

---

[40] *Ibid.*

[41] MacDonald, 'Fundamental Norms in Contemporary International Law' (1987) *CYIL 115, 138.*

[42] Explanation of *erga omnes* according to Byers, 'Conceptualising the Relationship between *Jus Cogens* and *Erga Omnes* Rules', *op cit*, p. 211. See Chapter 2 of this thesis.

[43] Article 40 of the Vienna Diplomatic Convention provides for inviolability of a diplomat who is in transit to take up or to return to his post, or when returning to his state.

[44] Byers, 'Conceptualising the Relationship between *Jus Cogens* and *Erga Omnes* Rules', *op cit*, p. 232.

The Implied Waiver Theory: A Viable Solution?

Having ascertained the hierarchical status of the immunity *ratione personae*, immunity *ratione materiae*, international customary crimes and universal jurisdiction, can it now be said that the implied waiver theory offers a viable solution to our problem? Using our model, we can apply the hierarchical status to the norms mentioned, and in so doing hopefully provide a way to apply the implied waiver theory. Thus: Prohibitions of the various international crimes are *jus cogens* norms, but the individual accountability aspect (universal jurisdiction) is customary. Consequently, in a situation where a sitting head of state or government or accredited diplomat is accused of committing an international customary crime, the act is *jus cogens* whereas personal accountability is customary. Personal accountability is tied to investigation, arrest and trial, which for a current state official will be relevant to immunity *ratione personae*.

Lord Hope in *Pinochet (No. 3)* points out that 'even in the field of such high crimes as have achieved the status of *jus cogens* under international customary law there is as yet no general agreement that they are outside the immunity to which former heads of state are entitled from the jurisdiction of foreign national courts'.[45] This statement can be analysed with reference to our model. A former head of state only enjoys immunity *ratione materiae*, and, according to our model, immunity *ratione materiae* is a norm of international customary law. However, international customary crimes are norms of *jus cogens* and take precedence over immunity *ratione materiae*. Accordingly, immunity *ratione materiae* cannot be granted where the individual is accused of having committed such crimes.

But our model raises the following question: Which rule takes priority, the prohibition of international crimes or inviolability, as both are *jus cogens* and *erga omnes*? In response to this question it must be noted that inviolability is primarily directed at a state's custodial enforcement jurisdiction whereas the norms of international customary crimes relate to proscriptive jurisdiction. It is unlikely that a conflict between the two doctrines will arise. Jurisdiction will clash with the doctrine of inviolability, as it is the enforcement part of the crimes that relates to immunity *ratione personae*. The jurisdiction attached to the *jus cogens* norms prohibiting international crimes is customary rather than *jus cogens*, thus immunity *ratione personae* takes precedence over it.

However, in effecting our model, it is possible to conclude that the implied waiver theory cannot be utilized to circumvent Article 98. Nonetheless, this hierarchical model is arguably a useful device that is capable of effecting the balance between international justice and inter-state relations.

According to the hierarchical status of the norms in our model, a sitting head of state or government, or an accredited diplomat, cannot be arrested, but his acts will not be immune. Although immune because he is inviolable, such person is still criminally responsible for his acts amounting to international crimes. This will not hinder his duties as head of state as he can travel without fear, knowing that he is

---

[45] *Pinochet (No. 3)*, p. 147.

The Need for Balance 145

inviolable, and that that inviolability as *jus cogens* and *erga omnes* is absolute.[46] When immunities and international crimes are structured in this way, Barker's argument that immunity '*ratione personae* and indeed, the consequent inviolability which flows from that immunity...be absolute even in the face of a claim of *jus cogens*' is substantiated. [47]

With regards to immunity *ratione materiae* and diplomats, it is arguable that as a diplomat carries out orders, his immunity *ratione materiae* should always subsist. Even if the acts in question are international crimes, the diplomat will simply be carrying out government instructions.[48] Although this point of view appears rational, it is even more logical to assume that governments cannot instruct their diplomats to act contrary to norms of *jus cogens*. If there is a *jus cogens* norm prohibiting a certain act, a diplomat carrying out orders contrary to this norm cannot be said to be acting officially for his state. It is recognized that a diplomat is aware that certain acts are internationally prohibited and cannot be absolved from responsibility based on the assumption that he was carrying out instructions.[49]

Even though it has been claimed in the past that the utility of theoretical priority determination is at best questionable, it is possible to achieve a balance between the pursuit of international justice and stable inter-state relations by differentiating the two immunities and placing them on a hierarchical scale alongside the norms prohibiting international crimes and universal jurisdiction.[50] Theoretical priority determination is, therefore, a potentially viable process. But this method is only possible if immunities are distinguished. There has not been a conscious effort to make a distinction between the two types of immunities and analyse how their differences can help achieve both international justice and stability. Zappalà attempted to make this distinction in his analysis of the *Qaddafi*

---

[46] The Belgian Supreme Court appears to have reached this conclusion in their recent decision regarding the case against Sharon. They held that the case against him could go on once he no longer has immunity, assuming the immunity they were referring to is *ratione personae*. See: Miles, 'Sharon Faces War Crimes Trial Once Out of Office' *The Independent*, 13 February 2003.

[47] Barker, '*Immunity Ratione Personae* and *Jus Cogens Norms – Approach With Caution*', *op cit*, p. 9.

[48] Lord Hutton looked at this issue in *Pinochet (No. 3)*, p. 159.

[49] Perhaps a more flexible approach is needed. Taking into consideration that diplomats follow orders, they cannot be said to be acting fully in their private capacity if ordered to commit an international crime. The act in question was not for their benefit. Perhaps the two-staged approach of public/private acts can be expanded to include a third category. Possibly, a diplomat's acts can be categorised into the existing two categories for the benefit of immunity *ratione materiae*: public, private. However, another sub-category could be used as a defence, that of delegated acts. By designating certain acts as delegated, a diplomat does not escape personal responsibility for the commission of international crimes, and the acts are still deemed unofficial. Reference to 'delegated' action will show that the diplomat was following orders of a private nature from the head of state or government, or indeed foreign minister.

[50] Ben-Asher, 'Human Rights Meets Diplomatic Immunities: Problems and Possible Solutions', *op cit*, p. 26.

146 *Immunity and International Criminal Law*

Case.[51] In fact, he correctly suggests that heads of state 'should not be arrested even if they are on a private visit' as this could 'destabilize international relations'.[52] It is suggested, however, that this destabilizing effect can be minimized if an internationally constituted police force arrests state officials. An international police force may be the only solution to the problem of Article 98.

An International Constabulary

The option of an international constabulary as outlined in this study is not a short-term option. The possibility of such an establishment being created is just that: a possibility, and as with most 'possibles' comes reality. It is suggested that sometime in the future this idea, like the ICC, will cease to be a distant possibility and become a reality.

A state with custody may find itself in a politically sensitive situation even where the ICC has obtained a waiver. However pleasing it would be to have a state put aside diplomatic relations in pursuit of justice, such a position is naïve. Diplomatic relations between states must be maintained. A state with custody should be allowed to demonstrate its willingness to support international justice as well as maintain friendly relations with the state whose national is sought by the ICC. In order to do so a state's legal enforcement mechanisms should not be the primary facilitators of the arrest, detention and surrender of a head of state or government, diplomat or other high-ranking government officials. It is suggested that in such circumstances states be given the opportunity to allow a specially created international police force to take control. It is further suggested that states ratifying the Rome Statute be given the chance to sign an additional protocol for the establishment of such a force.

As outlined in Chapter 3, international criminal courts should not be hampered by the doctrine of sovereignty in fulfilling their functions. Thus it is arguable that an international constabulary, set up and operating under the auspices of the ICC, would be capable of overriding notions of sovereignty. It is anticipated, therefore, that waivers and consent from states may not be required. Accordingly, Article 98 may never be utilized under this scheme.

The idea of establishing an international constabulary is not new. The London Assembly in their 1948 international criminal court draft convention included a provision for an international constabulary.[53] According to the draft's Article 25:

---

[51] *Qaddafi Case*, Zappalà, 'Do Heads of State in Office Enjoy Immunity from the Jurisdiction for International Crimes?', *op cit.*

[52] *Ibid*, p. 606, 607.

[53] Mentioned above p. 10.

The Need for Balance

1.   Near the Court there shall be a body of International Constabulary which will be charged with the execution of the orders of the Court and of the Procurator General.
2.   The members of this body shall be chosen by the Court among candidates belonging to different nationalities, in the manner proscribed for the nomination of judges.
3.   The H.C.P.s will confer upon the Constabulary the necessary power to call the assistance of the local police, when such assistance is necessary for the performance of its duties.[54]

In developing this idea, it is hoped that it can be shown that the creation of an international constabulary may be possible in the distant future. The establishment of the International Criminal Police Organization, or Interpol,[55] and the special police force in Bosnia Herzegovina[56] are developments that make the prospect of an international constabulary more than mere fiction.

The Establishment: Methods and Means

The constabulary could take two forms. It could be an independent body that operates outside the ICC or as an auxiliary organ. As an independent body the constabulary can undertake the necessary investigations, arrest, detention and surrender at the behest of a state that may receive a surrender request. If created as an auxiliary organ of the ICC, it could carry out the same function, but get surrender requests direct from the court itself. It is interesting to note that the

---

[54] H.C.P. refers to High Contracting Party. London Assembly Draft Convention for an International Criminal Court 1943. According to this draft convention, Article 10, the selection and appointment process was to mirror that for judges. Consequently a high contracting party could nominate a maximum of three candidates who need not be its nationals.   Appointments require joint decision of the HCPs with emphasis on fair representation.

1.   Each time a vacancy occurs, any H.C.P. in respect of which the present Convention is in force may nominate not more than three candidates for appointment as judges of the Court. The candidates may or may not be nationals of the nominating H.C.P.
2.   The International Criminal Court shall elect the judges from the persons so nominated.
3.   The appointment of the original judges shall be made by a joint decision of the H.C.P.s Such appointment shall be made regardless of the nationality of the judge, but it shall take into account that the Court should represent the principal legal systems of the world and that it should ensure a fair representation of the countries that have been occupied by the enemy. Such appointment shall be made not more than two months after the time when the present Convention has been signed by seven H.C..s.

[55] Interpol was founded in 1923 by police chiefs from 20 countries in a meeting in Vienna, Austria. Fooner, *Interpol Issues in World Crime and International Criminal Justice* (1989).

[56] The UN Special Police Force set up under the Dayton Accords. See below p. 153.

German idea of a Europol, as equivalent to the FBI, was not acceptable within the European Union. Although established it has no enforcement functions.[57]

As an autonomous organization, the constabulary can be established as an intergovernmental organization (IGO) or as a non-governmental organization (NGO). NGOs are bodies recognized by the United Nations as possessing special knowledge and technical skills of value to it in its work.[58] The UN's ECOSOC consults NGOs in areas with which they are concerned.[59] If the constabulary is to be of consequence then it cannot be set up as an NGO. As an IGO, however, its status will be superior in the international community, but it will have to fulfil the following issues:

(i)   It must be a permanent body instituted to carry on a continuing set of functions;

(ii)   voluntary membership of eligible parties;

(iii)   a basic instrument stating goals, structure and methods of operation;

(iv)   a permanent secretariat to carry on continuous administrative research, and information functions.[60]

Interpol is a good example of an IGO police force. It was established in Vienna in 1923 through a conference organized by the Austrian Chief of Police.[61] It was initially granted NGO status in 1948 by ECOSOC but sought to upgrade to an IGO in the 1970s. It was officially recognized as an IGO in 1971.[62] Interpol is unique, however, as it was not established via treaty. IGOs are typically launched by treaty.[63] By establishing IGOs by treaty, states make certain that as organizations they operate through consent, recommendation and cooperation.[64] Some IGOs, in particular specialized agencies, have a superior status to NGOs as they are related to the UN by special agreement, whereby they work with the UN and each other through ECOSOC.[65]

The constabulary will most definitely need to work with the UN and other IGOs rather than simply provide technical or special knowledge on a consultative basis. Accordingly it would need to be an IGO. But setting up an international constabulary as an IGO could prove problematic. Getting states to agree to a body

---

[57] Its mission is to assist the law enforcement authorities of member states in their fight against serious forms of organised crime. www.europol.net.

[58] *Everyman's United Nations* 7th Ed., p. 16.

[59] *Ibid.*

[60] Bennet, *International Organizations Principles and Issues* (1995), p. 3.

[61] Fooner, *Interpol Issues in World Crime and International Criminal Justice, op cit*, p. 7.

[62] Special Arrangement between the International Criminal Police Organization and the Economic and Social Council, ECOSOC (1971) E/RES/1579 (L).

[63] Examples of IGOs so established include the Council of Europe, the Customs Cooperative Council, the AU (or as previously known, Organization of African Unity), the International Civil Aviation Organization, etc.

[64] Bennet, *International Organizations Principles and Issues, op cit*, 3

[65] *Everyman's United Nations, op cit*, p. 16.

that will operate in their territory to investigate, arrest, detain and transfer state officials to the ICC will not be easy. In fact it may be impossible. That Interpol was created and still operates in the present day is not a clear indicator that states would be willing to establish an international constabulary along the lines mentioned.

However, if an international constabulary were set up, it is suggested that such a constabulary could only really be effective if it is attached to the ICC. There is one main reason for this assumption. States are not comfortable with international bodies that would, once established, erode their influence over their criminal jurisdiction. One only has to look at the USA's negative reaction to the ICC to detect this trend.[66] If the USA is uneasy about its citizens facing prosecutions based on ulterior motives in an international court that has inbuilt checks and balances drafted to prevent this from occurring, it is a foregone conclusion that it will be even more anxious of an international police force capable of arresting its officials abroad. Although the USA stands somewhat isolated in its total rejection of the ICC, it is assumed that other states will not be willing to see an international police force capable of arresting and detaining their leaders and officials abroad. A treaty that purports to give a body such powers will never command support and will ultimately fail. Hence, for practical reasons, the scale and scope of the constabulary has to be narrow. The constabulary must be linked to the ICC. Its purpose and functions have to focus solely on the ICC.

The International Constabulary as an Organ of the International Criminal Court

The proposal for the establishment of an international constabulary is feasible if it is part of the ICC. Police forces have been established as part of other projects. The best example is that of the civilian police force set up in the Republic of Bosnia and Herzegovina, the Federation of Bosnia Herzegovina and the Republic of Srpska under the Dayton Peace Accords.[67] The Accords called on the Security Council to set up an International Police Task Force (IPTF) to carry out a programme of assistance.[68] The police force is headed by a Commissioner who is appointed by the Secretary General in consultation with the Security Council.[69]

The IPTF was mandated to monitor and inspect judicial and law enforcement activities, advise and train local law enforcement personnel, analyse public security threats and offer the government advice on how to organize their

---

[66] See Bradley, 'The US Announces Intent Not to Ratify International Criminal Court Treaty (May 2002) www.asil.org/insights.

[67] The Dayton Accords were initialled by the Republic of Bosnia Herzegovina, the Republic of Croatia and the Federal Republic of Yugoslavia.

[68] Dayton Accords, Annex 11, Article 1(2). Article 3 outlines the programme of assistance; see Annex.

[69] Dayton Accords, Annex 11, Article 2, *ibid*. The activities of IPTF are coordinated by the High Representative, designated by the Security Council to coordinate and facilitate civilian aspects of the peace settlement. Annex 10.

150 *Immunity and International Criminal Law*

police forces and facilitate law enforcement improvement.[70] The IPTF objective was to help already established local police forces; consequently, it was not instituted to enforce local laws.[71] Members of the IPTF, under the terms of the Dayton Accords, are accorded the same status as officials of the UN.[72] They are immune from arrest and detention.[73] Waiver from the Secretary General is required.

Creating a police force connected to another undertaking makes the purpose and task of such a force easily discernible, thus alleviating state concerns as to the loss of their sovereignty. With these issues in mind it is possible to propose a draft protocol establishing the constabulary.

The Rome Statute does not specifically provide for future additions. However, it does permit amendments of an institutional nature. Proposals for modifications can be made at any time to the UN Secretary General by state parties or persons delegated by the court's Assembly of State Parties.[74] It is assumed that additions to the Rome Statute will follow the same procedure. Although championed as the best solution, it is acknowledged that it will still be difficult to establish an international constabulary.

A Draft Additional Protocol to the Rome Statute of The International Constabulary

| Article | 1 | An International Constabulary (The Constabulary) is established hereby as a permanent institution. |

The Relationship of the International Constabulary, the International Criminal Court and the United Nations

Article	2 (1)	The Constabulary shall be duly attached to the International Criminal Court (The Court) and shall according to the Court's Statute enter into relationship with the UN through the agreement to be approved by the Court's Assembly of State Parties (The Assembly) on its behalf.
	(2)	The responsibilities and duties of the Assembly outlined in the Court's Statutes, Article 112, shall apply to the Constabulary.
	(3)	The Constabulary shall, according to the Court's Statute, have its headquarters at The Hague in The

---

[70] Bair and Dziedzic, 'The International Police Task Force: Lessons from Bosnia' in *Policing the New World Disorder. Peace Operations and Public Security* (R.B. Oakley, M.J. Dziedzic and E.M. Goldberg eds.) (2002).

[71] *Ibid.*

[72] UN officials are accorded diplomatic immunity and privileges as provided for by the Convention on the Privileges and Immunities of the UN 1946 (1 UNTS 15).

[73] Convention on the Privileges and Immunities of the UN, Articles 18 and 19, *ibid.*

[74] Rome Statute, Article 122.

The Need for Balance

Netherlands, in accordance with the Court's Headquarters Agreement as approved by the Assembly.

The Purpose of the Constabulary

Article 3
The Constabulary is established to investigate individuals for and on behalf of the Court where so ordered by a Pre-Trial Chamber of the Court, pursuant to the provisions of the Court's Statute, Article 15.

Article 4
The Constabulary shall if so ordered by a Pre-Trial Chamber of the Court, commence proceedings to apprehend and detain named individual(s) in an arrest warrant pursuant to the Court's Statute, Article 58.

Article 5
The Constabulary shall in accordance with Article 59 of the Court's Statute effect the arrest and detention, and thereafter the transfer of the named individual(s) to the Court for trial.

Special Purpose of the International Constabulary

Article 6 (1)
The Constabulary shall deal primarily but not exclusively with individuals of status that the Custodian State is not willing or is unable to investigate, apprehend, detain and surrender to the Court.

(2)
The Constabulary's special purpose is designed primarily for facilitating the work of the Court. It shall not intervene or participate in the domestic issues pertaining to a state's enforcement jurisdiction.

Article 7
The Constabulary shall provide prison facilities in the territory of any member state for individuals sentenced by the Court where no state declares its willingness to accept the sentenced person due to his previous status, pursuant to Articles 103 and 104 of the Court's Statute. The decision as to where the convicted individual will be imprisoned shall be made by the Assembly.

The Composition of the Constabulary

Article 8
The Constabulary shall consist of:
1.   The President who shall also be the President of the Court;
2.   The Office of the Chief of Police;
3.   Country Stations.

152 *Immunity and International Criminal Law*

The Presidency

Article 9 The election and responsibilities of the President of the Constabulary shall correspond with the election and responsibilities of the President of the Court.

The Office of the Chief of Police

Article 10 (1) The Office of the Chief of Police shall be headed by the Chief of Police (The Chief) who shall have full authority over the management and administration of the Constabulary. He or she will have responsibility over all staff, facilities and resources pertaining to the Constabulary, assisted by 3 or more Deputies. The President, Chief and his or her Deputies shall be of different nationalities serving on a full-time basis.

(2) The Chief shall be elected by secret ballot by an absolute majority of the Members of the Assembly of State Parties. The Deputies shall be elected in the same manner drawn from a list provided by the Chief in consultation with the President.

(3) The Chief and his or her Deputies shall, unless a shorter time is decided at the time of election, hold office for a term of nine years and shall not be eligible for re-election during that time.

(4) The Chief and his or her Deputies shall be persons of high moral character, be highly competent in and have extensive experience in the police forces of their respective countries. They are obliged to conduct themselves in a manner that will not bring into question their impartiality.

(5) Any question as to their dismissal from office shall be determined by the Assembly of State Parties at the behest of the President.

Police Officers

Article 11(1) The Chief shall appoint all Police Officers for a maximum term of three years in each duty station.

(2) (a) The Chief and his or her Deputies shall appoint in each duty station an officer to head the team of officers (Team Leader). Officers shall be so recruited directly from Member States or through the United Nations office of the Personnel Management and Support

The Need for Balance 153

Service of the Field Administration and Logistics division in the Department of Peacekeeping Operations.

(b)   The Team Leader shall have the power to appoint all general staff as required to facilitate the work of the team in each station. Such staff shall be covered by Staff Regulations in accordance to Article 13(2).

(c)   The Chief shall ensure that his recruits have attained the high standards with the police force of their respective countries, having shown competence and integrity.

(3)   Any question as to dismissal of any Police Officer shall be decided by the President, the Chief and all his or her Deputies in a vote by majority.

Salaries and Allowances

Article   12   Salaries and allowances for the Chief, the Deputies and Police Officers shall be guided by Article 49 of the Court's Statute.

General Staff

Article   13 (1)   The Chief and his or her Deputies shall appoint all such qualified other staff as may be required in effecting their and their Officers' work.

(2)   The Chief and his or her Deputies shall decide all matters dealing with such staff, draft Staff Regulations, to include terms and conditions upon which staff shall be appointed, remunerated and dismissed, as shall be approved by the Assembly. Such Regulations shall not purport to accord Staff less rights than those accorded to the Court's staff.

Privileges and Immunities

Article   14   The Constabulary, as a body, shall enjoy in the territory of each State Party privileges and immunities as are necessary for the fulfilment of its purpose.

Article   15   The Chief and his or her Deputies, the Station Team Leader and all Police Officers shall enjoy, when engaged on or with respect to the work of the Constabulary, the same privileges and immunities as are accorded to heads of diplomatic missions and shall, after the expiry of their terms in office, continue to be accorded immunity from legal process of every kind in

154 Immunity and International Criminal Law

		respect of words spoken or written and acts performed by them in their official capacity.
Article	16 (1)	The Chief and his or her Deputies, the Team Leader and Police Officers shall be inviolable.
	(2)	All official vehicles, documents, correspondence and other materials shall be inviolable.
Article	17	Member States shall acknowledge that inviolability and immunities of their nationals in respect of acts undertaken at the behest of the Court will bar prosecution within their territories. Member States are obliged to work towards enacting special legislation or exemption orders for their nations working with the Constabulary to protect them from future prosecutions for such acts.
Article	18	Other non-national staff members of each Constabulary Mission shall enjoy privileges and immunities and facilities necessary for the performance of their functions in accordance with Article 48 of the Court's Statute.
Article	19	Without prejudice to Article 14 and 15, any injuries to persons and or damages to property caused by officers of the Constabulary during the course of their employment shall be fully compensated by the Constabulary with approval by the Assembly. All such claims shall be made to the Chief within two years of the date the act giving rise to the claim occurred.

Responsibilities of Member States

Article	20 (1)	Each Member State shall be obliged to provide office premises for the Constabulary within its territory.
	(a)	Official Constabulary premises shall be granted immunity from local jurisdiction. Local authorities shall at no time enter Constabulary official premises without the express consent of the Team Leader. Such permission shall not be granted without authorization from the Chief.
	(b)	Each Receiving State shall acknowledge its duty to protect the Constabulary and its Officers, official premises and vehicles from attack, be it verbal or physical.
Article	21	Member States shall, at the behest of the President ,initiate proceedings against Police Officers who are their nationals where the President in investigations with the Prosecutor of the Court has substantiated

The Need for Balance   155

| | | allegations of criminal conduct unconnected to the work of the Constabulary. |
| Article | 22 | Each Member State shall cooperate as much as is possible with the Constabulary in facilitating the investigation, apprehension and detention of foreign persons of status in accordance with the provisions of the Court's Statute in Articles 86-102. |

Financing

Article	23	Expenses of the Constabulary shall be included in the Court's expenses to be provided for under Article 115 of the Court's Statute.
	(1)	Without prejudice to Article 21, the Constabulary may receive and utilize as additional funds, voluntary contributions from international organizations, non-governmental organizations and private individuals in accordance with relevant criteria adopted by the Assembly.
	(2)	The Constabulary shall not in any circumstance accept contributions, be they monetary or other, from governments or corporations at any time without the prior approval and authorization of the Assembly.
Article	24	The Assembly shall establish a special compensatory fund for the purposes of claims made, pursuant to Article 18, by civilians and Officers.

Anticipated Problems

Getting states to agree to an international police force operating in their territories will be a difficult task. An international court drafted without primacy is an indication that states are still keen to maintain their sovereignty with regard to their criminal jurisdictions. Their national legal authorities are to be given first opportunity to investigate a case. It is possible to infer from this position that they will be reluctant to have a police force operating in their territories, irrespective of the fact that the mandate is restricted to ICC investigations and surrender requests. Even if states were to agree to the creation of such a body, other problems will inevitably arise.

Once the constabulary has set up offices within a state, it is probable that tensions between it and local police forces could ensue. It is possible that in some countries the constabulary will have good office premises and be better equipped than their local counterparts. Being so well provided for and having a lower workload could leave the constabulary open to criticism. It is anticipated that local police forces in such countries could end up resenting the constabulary and its officers for this reason. This could lead to a lack of cooperation between the local police force and the constabulary.

An even bigger problem could arise in a situation where a visiting head of state with an ICC indictment issued against him enters a member state's territory and is given local officers to protect him during his stay. Conflict could arise between the local police force who are responsible for his protection and officers of the constabulary who may attempt to effect an arrest warrant from the ICC. In such a situation, officers of the constabulary may feel reluctant to engage local officers, and the person in question could evade the surrender request.

Although the constabulary may be better equipped than its local counterparts, problems with regard to its funding will most definitely arise. The constabulary's budget to keep all stations operational will have to reflect its small workload. Thus the numbers of on-duty officers at each duty station will have to be small so as to justify keeping the station open. In fact it is questionable if duty stations will be required to be operational every day, or simply opened when it is anticipated that an immune individual wanted by the ICC will arrive in a given state. Perhaps, then, the constabulary could be set up at The Hague with its officers ready to fly out to a relevant country at short notice. But keeping officers on call everyday, when cases are limited, will prove expensive. Perhaps a list of officers attached to the constabulary could be drawn, and such officers, although continuing with their duties in their respective countries, could be called to attend to ICC duties at any moment. State parties will have to create the necessary environment in their territories to enable such officers to leave their jobs for the duration of their contract period with the ICC. The question outstanding is the amount of money they would be paid to act as ad hoc policemen for the constabulary. Its anticipated problems do not end here.

It will be a difficult task getting together a group of officers that have equivalent training and experience. Police forces around the world all have their own methods and means of policing. Thus finding an internationally standardized quality of policemen is impossible. Recruitment could therefore be difficult. Funding will be required to make sure that a training course is established to provide all constabulary officers with the necessary skills and training to be part of the constabulary, thus standardizing police practices with the force.

Finally, the issue of immunity *ratione personae* of the officers themselves in their duty stations could cause difficulties. Indeed, the problem of UN police officers and their capacity to evade justice has been a long-running problem in Bosnia. Human Rights Watch in its report on the trafficking of women in Bosnia credits this issue as a contributing factor in hindering cases against UN police officers who are involved, thus preventing justice from being done.[75]

---

[75] www.hrw.org.

The Constabulary and Article 98 of the International Criminal Court's Statute

The problems which the constabulary may face, as outlined above, will help make the international constabulary a weak force that will be tied to a potentially feeble institution. It is unlikely that the international constabulary will acquire greater operational powers than its founding institution. It would have been interesting to see how much power a police force attached to the Ad Hoc Tribunals would have had. If such a force existed, would it have been able to enter a state and arrest Milosevic on a state visit abroad? Certainly, with an international constabulary as envisaged here, such a situation would have proved impossible. However, the international constabulary appears to offer the best solution to the conflict between Articles 27 and 98.

Conclusion

It is suggested that Article 27 faces possible death if legal avenues are not devised to circumvent Article 98. In order for Article 27 to be of operative use the effects of Article 98 must be dampened. It is important that Article 27 be given the chance to work as a mechanism to pursue those responsible for committing international crimes irrespective of status, yet the need to maintain peaceful relations between states is also great. It is vital, therefore, to strike a balance between these two concerns.

In attempting to present issues that will enable such equilibrium, the opening task is the analysis of the ICC. It is important that the organ for which the articles under scrutiny refer to be fully understood. Created through a diplomatic conference, the ICC reflects the requirements of states for an internationally constituted criminal organ. Thus it is possible to state that the incorporation of Article 98 reflected the need by states for the court to respect the doctrine of sovereignty. However, it is also possible to say that adding Article 98 swung the balance in favour of peaceful inter-state relations in our equilibrium, over and above the need for international justice. In attempting to try and present a balance it is important to review international law principles pertinent to each article.

Articles 27 and 98 pertain to individuals over whom the court will have jurisdiction, hence international crimes and the notion of individual responsibility were analysed. International criminal law has at its heart the individual; however, Articles 27 and 98 focus on specific individuals who enjoy immunity from the jurisdiction of foreign states. Accordingly immunities and its constituent parts, *ratione personae* and *materiae*, have to be examined in great detail. It is essential to acquaint the reader with varying subjects and principles that assist any conclusions made. Thus, in Chapter 6 the legal means to circumvent Article 98 are articulated and it is concluded that the possible options presented, implied waiver theory and the international constabulary, cannot necessarily provide the much needed methods to legitimately evade Article 98 and ensure a balance between the two concerns.

The implied waiver theory does not provide a solution because immunity *ratione personae* for incumbent heads of state and government as well as diplomats remains absolute, and has the potential to become a norm of *jus cogens*. And it is with the absolute nature of immunity *ratione personae* as put forward by the ICJ in the *Arrest Warrant Case*, and its potential as a *jus cogens* norm, that this conclusion is reached. The international constabulary is rejected as a solution capable of balancing the concerns behind Articles 27 and 98, as it will suffer from weaknesses that may render it ineffective. Given the ICTY's Appeals Chamber's decision in *Blaskic Croatian Subpoena Decisions (Appeal)*, that international

Conclusion 159

criminal courts must respect the doctrine of sovereignty,[1] and the ICJ's recent ruling in the *Arrest Warrant Case* that inviolability is absolute even in the face of an international crime,[2] it would appear highly unlikely that even an internationally constituted police force would be able to effect the arrest of an inviolable person without consent or waiver.

The fundamental conclusion reached is, therefore, that any attempt to maintain the equilibrium between the pursuit of international justice and stable inter-state relations, and therefore ensure world peace, cannot disregard the absolute necessity for immunity *ratione personae* for those still in office. Immunity *ratione personae* is and must remain absolute.

Thus to conclude, it has to be noted that the only means by which persons of status can be called to account at the ICC is by the denial of immunity *ratione materiae*, and the arrest of the accused once he ceases to hold office. The need for international justice under Article 27 can be fulfilled by use of two separate routes. The first is through the hierarchy of norms system. According to this approach, norms prohibiting international customary crimes are ranked superior to immunity *ratione materiae* as norms of *jus cogens*. Thus immunity *ratione materiae* cannot subsist against a claim where an individual is accused of having committed international customary law crimes. The second approach involves the act of state doctrine and analysis of the functions of state officials. Consequently, it is possible to state that the commission of international crimes cannot form part of a state official's function. By custom or treaty, states as abstract entities prohibit these acts and a state official cannot thereafter claim to be acting for his state when committing such acts. It is proposed that the second approach is the best approach. The use of *jus cogens* is tenuous and, as explained in Chapter 2, can create false hopes. The argument that the commission of an international crime cannot be an act of state so as to attract immunity *ratione materiae* is more persuasive. It is not only persuasive but can incorporate international treaty-based crimes as well, something that the hierarchy of norms approach fails to do.

It is concluded, therefore, that international criminal law has eroded the absolute nature of sovereign and diplomatic immunity, but only with regard to *ratione materiae* for incumbent state officials. In future state officials will have to bear in mind that acts of state do not include the commission of international crimes, and that they are immune from prosecution for such crimes simply because they are still in office and have immunity *ratione personae*. Immunity for other official acts will still subsist.

---

[1] *Blaskic Croatian Subpoena Decisions (Appeal), op cit.*
[2] *Arrest Warrants Case, op cit.*

Appendix

Chronological Order of Events leading up to the Rome Statute

4 December 1989	General Assembly Resolution 44/39	Requests the ILC to address questions of the establishment of the ICC.
28 November 1990	General Assembly Resolution 45/41	ILC invited to consider further issues on the establishment of international criminal jurisdiction and the establishment of the ICC.
1990	ILC 42nd Session	Considers draft statute for the ICC (continues to do so until 1994).
9 December 1991	General Assembly Resolution 46/54	ILC invited to consider further issues on the establishment of international criminal jurisdiction and the establishment of the ICC.
25 November 1992	General Assembly Resolution 47/33	Requests ILC to develop draft statute as a matter of priority.
9 December 1993	General Assembly Resolution 48/31	Invites states to submit written comments on draft ICC statute.
1994	ILC 46th Session	Adopts a statute for the ICC and submits to the General Assembly.

Appendix

9 December 1994	General Assembly Resolution 49/53	Committee established to consider key substantive and administrative issues arising out of the ILC's draft statute and to think about arrangements for a diplomatic conference.
3-13 April, 14-25 August 1995	Ad Hoc Committee	Reviews issues arising out of the draft statute and looks at arrangement for the conference.
18 December 1995	General Assembly Resolution 50/46	Preparatory Committee established to discuss key substantive and administrative issues arising out of the draft statute, to look at drafting texts that will lead to more broadly acceptable consolidated contents for a convention for the ICC.
25 March-12 April and 12-30 August 1996	Preparatory Committee on the Establishment of an International Criminal Court	Discusses further issues arising out of the draft statute.
17 December 1996	General Assembly Resolution 51/207	The Preparatory Committee to meet in 1997 and 1998 to complete and submit a text to the conference.
11-21 February and 4-15 August 1997	Preparatory Committee	Work towards an acceptable consolidated text for the ICC Convention.
15 December 1997	General Assembly Resolution 52/160	Preparatory Committee requested to work as instructed under Res. 51/207 and to transmit to the

		conference at the end of its session a text of the draft convention.
3 April 1998	Preparatory Committee	Draft Convention completed and transmitted to the conference.
15 June-17 July 1998	UN Diplomatic Conference of Plenipotentiaries on the Establishment of the ICC	States participate in conference to produce convention for the ICC.
17 July 1998	Diplomatic Conference	Statute adopted and opened for signature 17 July-17 October 1998 in Italy, thereafter until 31 December 2000 at the UN headquarters in New York.

Events post Rome Statute

26 January 1999	General Assembly Resolution 53/105	Expresses satisfaction at the adoption of the ICC statute and requests Secretary General to convene preparatory commission to discuss was to enhance the court's effectiveness and its acceptance.
25 January 2000	General Assembly Resolution 54/105	Calls upon all states to consider signing and ratifying the Rome Statute.
12 December 2000	General Assembly Resolution 55/155/	Welcomes work done by preparatory commission.

Appendix 163

Chart of Amnesty International Annual Reports Information on Torture[1]

Year (Report pertains to previous year)	Number of States in Whose Territory People Reported Torture or Ill-treatment by Security Forces, Police or Other State Authorities
2003	106
2002	111
2001	125
2000	132
1999	125
1998	117
1997	124
1996	114

---

[1] Source of information: www.amnesty.org.uk. The numbers are from Amnesty International Annual Reports, only in relation to reported instances of torture/ill treatment.

Bibliography

Adair E.R., (1929) *The Extraterritoriality of Ambassadors in the Sixteenth and Seventeenth Centuries* (London: Longman).

Ago, R., (1957) 'Positive Law and International Law' *51 AJIL 691*.

Akehurst, M., (1974-1975) 'The Hierarchy of the Sources of International Law' *47 BYIL 273*.

Akehurst, M., (1974-1975) 'Custom as a Source of International Law' *47 BYIL 1*.

Austin, J., (1920) *Lectures on Jurisprudence or the Philosophy of Positive Law* (ed. R. Campbell) (5th edition) (London: John Murray).

Bair, A., and Dziedzic, M.J., (2002) 'The International Police Task Force: Lessons from Bosnia' in *Policing the New World Disorder. Peace Operations and Public Security* (eds. R.B. Oakley, M.J. Dziedzic and E.M. Goldberg) (Washington D.C.: Institute of National Strategic Studies).

Bancroft, P.A. and Bello, J.H., (ed.) (1996) 'Chile – Criminal Jurisdiction – Prosecution of Officials of Security Service for Assassination of Former Ambassador of Chile to the USA' *90 AJIL 290*.

Barker, J.C., (1995) 'The Theory and Practice of Diplomatic Law in the Renaissance and Classical Periods' *6 Diplomacy & Statecraft 593*.

Barker, J.C., (1996) *The Abuse of Diplomatic Privileges and Immunities. A Necessary Evil?* (Aldershot/Brookfield/Singapore/Sydney: Dartmouth Publishing Co. Ltd.).

Barker, J.C., (1999) 'The Future of Head of State Immunity after *ex Parte Pinochet*' *48 ICLQ 937*.

Barker, J.C., (2000) *International Law and International Relations* (London/New York: Continium).

Barker, J.C., (2002) *Immunity Ratione Personae and Jus Cogens Norms – Approach with Caution* In File With Author (ILA (British Branch) Conference Paper, April 2002, Oxford University).

Bassiouni, M.C., (2001) 'Universal Jurisdiction for International Crimes: Historical Perspectives and Contemporary Practice' *42 VJIL 81*.

Belsk, A.C., Merva, M. and Roht-Arriaza, N., (1989) 'Implied Waiver under the FSIA: A Proposed Exception to Immunity for Violations of Peremptory Norms of International Law' *77 Calif. L. Rev. 365*.

Ben-Asher, D., (2000) 'Human Rights Meets Diplomatic Immunities: Problems and Possible Solutions' *www.law.harvard.edu*.

Bennet, L.A., (1995) *International Organizations Principles and Issues* (New Jersey: Prentice Hall).

Berriedale-Keith, A., (1936) *The King and the Imperial Crown: The Powers and Duties of His Majesty* (London/New York/Toronto: Longmans, Green & Co.).

Best, G., (1994) *War and Law Since 1945* (Oxford: Clarendon Press).

Bird, R., (1983) *Osborn's Concise Law Dictionary* (7th edition) (London: Sweet & Maxwell).

Brackman, A.C., (1989) *The Other Nuremberg. The Untold Story of the Tokyo War Crimes Trials* (London: Collins).

Bradley, C.A., (May 2002) 'The US Announces Intent Not to Ratify International Criminal Court Treaty' *www.asil.org/insights*.

Bibliography

Brierly, J.L., (1963) (ed.) *The Law of Nations: An Introduction to the International Law of Peace* (6th edition) (Oxford: Clarendon Press).

Bröhmer, J., (1997) *State Immunity and the Violation of Human Rights* (The Hague/Boston/London: Martinus Nijhoff Publishers).

Brownlie, I., (1990) *Principles of Public International Law* (4th edition) (Oxford: Clarendon Press).

Byers, M., (1997) 'Conceptualising the Relationship between *Jus Cogens* and *Erga Omnes* Rules' *66 NJIL 211.*

Caron, D.D., (2002) 'The ILC Articles on State Responsibility: The Paradoxical Relationship between Form and Authority' *96 AJIL 857.*

Cassese, A. (1999) 'The Statute of the International Criminal Court: Some Preliminary Reflections' *10 EJIL 144.*

Cassese, A., (2000) *International Law* (Oxford: Oxford University Press).

Cassese, A., (2001) 'Terrorism is Also Disrupting Some Crucial Legal Categories of International Law' *12 EJIL 1993.*

Cassese, A., (2003) *International Criminal Law* (Oxford: Oxford University Press).

Christensen, G.A., (1988) '*Jus Cogens*: Guarding Interests Fundamental to International Society' *VJIL 585.*

Cicero, M.T., (1990) *On Duties* (eds. M.T. Griffin and E.M. Atkins) (Cambridge: Cambridge University Press).

von Clauswitz, C., (1993) *On War* (ed. and translated by M. Howard and P. Paret) (London: Everyman's Library).

CNN (23 January 2002) 'Belgium's Legal Trap for World Leaders' www.cnn.com

Craton, M., Walvin, J and Wright, D., (1976) *Slavery, Abolition and Emancipation* (London: Longman Group Ltd.).

Crawford, F.M., (1900) *Rulers of the South, Sicily, Calabria, Malta* Volume 2 (London: Macmillan & Co).

Crawford, F.M. and Cloud, R., (eds.) (1996) *Rome Statutes* (London: Institute of Classical Studies, School of Advanced Studies, University of London).

D'Amato, A., (1971) *The Concept of Custom in International Law* (Ithaca/London: Cornell University Press).

D'Amato, A., (1991) 'It's a Bird, It's a Plane, It's *Jus Cogens*' *6 Conn. JIL 1.*

Danilenko, G.M., (1991) 'International *Jus Cogens*: Issues of Law Making' *2 EJIL 42.*

De Souza, P., (1999) *Piracy in the Graeco-Roman World* (Cambridge: Cambridge University Press).

De Vitoria, F., (1917) *On the Law of War* (ed. E. Nys, translated by J. Pawley Bate) (Washington DC).

Deák, F., (1968) 'Organs of State in their Extraterritorial Relations: Immunity and Privileges of Organs of the State' in *Manual of Public International Law* (ed. M. Sørensen) (London: Macmillan Press).

Denza, E., (1998) *Diplomatic Law. A Commentary on the Vienna Convention on Diplomatic Relations* (Oxford: Clarendon Press).

Denza, E., (1999) '*Ex Parte Pinochet*: Lacuna or Leap?' *48 ICLQ 941.*

Dinstein, Y., (1966) 'Diplomatic Immunity from Jurisdiction *Ratione Materiae*' *15 ICLQ 76.*

Do Nascimento e Silva, G.E., (1972) *Diplomacy in International Law* (Leiden: A.W. Sijthoff).

Evans, M.D., (ed.) (2002) *Blackstone's International Law Documents* (5th edition) (Oxford: Oxford University Press).

Everyman's United Nations Structure, Functions and Work of the Organization and its Related Agencies During the Years 1945-1962 (United Nations: New York).

Faasbender, B., (1998) 'S v. Berlin Court of Appeal and District Court of Appeal Berlin-Tiergartan' *92 AJIL 74.*

Ferencz, B.B., (1980) *An International Criminal Court. A Step Toward World Peace* Volumes 1 & 2 (London: Oceana Publishing Inc.).

Ferencz, B.B., (1998) 'International Criminal Courts: The Legacy of Nuremberg' *10 Pace IL Rev. 203.*

Fife, R.E., (2000) 'The International Criminal Court Whence It Came, Where It Goes' *69 NJIL 63.*

Fooner, M., (1989) *Interpol Issues in World Crime and International Criminal Justice* (New York & London: Plenum Press).

Foreign Affairs Committee UK (1984-1985 session) *Diplomatic Immunity and Privileges. Government Report on the Review of the Vienna Convention on Diplomatic Relations and Reply to 'Abuse of Diplomatic Immunities and Privileges' First Report* (cmnd. 949.)

Fox, H., (2002) *The Law of State Immunity* (Oxford: Oxford University Press).

Friedland, M.L., (1969) *Double Jeopardy* (Oxford: Clarendon Press).

Garnett, R., (1997) 'The Defence of State Immunity for Acts of Torture' *Australian YBIL 97.*

Goodwin-Gill, G.S., (1999) 'Crime in International Law: Obligations *Erga Omnes* and the Duty to Prosecute' in *The Reality of International Law. Essays in Honour of Ian Brownlie* (eds. G.S Goodwin and S. Talmon) (Oxford: Clarendon Press).

Gore-Booth, P., (ed.) (1979) *Satow's Guide to Diplomatic Practice* (5th Edition) (London: Longman).

Grotius, H., (1901) *The Rights of War and Peace* (translated by A.C. Campbell) (Washington/London: Walter Dunne).

Haffke, C.W., (1994) 'The Torture Victim Protection Act: More Symbol than Substance' *43 Emory LJ 1469.*

Hamilton, K., and Langhorne, R., (1998) *The Practice of Diplomacy* (London: Routledge)

Hand, G.J., (3 December 2001) 'The Belgian Follies' *JMC.* www.enterstageright.com.

Harris, D.J. (ed) (1998) *Cases and Materials on International Law* (5th edition) (London: Sweet & Maxwell).

Harvard Draft Convention on Jurisdiction with Respect to Crime (1935) *29 AJIL 579.*

Harvard Research Draft in International Law: Diplomatic Privileges and Immunities (1932) *26 AJIL 15 Supp.*

Hegel, G.W.L., (1942) *The Philosophy of Right* (translated by T.M. Knox) (Oxford: Clarendon Press)

Henkin, L., (1978) *The Rights of Man Today* (London: Stevens & Co.).

Higgins, R., (1982) 'Certain Aspects of the Law of State Immunity' *29 NILR 265.*

Higgins, R., (1994) *Problems and Processes. International Law and How We Use It.* (Oxford: Oxford University Press).

Hinsley, F.H. (1986) *Sovereignty* (2nd edition) (Cambridge: Cambridge University Press)

Historical Survey of the Question of International Criminal Justice (1949) (New York: United Nations).

Hobbes, T., (1996) *Leviathan* (ed. R. Tuck) (Cambridge: Cambridge University Press).

Hurst, C., (1950) *International Law: Collected Papers* (London: Stevens & Sons Ltd.).

Hurwitz, L., (1981) *The State as Defendant: Governmental Accountability and the Redress of Individual Grievances* (London: Aldwych Press).

Jordan, J.B., (2000) 'Universal Jurisdiction in a Dangerous World: a Weapon for All Nations against International Crime' *9 MSU-DCL JIL 1.*

Jørgensen, N.H.B., (2000) *The Responsibility of States for International Crimes* (Oxford University Press).

Bibliography

Kaplan, M.A., and Katzenbach, N. de B., (1966) 'Resort to Force: War and Neutrality. The Strategy of World Order' in *International Law* (eds. R.A. Falk and S.H. Mendlovitz) Vol. 2 (New York: World Law Fund).

Kelly, M., (1999) 'The ICC: Case Studies "Ripe" for the ICC' *8 MSU-DCL JIL 21.*

Kelsen, H., (1945) *General Theory of Law and State* (translated by A. Wedberg) (New York: Russell & Russell).

Kelsen, H., (1966) *Principles of International Law* (2nd edition) (New York/Chicago/San Francisco/Toronto/London: Holt, Rinehart & Winston Inc.).

Kunz, J.L., (1947) 'Privileges and Immunities of International Organizations' *41 AJIL 828.*

Leich, M.N., (1984) 'Contemporary Practice of the United States Relating to International Law' *78 AJIL 658.*

Lemkin, R., (1944) *Axis Rule in Occupied Europe: Laws of Occupation, Analysis of Government Proposals for Redress* (Washington: Carnegie Endowment For World Peace).

Limbach, J., (2001) 'The Concept of the Supremacy of the Constitution' *64 MLR 1.*

Lopez, D.E., (2000) 'Not Twice for the Same: How the Dual Sovereignty Doctrine is Used to Circumvent *Non Bis In Idem*' *33 Van. JTL 263.*

MacDonald, R., (1987) 'Fundamental Norms in Contemporary International Law' *CYIL 115.*

Mair, L., (1964) *Primitive Government. A Study of Traditional Political Systems in Eastern Africa* (London: Scolar Press).

Malanczuk, P., (1997) *Akehurst's Modern Introduction to International Law* (London/New York: Routledge).

Maupas, S., (9 September 2000) *Judicial Diplomacy www.diplomatiejudiciaire.com.*

McClanahan, G.V., (1989) *Diplomatic Immunity: Principles, Practices, Problems* (London: Hurst & Company)

Meron, T., (1989) *Human Rights and Humanitarian Norms as Customary Law* (Oxford: Clarendon Press).

Meron, T., (1998) 'Crimes and Accountability in Shakespeare' *92 AJIL 1.*

Merrills, J.G., (1971) 'Recognition and Construction' *20 ICLQ 476.*

Miles, T., (13 February 2003) 'Sharon Faces War Crimes Trial Once Out of Office' *The Independent.*

Moore, J.B. (1970) *Digest of International Law* Vol. 1 (AMS edition) (New York: AMS Press Inc.).

Morris, V., and Bourloyannis-Vrailas, C., (1995) 'Current Development: The Work of the Sixth Committee at the Forty-Ninth Session of the UN General Assembly' *89 AJIL 607.*

Morrison, W., (1997) *Jurisprudence: From the Greeks to Post-Modernism* (London/Sydney: Cavendish Publishing Ltd.).

Nahlik, S.E., (1990) 'Development of Diplomatic. Law Selected Problems' *222 Hague Recueil des Cours 188.*

Nicolson, H., (1954) *Evolution of Diplomatic Method* (London: Constable & Co. Ltd.).

Nicolson, H., (1988) *Diplomacy* (Washington D.C.: Institute for the Study of Diplomacy).

Onuma, Y., (1986) 'The Tokyo Trial: Between Law and Politics' in *The Tokyo War Crimes Trial: An International Symposium* (eds. C. Hosoya, N. Ando, Y. Onuma and R. Linear) (Tokyo: Kodansha).

Oppenheim, L.F.L., (1995) *International Law A Treatise* Vol. 1 (eds. R. Jennings & A. Watts) (London: Longman).

Panhuys, H.F., (1964) 'In the Borderlands Between the Act of State Doctrine and Questions of Jurisdictional Immunities' *13 ICLQ 1193.*

Paust, J.J., (2000) 'The Reach of ICC Jurisdiction over Non-Signatory Nationals' *33 Van. JTL 1.*

Paust, J.J., Bassiouni, M.C., Scharf, M., Gurulé, J., Sadat, L., Zagaris, B. and Williams, S.A. (eds.) (2000) *International Criminal Law Cases and Materials* 2nd edition (Durham, North Carolina: Carolina Academic Press).

Pecoraro, T.W., (1988) 'Diplomatic Immunity: Application of the Restrictive Theory of Diplomatic Immunity. The Absinito Affair' *29 HILJ 533*.

Pennington, K., (1993) *The Prince and the Law, 1200-1600: Sovereignty and Rights in Western Legal Traditions* (Berkeley/Oxford: California University Press).

Ratner, S.R., and Abrams, J.S., (2001) *Accountability for Human Rights Atrocities in International Law: Beyond the Nuremberg Legacy* (Oxford: Oxford University Press).

Reports in the Sub-Committee on Diplomatic Immunity of Committee of Experts for Progressive Codification of International Law (1920) *20 AJIL 150 Supp.*

Roberts, A., (8 April 2002) 'Comment and Analysis' *The Guardian*.

Roberts, A. and Guelff, R., (eds.) (1989) *Documents on the Laws of War* (2nd edition) (Oxford: Clarendon Press).

Röling, B.V.A., (1993) *The Tokyo Trial and Beyond. Reflections of a Peacemonger* (ed. A. Cassese) (Cambridge: Polity Press).

Rosenne, S., (1962) *The World Court: What it Is and How it Works* (Dordrecht/Boston/London: Martinus Nijhoff Publishers).

Rubin, A.P., (2001) '*Actio Popularis, Jus Cogens* and Offenses *Erga Omnes*' *35 New England L. Rev. 265*.

Sarooshi, D., (1999) 'The Statute of the International Criminal Court' *48 ICLQ 387*.

Sarooshi, D., (1999) *The United Nations and the Development of Collective Security: The Delegation by the United Nations Security Council of its Chapter VII Powers* (Oxford: Clarendon Press).

Satow, E., (1922) *A Guide to Diplomatic Practice* (2nd edition) (London: Longmans, Green & Co.).

Schabas, W.A., (2000) *Genocide in International Law* (Cambridge: Cambridge University Press).

Schabas, W.A., (2001) *An Introduction to the International Criminal Court* (Cambridge: Cambridge University Press).

Schreuer, C.H., (1988) *State Immunity: Some Recent Developments* (Cambridge: Grotius).

Schwarzenberger, G., (1971) *International Law and Order* (London: Stevens & Sons).

Sen, B., (1979) *A Diplomat's Handbook of International Law and Practice* (the Hague/Boston/London: Martinus Nijhoff).

Shaw, M.N., (1997) *International Law* (4th edition) (Cambridge: Cambridge University Press).

Shearer, I.A., (ed.) (1994) *Starke's International Law* (11th edition) (London: Butterworths).

Sinclair, I., (1980) 'The Law of Sovereign Immunity. Recent Developments' *167 Hague Recueil des Cours 131*.

Tomuschat, C., (1999) 'International Law: Ensuring the Survival of the Eve of a New Century' *281 Hague Recueil des Cours 13*.

Turpil, M.E., and Sands, P., (1988) 'Peremptory International Law and Sovereignty: Some Questions' *3 Conn. JIL 364*.

Warbrick, C., (1996) 'Co-Operation with the International Criminal Tribunal for Yugoslavia' *45 ICLQ 947*.

Watts, A., (1994) 'The Legal Position in International Law of Heads of State, Heads of Government and Foreign Ministers' *247 Hague Recueil des Cours 13*.

Williams Walsh, M., (30th August 1995) 'A Tribunal in a Time of Atrocities' *Los Angeles Times* (www.latimes.com).

Wilson, C.E., (1967) *Diplomatic Privileges and Immunities* (Arizona: The University of Arizona Press).

Woolsey, L.H., (1926) 'The Non-Recognition of the Chammorro Government in Nicaragua' *20 AJIL 543.*

Young, E., (1964) 'The Development of the Law of Diplomatic Relations' *BYIL 141.*

Zappalà, S., (2001) 'Do Heads of State in Office Enjoy Immunity from the Jurisdiction for International Crimes? The Ghaddafi Case before the French Cour de Cassation' *12 EJIL 595.*

Index

Achille Lauro Case 80
acts of state 2, 3, 47, 98, 124-6, 129, 131-4, 159
Ad Hoc Tribunals 15, 16, 20, 21, 26, 27, 29, 30, 31, 33-5, 87, 90, 157
aggression 9, 13, 14, 16, 36, 41, 43, 50-4, 67, 111; see also crimes against peace
aircraft hijacking 36, 44, 49
sabotage 44
Al Adsani Case 61, 62, 102-4, 109,
ambassador 86, 94, 95, 99, 100-2, 120-3, 133, 137
Amerada Hess Case 102-4
Amnesty International 39, 66, 83
apartheid 44, 62, 67
armed conflict 43, 50, 51, 54, 56, 57, 59, 78, 121
arrest warrant(s) 1, 4-6, 29, 31, 89, 111, 112, 157
Arrest Warrant Case 4, 5, 89, 112, 113, 122, 142, 158, 159
Asylum Case 37
Austin 70
aut dedere aut judicare 45, 46, 51, 75

Barbie Case 55, 57
Barcelona Traction Case 60, 111
Belgium 4, 5, 34, 44, 45, 51, 60, 82, 83, 84, 86, 89, 110, 111, 128, 141, 142
Blaskic Case 28, 31, 32, 90, 158, 159
Bosnia and Herzegovina (Genocide) Case 49, 89
Bodin 69, 93, 106
Bynkershoek 69, 70, 95

Caroline Case 120
Chile 1, 47, 86, 102, 129
Cicero 42, 68
crimes against humanity 1, 10, 36, 41, 43, 49, 50, 53, 56-9, 74, 76-8, 82, 88, 128, 141
crimes against peace 10, 36, 43, 50, 51-53, 57

Cutting Case 79

delicta juris gentium 76
diplomatic immunity 2, 5, 30, 94, 95, 99, 101, 110, 120, 122, 123, 125, 131-4, 136-7, 142, 143, 151, 159; see also immunity *ratione materiae*, immunity *ratione personae*
extraterritoriality 95, 100
diplomatic law 94-6, 99, 100, 117, 120, 123
double jeopardy 84-8; see also *non bis in idem*
drugs 36, 44, 51, 119, 130, 137
trafficking 51, 74, 116, 130
Duke of Hagenbach 73

ECHR, see European Court of Human Rights
Eichmann Case 21, 49, 50, 59, 76, 78-80, 128
erga omnes 36, 60-6, 111, 143-5; see also *loci standii*
European Court of Human Rights 61, 103, 109
extradition 36, 80-4, 86

Fisheries Case 39, 40
force majeure 122
France 18, 44, 51, 58, 73, 81, 89, 98, 99, 137
Furundzija Case 61, 66

General Assembly 11-14, 48, 53
Geneva Conventions 12, 43, 50, 54-6
Additional Protocols of 1957 50, 54
common Article 3 50, 55, 56
grave breaches 50, 55
genocide 10, 11, 14, 21, 36, 41, 43, 49, 50, 56, 58-60, 62, 67, 72, 77, 81, 83, 88, 89, 92, 98, 111, 131
Armenians 58
Germany 10, 20, 21, 32, 33, 38, 44, 53, 72, 76-8, 81, 98, 122, 123, 138

Treaty of Peace 1897 53
   Leipzig Trials 72
Goering at al 128
Grotius 119, 120

Habre Case 74, 75, 77
Hague Conventions 43, 54
   Martens Clause 54
head of state immunity 94, 106, 112, 115, 116, 126-130; see also immunity *ratione materiae*, immunity *ratione personae*
Hostages Case 121
hostage taking 47, 80
hierarchy of norms 60, 136, 139, 141, 159
Hegel 4, 6, 63, 68, 126, 129, 135
Hobbes 3, 93, 96, 106, 107
   social contract 3, 107
von Hohenstaufen 72, 73
human rights 22, 37, 41, 49, 61-6, 67, 70, 71, 72, 74, 103, 111, 143
   Human Rights Watch 74, 156

ICC, see International Criminal Court
ICJ, see International Court of Justice
ICRC, see International Committee of the Red Cross
ICTY, see International Criminal Tribunal for the Former Yugoslavia
ICTR, see International Criminal Tribunal for Rwanda
ILC, see International Law Commission
immunities 2, 4, 6, 7, 30, 31, 34, 35, 90-3, 95, 96, 99-102, 104, 108-110, 117, 118, 121, 122, 125, 132-4, 136-140, 143, 145-7, 150, 153, 154, 158
immunity 2, 3, 14, 31, 33-5, 37, 39, 40, 47, 65, 89, 90, 92-6, 96-110, 112-119, 121-3, 125-134, 154, 158, 159
   ratione materiae 47, 109, 110, 123-6, 129, 130-3, 141-5, 159
   ratione personae 109-111, 113-117, 122, 123, 125, 126, 133-6, 141-6, 156, 159
impunity 105
indictment(s) 29, 30, 80, 82, 85, 91, 157
individual accountability 53, 66, 72, 73, 89, 90, 91, 135, 144

individual responsibility 53, 61, 75, 89, 90, 126, 127, 129, 158
International Committee of the Red Cross 59
international constabulary 9, 137, 146-150, 157, 158
International Court of Justice 4, 5, 13, 31-3, 37-40, 49, 60, 88-91, 111-3, 117, 121, 139, 140, 142, 158, 159
   Pakistan and Bangladesh Incident 13, 88
international crimes 1, 6-8, 10-12, 14-16, 20, 22, 23, 34-7, 40, 41, 43, 45, 48-51, 57-61, 64, 66, 67, 71, 72, 74-77, 80, 83, 88, 89, 91, 92, 104, 105, 111, 121, 127-9, 131, 132, 134-136, 138, 141, 142, 144-147, 158, 159
international criminal court, the 1, 4, 5, 8, 14, 15, 18-21, 24, 27, 28, 30, 31, 33, 49, 50, 57, 58, 59, 149, 150, 157
   admissibility 23-6, 87
   Assembly of State Parties 150, 152
   complementarity 23, 86, 87
   Diplomatic Conference 1, 14, 15, 18, 23, 26, 59, 158
   draft statute 13
   Rome Statute 1, 2, 5, 6, 8, 14, 15, 18-20, 24, 25, 27, 29-31, 36, 41, 42, 50, 51, 53, 54, 56-9, 78, 86, 87, 92, 108, 136, 146, 150
   surrender request 35, 92, 108, 147, 155
International Criminal Court for Rwanda 15, 21, 27-31, 34, 50, 56, 57, 82, 87, 92
International Criminal Court for the Former Yugoslavia 14-17, 20-22, 27-34, 50, 55, 57, 61, 62, 86, 87, 90
international customary law 2, 5, 36, 37, 41, 43, 47-50, 55, 65, 76, 77, 100, 108, 128, 131, 141-4, 159
   opinio juris 37-40, 64-6
   state practice 37-9, 65, 66, 69, 70, 135
international humanitarian law 54, 87
international justice 7, 23, 27, 35, 135, 144-146, 158, 159
International Law Commission 11-14, 53, 54, 60-2, 64, 67, 98, 104, 118, 120

172   *Immunity and International Criminal Law*

international peace and security 6, 15, 17, 18, 22, 28, 135; see also Security Council

international tribunals 15, 20, 23, 33, 50, 87-90, 92; see also ICTY, ICTR, Nuremberg and Tokyo

international treaty crimes 37, 44, 45, 49, 50, 128

inviolability 3-6, 94, 95, 99-101, 108, 110-113, 115, 117-121, 126, 134, 142-145, 154, 159; see also immunity *ratione personae*

Israel 21, 34, 55, 76-80

jus in bello 43, 51, 54; see also war crimes

jus ad bellum 43, 51, 53; see also aggression, crimes against peace

jus cogens 53, 60-66, 103, 109, 138-145, 158, 159; see also peremptory norms

Kelsen 125-7, 139

Kellog-Briand Pact 52, 53

Lafontant Case 115, 116

LaGrand Case 32

League of Nations 9, 45, 52, 95

Lemkin 58

Letelier Case (Chile) 86

Letelier Case (USA) 103

Locke 107

Lotus Case 73, 81

locus standi 60, 143

London International Assembly 9

Mexico 80, 83

Milosevic 30, 34, 157

natural law(s) 63, 64, 68-71, 96, 105, 106, 142

Nazi(s) 55, 58, 71, 76, 77, 89,

Nicaragua Case 37-40, 139

non bis in idem 84-7; see also double jeopardy

non-justiciable(ity) 110, 123, 130, 132

Noriega 115, 116, 130

North Sea Continental Shelf Case 38, 39

Ntuyahaga Case 82-4, 86, 87

Nuremberg 8, 10, 11, 15, 20, 23, 42, 50, 52, 53, 55-7, 72, 89, 128

PCIJ, see Permanent Court of International Justice

par in parem non habet imperium 93

persona non grata 119, 123, 137, 138

Peace of Westphalia 58

Permanent Court of International Justice 3, 81

Pinochet Case 1, 45-7, 61, 66, 74, 94, 109, 110, 127-130, 141, 145, 145

piracy 41-3, 45, 47, 49, 50, 80

positivism 68-70

peremptory norm(s) 62, 65, 138; see also *jus cogens*

prisoners of war 43, 54, 55, 56

Pufendorf 69

recognition, international law doctrine of 113-116

Reparations Case 32, 91

Rezaq Case 47, 48

Roman(s) 41, 42, 43, 69, 84, 95, 106
    Lex de provinciis praetoriis 42

paganism 69

rex gratia dei 105-7

rex gratia populi 106

St Augustine 69

Schooner Exchange Case 96

Second World War 8, 9, 12, 20, 42, 52, 55, 58, 71

Security Council 14-19, 28, 29, 31, 34, 91, 149

Self-defence 120

Sharon 35, 77, 110, 145

Siderman de Blake Case 61, 103, 138, 139, 141

slavery 44, 45, 57, 62, 67, 111; see also international treaty crimes

sovereign(s) 3, 4, 6, 12, 22, 29, 31, 33, 43, 44, 49, 52, 63, 69, 73, 92, 93-96, 100, 105-109, 113, 114, 118-120, 124, 126, 127, 130, 135, 139

sovereignty 3, 11-13, 15, 21-3, 35, 43, 52, 69, 73, 84, 88-91, 93, 94, 96, 104-6, 114, 141, 146, 150, 155, 158, 159

Index

173

sovereign immunity 93, 94, 97, 105, 107, 112, 115, 126, 138; see also head of state immunity
state immunity 39, 40, 65, 93, 94, 97-9, 103, 104, 109, 111, 124, 127
restrictive doctrine 97, 98, 102
state jurisdiction 34, 48; see also universal jurisdiction
state responsibility 61, 67, 98, 104
civil reparations 131
subpoena 28, 31, 32, 33, 90, 91, 158, 159

Tachiona 112, 113, 122
Tanzania 80, 82, 83, 84, 86, 102, 139
terrorism 9, 12, 48-50, 51, 57, 80, 83, 128
Thucydides 41
Tokyo Tribunal 10, 15, 20, 50, 52, 53, 57, 89, 90
torture 39-41, 43, 44, 46, 47, 50, 55-7, 59, 61, 62, 65, 66, 74, 75, 77, 78, 83, 103, 104, 109, 129-131, 138, 139, 141
treaty obligations 19
lex specialis 59, 139

UK, see United Kingdom
UN, see United Nations
US, see United States
USA, see United States
United Kingdom 2, 4-6, 31, 39, 40, 44, 46, 47, 47, 61, 83, 85, 88, 95-8, 102,

103, 105, 115, 116, 118, 119, 132, 137
Foreign Affairs Committee 118, 132
United Nations 8-10, 14-20, 29, 32, 38, 44, 48-50, 53, 58, 62, 89, 135, 147, 148, 150, 152, 156; see also General Assembly, Security Council
United States 5,8, 10, 18, 31-3, 37, 44, 47, 49, 51, 54, 79, 80, 84-6, 94, 96, 98, 101-4, 111-113, 115-118, 121, 122, 124, 130, 133, 137, 138-140, 142, 149
universal jurisdiction 27, 37, 42, 43, 45-50, 57, 61, 66, 74, 77, 78, 81-3, 141, 142, 144, 145; see also state jurisdiction
Usama bin Laden 80

Vattel 69, 99

waiver, of immunity 118, 134, 136-8, 150; see also diplomatic immunity
war crimes 9, 10 , 34, 36, 41, 43, 50, 54-7, 59, 72, 77, 145

Yunis Case 47, 48

Zanu-PF 112, 122; see also Tachiona Case
Zeus 95
Zouche 69